From Bursar to School
Business Manager

From Bursar to School Business Manager

Reengineering leadership for resource management

■ ■ ■

FERGUS O'SULLIVAN, ANGELA THODY
AND ELIZABETH WOOD

An imprint of **Pearson Education**

London · New York · San Francisco · Toronto · Sydney ·
Tokyo · Singapore · Hong Kong · Cape Town · Madrid ·
Paris · Milan · Munich · Amsterdam

PEARSON EDUCATION LIMITED

Head Office:
Edinburgh Gate
Harlow CM20 2JE
Tel: +44 (0)1279 623623
Fax: +44 (0)1279 431059

London Office:
128 Long Acre
London WC2E 9AN
Tel: +44 (0)20 7447 2000
Fax: +44 (0)20 7240 5771
www.business-minds.com

First published in Great Britain in 2000

© Pearson Education Limited 2000

The right of Fergus O'Sullivan, Angela Thody and Elizabeth Wood
to be identified as authors of this work has been asserted by them
in accordance with the Copyright, Designs and Patents Act 1988.

ISBN 0 273 64325 8

British Library Cataloguing in Publication Data
A CIP catalogue record for this book can be obtained from the British Library

10 9 8 7 6 5 4 3 2

Typeset by Pantek Arts
Printed and bound in Great Britain

The Publishers' policy is to use paper manufactured from sustainable forests

About the Authors

■ ■ ■

Fergus O'Sullivan. Fergus is Director of Bursarship Development in the International Educational Leadership Centre at the University of Lincolnshire and Humberside, England, where he has developed, and leads, the first MBA for school bursars. He is joint director of the IELC's research project on school educational resource management and its future. His previous experience was as deputy head of a large comprehensive school succeeded by senior Local Education Authority (LEA) officer and adviser posts and as course leader in higher education. His research interests are in schools as learning organisations and in professional development for teachers and school business managers. He lectures widely in the UK and is active in professional associations for education management and for teachers' professional development. He has published two books, numerous articles and regularly presents conference papers in the UK and the USA.

Angela Thody. Angela is Professor of Educational Leadership at the International Educational Leadership Centre and Faculty of Business and Management Research Director at the University of Lincolnshire and Humberside, England. She leads the taught and research doctoral programmes there in educational leadership and is joint director of the IELC's research project on school educational resource management and its future. She has researched and published extensively in leadership issues, including her doctorate in school governance, six books, fifty articles and numerous conference presentations. She is invited to lecture worldwide, was a Visiting Professor at the Queensland University of Technology and is an accredited member of the Australian Council for Educational Administration. She is the first female President of the Commonwealth Council for Educational Administration and Management, is a member of the International Committee of the British Educational Management and Administration Society, was a Council member of the latter for three years and editor of one of its journals, *Management in Education*, for five years.

Elizabeth Wood. Elizabeth is a researcher in the International Educational Leadership Centre at the University of Lincolnshire and Humberside investigating the role of bursars in schools. She has published articles and presented conference papers on the topic. Before joining the International Educational Leadership Centre in 1995 as the Centre administrator, she spent 15 years in industry as a partner of a small manufacturing business employing 20 people. She has completed the Centre's MBA in Education Management for bursars and her PhD studies are concentrating on the emergence of new professions taking bursars as a case study. She is a tutor on the MBA in Education Management for bursars and evaluates assessor training on the National Bursars Association licentiate registration scheme. She has eight years' experience as a school governor as either the deputy or chair.

Contents

■ ■ ■

Series Editors' Foreword ix

Acknowledgements x

Preface xi

Abbreviations xii

Structure of the Book xiv

Part One
School Business Mangement: the Need for Development 1

  1 The Educational Context 3

Part Two
Launching Development: Analysing the Tasks 17

  2 The Rise of the School Business Manager 19
  3 What Is the School Business Manager Expected to Do? 29
  4 What Do School Business Managers Actually Do? 43
  5 Coming from . . . Going to? The Career of the School
    Business Manager 51
  6 Roles and Relationships 62

Part Three
Continuing Development: Case Studies of Effective Practice 75

  7 Strategic Planning 77
  8 Support Staff 96
  9 Sites and Equipment 112
10 School Image 129
11 Learning: the Bursar and Aspects of the Curriculum 149

Part Four
Future Development: Leading Resource Management for the Learning Community *167*

12 The Past and the Future *169*
13 The Professionalisation of Bursarship *183*
14 Leading Onwards *198*

Appendix I: Research Methodology 210

Appendix II: National Standards for School Bursars 222

Appendix III: 231

References 232

Index 237

Series Editors' Foreword

■ ■ ■

In a turbulent educational environment it is important that schools focus on the core purpose of effective student learning and development.

A key aspect of delivering effective learning is the efficient management of resources. Directing resources to the learning process is a pivotal role in self-managing schools. The role of the school bursar in the senior leadership team in a school has grown in significance in both the state and private sector during the 1980s and 1990s.

Reconceptualising the role of the school bursar into the educational resource manager is a major challenge for those schools who wish to link curriculum and resources into an effective learning strategy.

This book is ground breaking in the scope and perception of its analysis of the role of resource managers in schools. It should provide both insights to evaluate current management practice and a framework for strategic rethinking in the deployment of senior staff in schools.

Professor Brent Davies
Director, the International Educational Leadership Centre

Professor John West-Burnham
Director of the MBA Educational Leadership and Management Programmes

University of Lincolnshire and Humberside

Acknowledgements

■　■　■

We would like to thank the following people, schools and organisations for their contributions, suggestions and encouragement during the writing of this book.

Avon Valley School
Blenheim Primary School
Carter Community School
Coopers School
Eiras High School
Hayes School
International Educational Leadership Centre, University of Lincolnshire and Humberside
Ipswich High School for Girls, Girls' Day School Trust
Management Information Systems, Leeds Local Education Authority
St Alban's RC High School
St Mary and St Joseph's School
St Laurence School
The Independent Schools' Bursars Association
The National Bursars Association
United World College of the Atlantic
Waltham Holy Cross School
Gareth Cheesman, Bursar
Sue Connell, Bursar
Mary Cook, Bursar
Professor Brent Davies (IELC)
Tim Ellis, Bursar
Professor Ron Everett, Illinois Association of School Business Officials
Julia Goodfellow, IELC
Janice Grant, Department for Education and Employment (DfEE)
Stephen Harrison, Teacher Training Agency (TTA)
John Hillier, Bursar
Professor Richard King, University of Northern Colorado
Alison Martin, Bursar
Everette Maynard, Bursar
David Milsom, Bursar
Lindsay Nunn, Bursar
Anne-Marie Parkes, Bursar
Irene Scott, Bursar
Angela Smith, Bursar
Professor John West-Burnham, IELC
Sue Whyler, Bursar

The authors would also like to thank their families for their support and encouragement and for putting up with late nights and having to cook their own meals – Heather, Laura and Duncan O'Sullivan, Roy, Serena and Amber Thody and Rob, Richard and James Wood and Emmy Thut.

Preface

■ ■ ■

This is the first book about school business managers, usually known as 'bursars' but also having a range of titles, such as Administration Officers, Business Directors or General Managers. It is a book about the practice of 'bursarship', about what is going on now, about what could be happening and what ought to be happening. School business management is a burgeoning area if measured only by the growing quantity of bursarship appointments in schools, but its importance lies also in its quality. It is growing in significance too. Business management in schools is no longer perceived as only about making the books balance. It has already gone beyond that for many bursars whose role is to give financial information to guide strategic decisions. More than that, bursars are fully operational members of senior management teams in schools as effective direction and management of resources have become recognised as vital to students' success and improved achievements.

Our aim in this book is to record the experiences of bursars themselves and present the outcomes of a research project about bursars. This combines the views of 'outsiders', the researchers, who watched bursars at work, interviewed them and studied literature and school sources about them (Part Two) and the views of the 'insiders', the bursars themselves, about what they do and how they do it (Part Three). This creates a rounded picture of the present on which has been based the predictions and suggestions for the future (Part Four).

For bursars, for whom there are no other published sources of information on their profession, this book offers a chance to see how they compare with others in their field. Just as significantly, for school headteachers/principals, senior management teams and governors the book offers insights into how other schools are operating their business and teaching support services. For both groups, there is material to suggest routes for development. This is particularly important since one of the issues highlighted both in the research and in practice has been that of relationships between the bursarship role and that of the other school managers and governors.

The book uses examples from English and Welsh state and independent schools but its findings are relevant to all areas of the world where self-managed schools have emerged, such as New Zealand, Australia, Hong Kong, Singapore and the USA.

Fergus O'Sullivan, Angela Thody and Elizabeth Wood

Abbreviations

■ ■ ■

A-level	Advanced Level General Certificate of Education
AAT	Association of Accounting Technicians
AO-level	Advanced Ordinary Level General Certificate of Education
BEd	Bachelor of Education
BTEC National	Business and Technical Education Council National Diploma
CAME	Cognitive Acceleration through Mathematics Education
CASE	Cognitive Acceleration through Science Education
CAT	Cognitive Ability Test
CATS	Credit Accumulation and Transfer Scheme
CD	Compact Disk
CD-ROM	Compact Disk Read-only Memory
CDT	Craft, Design and Technology
CMS	Certificate of Management Studies
COPAC	Unified access to some of the catalogues of the largest research libraries in the UK and Ireland
DfEE	Department for Education and Employment
DMS	Diploma of Management Studies
DT	Design and Technology
EdD	Doctorate in Education
ERM	Education Resource Manager
EU	European Union
FAS	Funding Agency for Schools
FE	Further Education
F/T	Full Time
FTE	Full-time Equivalant
GCSE	General Certificate of Secondary Education
GDST	Girls' Day Schools Trust
GEST	Grants for Education Support and Training
GM	Grant Maintained
GNVQ	General National Vocational Qualification
HE	Higher Education
HEADLAMP	Headteachers' Leadership and Management Programme
HoC	House of Commons
HMI	Her Majesty's Inspectorate
HNC	Higher National Certificate
HND	Higher National Diploma
HRM	Human Resource Management
ICT	Information and Communications Technology
IELC	International Educational Leadership Centre

IIP	Investors in People
ILS	Integrated Learning System
INSET	In-Service Education and Training
IPD	Institute of Personnel Development
ISBA	Independent Schools' Bursars Association
IT	Information Technology
LEA	Local Education Authority
LM	Locally Managed/Local Management/Locally Maintained
LMS	Local Management of Schools
LNBA	Licentiate of National Bursars Association
MCI	Management Charter Initiative
MBA	Master of Business Administration
MPhil	Master of Philosophy
NAHT	National Association of Headteachers
NBA	National Bursars Association
NCET	National Council for Educational Technology
NCT	New Careers Training
NPQH	National Professional Qualification for Headship
NVQ	National Vocational Qualifications
O-Level	Ordinary Level General Certificate of Education
Ofsted	Office for Standards in Education
ONC	Ordinary National Certificate
PE	Physical Education
PEST	Political, Economic, Socio-cultural, Technological (analysis)
PESTLE	Political, Economic, Social, Technological, Legal and Ethical (analysis)
PhD	Doctor of Philosophy
PSHE	Personal, Social and Health Education
P/T	Part Time
PTA	Parent Teachers Association
RSA	Royal Society of Arts
SAT	Standard Assessment Task
SBM	Site-Based Management
SEN	Special Educational Needs
SENCO	Special Needs Co-ordinator
SHA	Secondary Heads Association
SMT	Senior Management Team
SPSS	Statistical Package for the Social Sciences
SRB	Single Regeneration Budget
SWOT	Strengths, Weaknesses, Opportunities and Threats (analysis)
TEC	Training Enterprise Council
TES	*Times Educational Supplement*
TTA	Teacher Training Agency
TVEI	Technical and Vocational Education Initiative
QSR NUDIST	Non-numerical Data Indexing, Structuring and Theorising (qualitative software analysis package)
UBI	Understanding British Industry
UK	United Kingdom
USA	United States of America

Structure of the Book

■ ■ ■

The book is divided into four sections.

- Part One explains the context which has given rise to the need for leadership and management of the resources which indirectly support teaching and learning.
- Part Two relates the tasks, roles, relationships and careers of school business management and managers.
- Part Three describes and comments on the practice of school business management, using examples provided by bursars from a wide range of primary and secondary schools from both the state and independent sectors.
- Part Four suggests the future directions and organisation of school business management.

Part One

■ ■ ■

School Business Management: the Need for Development

1

■ ■ ■

The Educational Context

Introduction

This book is written at a key point in the development of state education in the UK. Since the 1988 Education Reform Act and the introduction of local management of schools (LMS) and grant maintained (GM) initiatives there has been an unprecedented transfer of education funding to school site level. This has been paralleled by a burgeoning and bewildering increase in the special status of schools – city technology colleges, magnet schools, specialist schools, technology schools, beacon schools – all of which have increased the administrative load of senior management.

The solution to this increased administration in many schools has been the appointment of a person charged specifically with the responsibility of managing it. Such persons enjoy a wide variety of titles but the most commonly found is that of bursar. We will debate the suitability of this title and the various options later in this book, suffice it to say at this point, we will define the bursar as:

The person appointed to manage educational resources and lead the support services in schools

What sort of person, therefore, is this book primarily for and about? In our research we have found no recent text written for such a person in state schools, although there is a chapter in a book for the independent sector examining the responsibilities of the bursar (Boyd, 1998). Private schools have had bursars for hundreds of years, however, the bursar is a relatively new phenomenon in the state sector. In this book, therefore, we have mapped out the roles and responsibilities of school bursars, reporting on research we have carried out in the field, presenting illustrative case studies of what bursars do and, finally, speculating on how the role might develop in the future. In this endeavour we are writing for those who are school bursars, their senior management colleagues and LEA education officers, as well as anybody who is interested in the way in which schools have handled, and will handle, the administrative function in schools.

At this point it is useful to draw a pen picture of the sort of person who takes on the role of school bursar. Such a person is usually in the middle years of life, often having had a break in their career either to have children or in the pursuance of another career path, originally a specialist in finance/office administration but now with a wide responsibility for school business management including finance, sites and premises, personnel matters, administration and leading the support services team. Incidentally, this last group is often referred to as the 'non-teaching staff', however, it is invidious for such a vital group to be defined by what they *don't* do (one might as well call teachers 'non-administrative staff') so we will adopt the convention of support staff. The bursar will commonly be closely connected to the senior management team (SMT), if not actually a member, and the governing body, if not the clerk to the governors. Their relationship with other senior staff will usually be that of business adviser but, with the increasing devolution of curriculum initiatives (for example, literacy and numeracy hours in primary schools and other Standards Fund items in secondary schools) they are having to get involved in the core business of teaching and learning. With the change in the funding regime (Fair Funding) from April 1999 and the status of schools in September 1999, this aspect has grown in importance.

So what has led to the rise of such a post in state schools at a time when government's declared priority of 'education, education, education' has been to ensure that the vast bulk of funding gets spent on raising the standards of children's achievements? It is an exploration of these trends and developments which prompted this book. In the next section we map out the main strands of policy which lie behind the appointment of bursars to state schools. We consider site-level resource management (the bursar's environment), the roles of headteachers, senior management teams, school governors and support staff (the bursar's colleagues) and professionalisation (the bursar's career) between 1985 and 2000. This therefore establishes the starting point for bursarship in 2000, and the chapter concludes with our views of the current models for bursarship and thus the implications for the school bursar.

The educational context

The final 15 years of the twentieth century saw major changes in the UK's educational policy, which have also been paralleled in Australia, New Zealand, Hong Kong, Singapore and the USA. These changes focused on two apparently opposing strands of centralisation of curriculum and teacher development and of devolution of management to schools. Both strands were overtly aimed at improving standards in schools.

Centralisation

- A National Curriculum for school subjects; standards of curriculum achievement to be raised to nationally determined targets; achievements to be inspected by a much enlarged national inspectorate.
- An emergent national pedagogy through designated national literacy and numeracy hours.
- National standards for initial teacher education and for other grades of school staff, including aspiring and serving headteachers.
- National restructuring of the teaching profession, national introduction of performance-related pay, strengthening of national agencies in the leadership of the teaching profession and the establishment of the General Teaching Council.
- Several national 'reformattings' of the system of schooling with optional possibilities for schools of becoming directly centrally funded rather than locally funded, of acquiring joint state and private funding and of being designated as specialist schools in particular subjects.

Devolution

- All schools became self-managing with responsibilities for deciding their own allocations of all expenditure, including staff salaries, and for remaining solvent.
- Governors (a committee of outsiders to advise each school) given increased powers.
- Each school to market itself in response to parental rights to have some influence in the choice of the school their children attend. Those opting for a particular school are vital as state funding is linked to pupil numbers.
- Each school to provide its own administrative services to replace those previously available from LEAs.

Both policy strands supported the appointment of 'bursars' in state schools to:

1 relieve headteachers and deputies of the additional work devolved to them by site-based management;
2 free time for headteachers to devote their specialist professionalism to new curriculum and pedagogic demands;
3 provide specialist knowledge in schools, which educational professionals did not have for their newly devolved administrative functions.

As we note in the introduction to this chapter, bursars were initially appointed to administrative/accountancy roles but gradually began to develop into a wider remit of school business management. We now explore the present situation in schools and the implications for bursars of a number of reports and consultations on the role of headteachers in the context of site-level management.

5

Site-level resource management

The movement from centralised resource management by the LEAs to site-based management began slowly. Schools were given a greater level of autonomy over their staff appointments and budgets, and were then encouraged to take even greater control through GM status. The number of schools opting for grant maintained status, however, did not reach the levels anticipated by the Conservative government of the time, although there were obvious financial benefits involved. Many schools continued to rely on the LEAs to provide them with resources and services. When a Labour government was elected in 1997, it was unclear as to whether management would revert back to the LEAs or remain with the schools. It was equally unclear whether GM schools would retain their status.

The question of how the supposed benefits of the 'flagship reforms' of the Conservative government such as GM status, city technology colleges and magnet schools could be transferred to all schools became a key issue for the incoming Labour government, to such an extent that the Secretary of State promised to resign if standards did not reach targets by 2002 (in time for the next election).

Although the new government had its fair share of imperatives and a huge mandate from the electorate, there was a period of consolidation and research in the first 18 months which saw the setting up of a number of fact-finding and policy-testing activities. The role of headteachers came under particular scrutiny through the House of Commons Select Committee on Education and Employment, which spent a substantial part of 1998 receiving evidence from the profession, trainers, researchers and managers in industry and commerce.

The conundrum of what to do about GM status was resolved through a consultation paper issued in spring 1998 euphemistically entitled 'Fair Funding' (DfEE, 1998a) which planned to increase the pressure on LEAs as providers of support services such as curriculum advice, financial, personnel and legal services, sites and premises maintenance, and special educational needs. This had the effect of transferring the benefit of site-based funding and management to all schools that wished it while simultaneously bringing former GM schools into the same funding regime as locally managed (LM) schools. Interestingly, the end of the consultation process was signalled by a letter, rather than a formal policy document, from the DfEE to Chief Education Officers (DfEE, 1998b) laying out the range of policy directions the government was intending to implement.

Alongside this, the government itself was developing its blueprint for the structure, remuneration and development of the teaching profession which first appeared in the form of the Green Paper 'Meeting the Challenge' (DfEE, 1998c). This is a many faceted and far-reaching document but its relevance here is the messages it contains for the development of the role of headteachers, support staff and school bursars.

In the winter of 1998/9, these various strands culminated in the publication of a number of key documents in support of the government's objective of raising standards in schools, all of which will have a significant impact on the role of bursars. The context for these reports is set out in the House of Commons Education and Employment Committee's (HoC) report:

> Schools will continue to face changing expectations, including the need to ensure higher standards of achievement, collect and analyse more data about children's achievement, offer a wider range of services, adapt educational provision to the needs of the local community and provide education in a range of settings. The rapidly-growing use of information and communication technology (ICT) is also creating new challenges for schools. It follows from all this that the future task of the headteacher is perhaps even more challenging than it is at present.
>
> (HoC, 1998: para. 55)

Although the key role of the headteacher is reaffirmed here, the same report also acknowledges that there has been a huge increase in the number and level of responsibilities which devolve to headteachers and they will need to draw on a wider range of senior staff to successfully deliver both effective leadership and higher standards of achievement in the children in their care:

> not all of these tasks need be carried out by the headteacher ... [they] should be prepared to delegate tasks to other members of staff – both teachers and others – in order to free up time for their key duties.   (Ibid.: para. 77)

The Green Paper also develops this notion of a team approach to senior leadership:

> While heads are of crucial importance, leadership in schools is often shared and studies show that this shared leadership responsibility is a characteristic of successful heads. In many schools the members of the senior management teams help heads give strategic direction in schools.   (DfEE, 1998c: para. 48)

This recognition of the role that senior school leaders play as a team is important for the future of school bursarship. As has been highlighted above, schools have received more and more delegated responsibilities since 1985. The initial response of headteachers and governing bodies was to retain these as they felt class teachers and middle managers had enough to do in implementing the National Curriculum and its assessment, teacher appraisal, records of achievement and all the other initiatives in the Education Reform Act 1988. The development of senior management teams has been one way of ensuring that the headteacher (and governors) are able to retain an overview of the strategic direction of the school as well as enabling senior teachers to develop the specialist expertise required in curriculum and pastoral aspects. However, even a team approach to coping with the increasing levels of delegation has been insufficient to deal adequately with the additional administrative load and enable senior leaders to focus on a more strategic approach. This is confirmed in the evidence from the Education and Employment Committee report which states that school bursars are seen as a:

> *seriously under-utilised resource. Their potential contribution as senior managers has significant implications for the future role of headteacher.* (HoC, 1998: para. 45)

Indeed this message is further reinforced by the government's response to the Education and Employment Committee report:

> *We also acknowledge that sharing services between schools can help free heads to concentrate on raising standards ... some schools might want to go further and offer a wider range of facilities on one site, overseen by a single estate manager.*
> (HoC, 1999: para. 7)

and:

> *we will give full consideration to the Committee's recommendations on the role and contribution of other senior staff including senior administrators ... as we take forward the Green Paper consultation.* (HoC, 1999: para. 8)

The challenge to schools which stretches headteachers and their SMT are the decisions, which need to be taken under the Fair Funding regulations (DfEE, 1998a; 1998b). This resulted in the further delegation to schools of £1 billion for services for which governors have responsibility and which senior staff have to manage. Although it is based broadly on the previous arrangements, central LEA budgets are strictly defined to maximise delegation to schools with the strategic role limited to statutory functions and the LEA's Education Action Plan. All other central LEA services such as building repairs and maintenance, school meals, central support/ancillary services, staff costs, advisory/inspection (not related to Education Action Plans), insurance, library/museums (not primary schools), have to be delegated. Along with the publication of LEA budget plans/out-turns, league tables and inspections this has the potential effect of reducing the influence of the LEA and giving all schools the option of the advantages of full control over site-level resources that the former GM schools enjoyed.

One of the hypotheses underlying this research is that the nature of the bursar's role will change and develop as more schools begin to enjoy the level of autonomy previously exclusive to independent and GM schools. Under such a funding regime the importance of a business manager at school level cannot be overestimated. The next section will examine the changing roles of those with whom the bursar has the closest relationships in site-level resource management.

Headteachers, senior management teams, governors and support staff

Heads, their senior management teams (SMTs) and governing bodies are having to think in commercial terms. They are increasingly engaging in negotiations with industrial and commercial organisations in order to expand their resources. They are renting their buildings and charging for services. They are seeking sponsorship from industry and local businesses for both capital expenditure and to meet running costs. (Evetts, 1996: 124)

The emergence of self-managing schools increased the business and commercial imperative as Evett's views underline. It may be significant, however, that even as late as 1996, the bursar did not merit a separate mention in Evett's list of those responsible in schools for participating in leading these developments. There was, however, the scope for the emergence and potential evolution of the bursars' roles from financial and administration responsibilities to resource management in the widest sense, including the seeking out and acquisition of additional (often non-public) funds (Swanson and King, 1997, ch. 7). That evolution could not operate in isolation but depended on how other roles in schools were developing concurrently. These form the subject of this part of the chapter.

Headteachers and senior management teams

In 2000, the knowledge industry was estimated to involve over 60 per cent of the population. In the circumstances, those with the keys to knowledge, such as headteachers and their senior teams, were potentially influential and powerful. Headteachers and their SMTs are highly qualified knowledge workers, with at least one if not two degrees, specialist teaching qualifications and salaries usually far in excess of those of bursars. In 1997–9, the government appeared to recognise the importance of school leaders by increasing headteachers' salaries and announcing the establishment of an élite headteachers' leadership college and a national training scheme for those in SMTs aspiring to headship.

At the same time as headteachers and their SMTs became responsible for management of the school business they also acquired 1980s' expectations that they would become visionary leaders (Peters and Waterman, 1982; Mortimore *et al.*, 1988) and 1990s' expectations that this would develop schools into learning organisations, managing change in times of chaos and ambiguity (Fullan, 1993), facilitating an atmosphere of 'reflection, open dialogue [and] mutual respect for ideas' (MacBeath *et al.*, 1998: 28). This respect for ideas is not just of those from within the school but from an extensive range of increasingly demanding external stakeholders whose views may be sought and incorporated into school policy. Meanwhile, headteachers and senior staff had to adapt to a technologically literate society and also ensure that their schools, their staff and students also did so. More recent imperatives presided over by headteachers included raising the quality of their schools and the results of their pupils, both of which were publicly reported in national league tables.

In all of these enormously exciting and demanding roles, the headteacher appeared to be pre-eminent and absolutely essential as evidenced in the government's response to the Ninth Report from the Education and Employment Committee of the House of Commons on the role of headteachers, which stated that:

> the impact of a talented and effective head is marked ... [our] central theme is strengthening leadership in schools ... the contribution of the headteacher is pivotal. (HoC, 1999: paras 1 and 3)

If, as stated above, the headteacher's role is central to effective school development, it is interesting to note that as long ago as 1973, it was regarded as 'a matter for concern that there are still far too many headteachers who carry too great a responsibility for their school's success on their own shoulders'. (Hughes, 1973: 179) This consideration was voiced before the deluge of responsibilities arising from the trends discussed at the beginning of the chapter and as a consequence is even more appropriate at the beginning of the twenty-first century. Indeed, it has been noted above that the emphasis, although still acknowledging the headteacher as crucial, has moved from a single omniscient to a team approach to school leadership, partly prompted by the huge increase in responsibilities that site based management brings.

We thus see, at the turn of the century, a senior school management team having three main constituents – the headteacher, deputy/assistant heads and the bursar, as leader of the support staff (*see* Figure 1.1).

Governors

By 2000, education professionals in schools in many Commonwealth and European countries were directly advised by volunteer boards of governors consisting of parents, teachers, members of the immediate community of the school, students, support staff, business people and political representatives. In England and Wales, the governing bodies attached to each school included all of these except students and support staff (after 1998, it became possible to elect a representative from among the support staff). Since 1986, central government had increased governors' powers to cover almost full responsibility for all aspects of school life including strategic planning, the budget, headteacher and teacher appointments and dismissals, setting staff salaries and numbers, accountability to parents, pupil exclusions and standards of pupil achievements. Thus, each school had a volunteer, largely untrained (Thody,

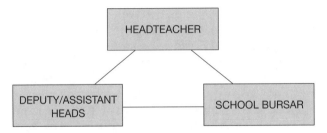

Figure 1.1 The senior management team

1998), non-educational specialist body 'technically' in a position of leadership over both teaching and learning, and over the business of running it, as well as fulfilling some of the tasks previously undertaken by central, regional or local authorities, just as the bursars were doing. The governing body legally shared the responsibilities of school leadership with headteachers (DfEE, 1996) but the division of labour was not clear and was largely dependent upon the personalities and managerial skills of headteachers and governors. By 2000, the education professionals appeared largely to dominate the relationship (Earley and Creese, 1998; Thody, 1999).

State school bursars were often the legal clerks to their governing bodies, a position that required them to prepare agendas and reports, write letters on behalf of the governing body and provide advice as requested. In theory, this put them in the possibly difficult position of being 'servant' to two masters, the headteacher and the governors, with the governors being the head-teacher's employers. Where they were not the clerks, the usual format of a bursar's job description might include such phraseology as: 'The bursar is responsible to, and working to instructions from, the headteacher and through him, the governing body' (Roman Catholic secondary school, 1998). This made the line of command clear until one realises that the same bursar also had a duty to advise the governors as required on such matters as investment and financial policy and the development of a business plan, both major areas of the headteacher's responsibilities. Suppose the views of governors and head-teacher conflicted? Where then would the bursar be positioned?

In the independent sector, the relationship between bursars and governors was clearer. Governors were more akin to a company board of directors and the bursar to a company secretary, but even in these circumstances the situa-tion could be complex (Partington *et al.*, 1998). The bursar would be adviser to the headteacher on a day-to-day basis and to the governors for the longer-term strategies. It was, however, with the headteacher that a bursar would meet most frequently and with whom, therefore, the personal contact was likely to be stronger. A significantly higher percentage of business people would be on the governing bodies of independent schools thus making a close interest in, and knowledge of, the bursar's work likely.

Similarities in business backgrounds between governors and bursars might make them likely to inter-relate well in independent schools and in state schools where the numbers of business governors were encouraged to grow after 1998. Likewise, governors and bursars might ally through feeling similarly disadvantaged when interacting with education professionals since few governors or bursars are able to match the teaching expertise of the headteacher and teaching staff. A unity of governors and the bursar might therefore be feasible and might operate to lessen the dominance of governing bodies by headteachers. There was no evidence that this had happened by 2000 so these comments can be only speculative.

Support staff

One of the issues in the relationships between bursars and headteachers, governors and the SMT, arose from the position of bursars in connection with the other support staff. Her Majesty's Inspectorate (HMI), in 1992, pointed out that the introduction of the National Curriculum 'focused attention on the potential of deploying more, and better trained, paid non-teaching staff in schools to support the work of the teacher' (HMI, 1992: vii). The work of teachers would be severely hampered, concluded their report, without secretaries, clerical assistants and bursars who undertook a mass of valuable, but time-consuming, administration. For those roles, it was no longer sufficient to regard them as part time with long school holidays (Stevens, 1992).

The enhancement of the significance of support staff was accompanied by a growth in their numbers. The Secondary Heads' Association (SHA) reported in 1991 that 78 per cent of all schools had increased the numbers of non-teaching staff or were planning to do so and almost the same percentage had increased the hours of work for support staff. A 1992 survey of 650 schools found that an LEA 11–18 school would be expected to have one clerk for 233 pupils and one technician for 197 pupils (Warrington, 1992). Grant maintained schools had more. Salaries had risen, or rises were in train, in 82 per cent of schools (Emerson and Goddard, 1993: 41). In a 15-school survey reported in 1996, an average of 62 per cent of staff in special schools were not teachers (range, 56–70 per cent), 57 per cent in primary schools (range, 36–77 per cent) and 33 per cent in secondary schools (range, 22–57 per cent) (Thomas and Martin, 1996).

With this significant increase in support staff, their management and leadership became more important to schools. Some support staff would see themselves, and their status, as being associated with line management by education professionals (e.g. classroom assistants, laboratory technicians, librarians); others seemed more immediately to be under the direction of a business professional (office staff, receptionists, cleaners, grounds maintenance). To manage both jointly might offend some and could create a large personnel division (even in a primary school); to manage them separately could emphasise the centrality of the core providers of teaching and learning. There was 'a strong case for drawing the support staff together under a single structure', argued Emerson and Goddard (1993: 50). Such a singular structure lent itself to leadership by a bursar, recommended as a means of reducing headteachers' workloads and of ensuring that support staff issues were properly represented and understood (Markham, 1990). How the professionalisation of bursarship responded to these expectations forms the subject of the next part of this chapter.

Professionalisation

When state schools identified the need for a manager of resources in the form of the bursar during the mid to late 1980s there was no established career route for them. The roles, competencies, skills and levels of operation required were also not well defined. The best known model was that of the bursar in independent schools or the company secretary in the private sector but neither of these seemed appropriate for adoption by state schools. As a consequence, each school identified its own bursarial needs and developed job descriptions accordingly. Most bursars were initially appointed to fill the role of the school's financial expert, but others were essentially office managers or marketing experts who were expected to generate increased income for the school. In the larger schools, some bursars were appointed to manage the finance, premises and administration officers, and became members of the SMT and advisers to the governing body. In these cases the bursar developed a role more akin to bursars in independent schools.

As the bursar's post was new to state schools, early appointees came from a variety of career backgrounds:

- school secretaries;
- ex-LEA employees;
- employees from commerce and industry such as secretaries, accountants, general managers or consultants;
- retiring forces' personnel for example regimental sergeant major, education officer or station commander.

Each type of appointment brought different ranges of expertise with them. School secretaries and ex-LEA employees had some understanding of education at site or local government level and, like commerce and industry employees, had functional skills in areas of bursarial responsibility such as finance or personnel. School secretaries, ex-LEA employees and some commerce/industry employees had previously operated as clerical administrators. Ex-forces' personnel had developed leadership skills and some, in common with certain commerce/industry employees, also had management training. Whatever their previous career, site based management meant all new bursars had to develop into the role alongside the headteacher. This variation in career origins, expertise and levels of operation meant that bursars' qualifications ranged from basic school leaving certificates such as Ordinary Level General Certificate of Education (O-levels) or General Certificates of Secondary Education (GCSEs) to postgraduate degrees and encompassed accounting, secretarial, engineering and health and safety professional qualifications to name but a few.

For many new bursars, therefore, this was a second career and as the levels and scope of responsibility were not clear on appointment there were many instances of mismatching the person with the post. As the role developed, areas of responsibility grew and training was required to fill the gaps in expertise at functional and operational level. Bursars required an understanding of accounting, contract management, personnel management, site management, health and safety, marketing, ICT, current educational issues and a basic understanding of learning. Management and leadership issues also needed addressing. Training in post, however, generally either lacked coherence or was non-existent. Local Education Authorities provided functional courses in areas such as computer skills and finance and, sometimes, bursars were invited to attend the school's INSET day if training was felt to be relevant. The Grant Maintained Schools Centre did acknowledge that there was a need to debate current issues and ran an annual conference for senior teaching staff and bursars on subjects identified by focus groups. One-day courses, however, were not run specifically for bursars although they did attend those focusing on relevant issues such as financial developments in education and appraisal for support staff. In general, bursars had to gain their qualifications through management courses not targeted at school contexts.

By the end of the twentieth century the role of the bursar was still developing and there was as yet no agreement about the best terms to use for the post, the range of responsibilities, or the status of the bursar in the school. Bursars were being recruited from all walks of life and schools were beginning to ask for first degrees and management qualifications. In state schools, bursars recognised the need for professional development and established their own professional association, the National Bursars Association (NBA), alongside the Independent Schools Bursars' Association (ISBA). A framework for the skills, competencies and responsibilities of bursars was developed and the government provided research funding with which to test it (see Appendix II). Individual bursars could join the NBA or, through their school membership, gain access to the ISBA thus benefiting from these support networks. More experienced bursars could become licentiates of the NBA after passing a rigorous, masters'- level, professional assessment programme. Self-development and specialist training courses were also developed, which progressed from National Vocational Qualifications (NVQs) to masters'-level degrees and educational doctorates. So, by the end of the 1990s the groundwork for the major elements of the new profession of school bursar had been laid.

Towards a reconceptualisation of school business management

By the mid-1990s the hopes for the effectiveness of bursarship were beginning to be realised. The site-based management movement, both in the UK and in parts of countries such as Australia, New Zealand and the USA, had devolved huge responsibilities to the school site level and headteachers had to develop strategies to cope with this increasing load. This led to the appointment of increasing numbers of administrative, technical and teaching support staff and, in turn, to the appointment of a senior manager to lead this team of para-professionals – the bursar. Bursarship, like other emerging professions, faced rising expectations (Foreman, 1997: 203) but the 'down-side' of the continued reliance on the bursar to carry the administration load could be overworked bursars (Mortimore *et al.*, 1995: 53–5), hence the establishment of the National Bursars Association, the national standards and the licentiate scheme.

The scene was thus set for the state school bursar of the twenty-first century to develop a role that could range from that of administrator/finance officer through to school business manager. In the former case the bursar would have very little senior management influence but specific expertise in respect of resource management in schools, however, the school business manager would, by contrast, fully understand the learning environment and know how best to resource it effectively and economically. Such a person would be capable of acting in a top management capacity and, if necessary, substituting for the headteacher (Whitehead, M., 1997).

From the context of site-based management outlined in this introductory chapter, we identify four models which represent the range of likely bursarship responses in schools to the issues of the management and leadership of administration and support service functions in the 1990s and beyond the year 2000.

1 *Administration manager*: the bursar as outside the SMT, seen as an administrator servicing the needs of teaching and management staff on request. Bursars are regarded as not having any relevant expertise in understanding the learning processes as they are not teachers, though they may be able to provide information pertinent to educational decisions.

2 *Support services manager*: the bursar as an adviser to the SMT still regarded as a subordinate to teaching staff. In such schools, there are battles being fought over the establishment of status for bursars as formal participants in the strategic direction team. The status is in process of establishment and there is incremental, minor change; the bursar is usually, but not invariably, the leader of the support staff.

3 *School business manager*: the bursar as a fully functional and accepted part of the SMT, operating as part of the strategic direction team, attending all meetings and making a valued contribution to all school management processes through offering additional perspectives. The bursarship role is in internal turbulence since the majority of its functions are at management level, though conjoint with some leadership roles. The bursar is leader of the support staff with some human resource management responsibilities for teaching staff. A key part of the role is managing outsourced contracts.

4 *Education resource manager*: a new species of educational leader, emerging from a background previously little expected to operate successfully in school senior posts. The bursarship role is an integral part of the SMT, with a post equivalent to, or higher than, that of a deputy head. The bursar has responsibility for all human resource management as well as all functions that affect the provision of a high-quality learning environment.

The models above largely concern the structure of bursarship and its relationship with other managers and leaders in the school. Underpinning them all is the role of the bursarship in the success of teaching and learning in the school. We have used the term 'business manager' in the title for this book. Given the usual connotations of the word, business may seem somehow separate from education, that part of the work concerned with finance and marketing for example. There is no separation intended. The proper 'business' of schools is that of teaching and learning.

In Parts Two and Three of this book, we offer the evidence we found for these models and for the increasing awareness of the centrality of bursars' functions to the core business of teaching and learning. From your own standpoint you may wish to compare and contrast these with developments in your own school, or other schools you know, and to reflect on which might be the preferred options in your own circumstances beyond AD 2000. Finally, Part Four offers suggestions for implementing various chosen models and explores the scenarios for developing the role into the future.

Part Two

■ ■ ■

Launching Development: Analysing the Tasks

2
■ ■ ■

The Rise of the School Business Manager

Introduction

> *A few weeks ago I was a Group Captain, directing a station with 5000 people under my leadership. I was God. Now I'm just a negative – a non-teacher.*
>
> (Bursar, secondary school, London, 1996)

This bursar's view of his lack of status, made evident in his negative title, is underlined by the virtual absence of any literature on bursars. There are no major published sources solely devoted to bursarship. This book arises from what appears to be the first research project on bursars and the first collected case studies of bursars and their practice. Bursarship appears briefly in texts on support staff in school management but it is an elusive butterfly. Bursars flit briefly across a page and disappear again before one has time to appreciate the markings on the wings and the significance of the flight trajectory. This chapter summarises these brief mentions that have appeared in the literature on support staff. It aims to show the point at which bursarship was placed in the years before this book began to be prepared in 1998.

The mentions of bursarship in earlier literature may be few but all agree its importance in the effective management of educational resourcing. This chapter investigates these assessments of bursars' developments in roles, importance and relationships with other staff. Finally the progress of bursarship is noted in its suggested training. We begin by reflecting on the naming of the bursar and on a brief, historical digression.

Naming the bursar

To find a commonly accepted title could be a first stage on the road to signifying a new status for bursarship. There is, as yet, no commonly accepted title which is used consistently, either for bursarship itself or for their genus of 'non-teachers'. This latter was the designation adopted in the first studies of this group in England and Wales (Riches, 1981; 1984). Riches included bursars and secretaries and defined the non-teaching staff collectively as those administering the offices, assisting with financial management and helping to run school services. The 'non-teacher' description may have been adequate when teachers comprised the majority of staff and teachers did most managerial tasks. Is it any longer adequate when, by 1996, for example, non-teaching staff were found to comprise 51 per cent of all staff in a sample of 63 Northamptonshire primary, secondary and special schools (Raddan, 1995)?

The increasing numbers of administrative, clerical, service and technician staff make their presence immediately noticeable in schools and there is flourishing specialisation. Terms used to refer to this whole group, which contains the bursar, include associate staff, ancillary staff, non-teaching staff, clerical and technician staff *inter alia*. The major 1990s' text on support staff, Mortimore *et al.* (1995), deliberately rejects the term, 'non-teaching staff'. Instead, they adopt 'associate staff' but still define them as all those 'who are not teachers' (*ibid.*: 1). Some support staff researched by the Mortimore team resented this designation of 'associate'. They thought it implied less than full membership of, and therefore significance to, their schools. Within the support staff grouping, titles for the bursarship role recorded in Mortimore *et al.* (1995) included 'Director' (of Administration or Finance or Personnel), 'Senior Administrator', 'Office Manager', 'Deputy Head for Buildings and Resources', 'Senior Clerical Assistant', 'Finance and Administration Manager' or ' Premises Manager'. In the Mortimore study, and in all other literature, the most commonly accepted title was still that of 'bursar', as we also found among the group studied for this book. This title has, therefore, been used throughout this chapter. It does at least have historical authenticity as our next section of this chapter demonstrates.

The bursar in history

Bursars do not seem to have attracted biographers or novelists as have headteachers or teachers. Just one 'non-text book' account of bursarship has been found – a biography of Robert Somervell who, for 33 years, 1887–1920, combined the offices of bursar and master at the independent, Harrow School (Somervell, 1935). Somervell's career seemed to parallel the development that many bursars in late twentieth-century state schools have followed, as their schools have become self-managing. First, Robert Somervell's workload increased very quickly after his bursarship appointment. He began to relieve teachers of a substantial number of non-teaching duties. At the same time, his post developed from a type of accounts clerk to that of a financial manager, advising on school development and dealing with estates and contractors. It was:

> *Impossible to estimate the hours he worked. Except for an hour after dinner in the evening, one hardly ever saw him in an armchair ... At about 9 pm., every evening in term time and often in the holidays, he would go back to his desk and stay there till bed-time.* (Somervell, 1935: 87)

When he retired, the increased workload led to the separation of the bursar-ship from the teaching role with which Somervell had combined it. The modern bursarship equivalent would be the appointment of deputy bursars to run the operational accounting functions as the bursar moves to management and strategic leadership.

Robert Somervell was well placed to make this same move. His biography noted his central position since he had contacts with everybody. His colleagues were always in and out of his office, he was the paymaster of the school servants and the expert adviser to the headmaster. He was the only staff member with close contacts with the school governors (Somervell, 1935: 85). Despite the growth in the importance of the post, though, his status was not reflected in his surroundings. He did not have an office but used a desk in the corner of his home dining room. Most modern state school bursar will recognise the 'make-do' philosophy of bursar's offices!

Roles and importance of bursars

The development of state schools as autonomous businesses has brought the development of major roles for bursars as outlined in Chapter 1. Despite this, there has been little consideration of the bursarship role in studies on general school management such as that by Dean (1995). Her advice to headteachers on structuring management teams does not mention support staff at all. They are also excluded from those groups Dean regarded as important to a headteacher in the management of change (Dean, 1995: 93). The seminal source on support staff in schools, Mortimore, Mortimore and Thomas (1995) does not devote extensive, nor particular commentary to bursarship. Publications on school leadership and management from the late 1980s onwards, usually include brief, separate mentions of bursars among the support staff but the coverage of non-teaching roles in such texts is never copious (Harrison and Gill, 1992; Emerson and Goddard, 1993; Dean, 1993, 1995; Thomas and Martin, 1994, 1996; Wallace and Hall, 1994; Fidler *et al.*, 1997; Bush and Middlewood, 1997). This omission in books on primary school management could be explained in that primary schools are less likely to have bursars than are secondary schools (Markham, 1990; Harrison and Gill, 1992: 54, 94–5) but the neglect of consideration in books on secondary school management is less justifiable.

All sources agree that support staff in general, and bursars in particular, are vitally significant. This belief is belied, however, by the scarcity of text devoted to the managerial issues concerning support staff or bursars, in comparison with that devoted to those of the teaching staff. None the less, the accord among writers about support staff shows that support staff are appreciated if only because their employment might save money (Szemeremyi, 1991: 109–10; Thomas and Martin, 1994: 35). This view is unlikely to be appreciated by bursars who, like other support staff are reported to feel overworked, undervalued and underpaid (Warrington, 1992). It seems that suggestions to recognise, overtly and fully, the value of support staff have not been adopted (Reid *et al.*, 1988).

Dean (1995), for example, inadvertently demonstrates how valuable a bursar could be in primary schools. She advises headteachers to undertake tasks, such as setting up a filing system (Dean, 1995: 109). How much more of the headteacher's time could be devoted to instructional leadership if the filing establishment were left to the office management of a bursar? Teachers too need deflection from the clerical tasks which occupy many of them (Mortimore *et al.*, 1992: para 6.33). Such diversion of responsibility to a bursar is fleetingly proposed in Harrison and Gill (1992: 53–4). They list the non-curricular tasks of school management and propose four models for distributing them, one of which is a bursarship, albeit with the actual post shared among several primary schools, an idea also suggested by Knight (1993), and by Bullock and Thomas (1997). This sharing of a peripatetic bursar is reported briefly by Webb and Vulliamy (1996) but their listing of the tasks of primary headship and deputy headship demonstrates that many undertake tasks which could be done by a bursar. This involvement of the bursar in the full range of activities not directly associated with teaching is outlined in the only article located which focuses solely on bursarship and is written by a school bursar (Markham, 1990).

Bursars could greatly relieve the workloads of headteachers and teachers, allowing them to concentrate on instructional matters (Harrold and Hough, 1988: 14; Markham, 1990; Bowe *et al.*, 1992: 154). Particular examples lend force to the general importance ascribed to bursarship:

> *We have the advantage of a high finance man as bursar ... he has brought us his wisdom and we have benefitted greatly.*
> (Chair of secondary school governing body, quoted in Bolam *et al.*, 1993: 94)

Writing from experience as a bursar, Markham's description of bursarship tasks (personnel, finance, premises, governors and administration) clearly shows how a role as financial director can emerge from a merely administrative role (Markham, 1990: 13). Within definitions of school administrative tasks for both primary and secondary schools can be found those commonly assumed to be appropriate to bursarship though not ascribed particularly to it. These included responsibilities for administration, managing school income and expenditure, sites and health and safety (Dean, 1993; 1995). This list also includes tasks often reserved to teachers, such as examination administration and the provision of curriculum materials, thus indicating the potential for overlap with areas previously reserved to the professional educators.

The beginnings of overlap with headteachers' or deputy heads' roles as leader of the teaching staff is foreseen by Markham (1990). He cautiously expressed this as *potential* for coping with *some* teachers' issues and for acting in an *advisory* capacity on pay and conditions of service for all staff. This contrasts with Potter and Powell's suggestions (1992: 69) that the bursar should 'run all the details ... [save the headteacher from getting] bogged down in pence or in budget tabulations and minutiae'. This operational role is also suggested by Spencer who sees the bursar as reducing 'the routine administrative load' (Spencer, 1991: 85). Knight regards this restriction of the role as too narrow. He proposes that finance, office management and purchasing functions should be extended to include all financial administration, fund raising and income generation, premises management, grounds maintenance, cleaning, heating and lighting, responsibility for furniture and equipment, office management, reprographics, purchasing advice and policy, management of all non-teaching personnel, community use of premises, catering, transport and vehicles (Knight, 1993: 49–50).

By the mid-1990s, task lists for bursars were longer, better defined and moving away from the minutiae. Most of those studied by Mortimore *et al.* (1995) could be seen as the 'technical, specialist' tasks not directly involved in the delivery of teaching. Within these there was evidence of leadership roles developing and of the possession of specialist knowledge which headteachers were unlikely to be able to, or want to, emulate. In many cases, bursarship tasks were those originally held by headteachers, if only vestigially in the early days of site-based management. Bursars' leadership roles also developed as the workload increased and assistant bursar posts were needed thus giving them their own staff 'empires' (Nathan, 1996: 234–5).

The developing profession of bursar as the leader of the support staff raised the profile of support staff in general (Mortimore *et al.*, 1995; Nathan, 1996: 220). The value of bursarship was evident from the Mortimore *et al.* studies (1995), where bursarship task lists were extensive and the benefits these conferred on teaching staff were clearly noted (*ibid.*: 53–5, 95–9, 109–14, 118–20, 121–7). While their book is concerned with support staff in general, their case studies indicate an increasingly noteworthy role for bursars and for bursars' incorporation into SMTs. These changes appeared to be recognised in the decreasing differentials between the pay of bursars and of teachers (Bush and Middlewood, 1997: 9).

The bursar's role in the SMT is less evident in Wallace and Hall's 1994 book on teamwork in SMTs since four of their six schools studied did not have a bursar in their SMT. A later Hall study (1997a), relating to staff management in general, briefly noted the involvement of both bursar and caretaker in the consultations at a school pursuing its Investors in People (IIP) award. Overall, however, the impression left from all these studies is that the status accorded to non-teaching staff in practice, including bursars, appears to be not much higher than it was at the time of the 1981 Riches study. This status hinges on the relationships between teachers and non-teachers, which is discussed next.

Relationships of bursars

Sources indicate that teachers may be less than enamoured of accepting non-teaching staff as equals in the leadership of schools (Emerson and Goddard, 1993: 54; Thomas and Martin, 1994: 92–3; Mortimore *et al.*, 1995: 69; Nathan, 1996: 219–20, 234–5). Could bursarship threaten the hegemony of the head-teacher and/or the teaching staff?

Relationships between bursars and SMTs are discussed in many of the Mortimore *et al.* (1995) case studies and arise in the conversations with secondary headteachers orchestrated by Ribbins and Marland (1994), in the SMTs discussed by Wallace and Hall (1994), and in the examples quoted in Thomas and Martin (1994), and in Nathan (1996). All indicate that schools can be classified into the styles of relationships with their bursars outlined in our model of the developing educational resource manager which opened this book (though none of the books cited suggested this model themselves). No one stage of our model is yet dominant. Despite this variation, Nathan concludes that, 'the bursar has become a pivotal figure in the daily running of the school' (Nathan, 1996: 220).

This pivotal position is recognised by Emerson and Goddard (1993: 52) as possibly destabilising school relationships. They speculate on whether or not a bursar can be recognised as a senior manager. Some schools accorded that recognition in the early 1990s when, for example, Langshurst City Technology College appointed only one deputy head – a Director of Administration and Finance (Ribbins and Marland, 1994: 27). Markham's 1990 experiences show how status as a financial director is emerging. Such status, he suggests leads to closer links between bursar and governors, further enhanced where bursars act as clerks to their governing bodies (Markham, 1990: 13). Bursars thus reach governors without having to use the headteacher as intermediary and, as clerks with legal knowledge, can act like a company secretary. The importance of the developing links between bursars and governors was confirmed by Mortimore *et al.* (1995: 35, 95, 149). Bursars' flexible time enables them to investigate new initiatives (Markham, 1990: 13) thus giving them the 'potential of becoming a main policy maker' (Hall, 1997b: 68).

The quality of relationships among support staff and between teachers and support staff is recognised as vital to maintaining a good school climate (Bolam *et al.*, 1993: 70). A positive, creative tension between headteacher and bursar is vital to make things happen (Mavor, 1993: 74). This climate is seen as particularly important in relation to a school's customers and there is recognition of the value of support staff being aware of a school's aims so that they become good ambassadors, and salespersons, for a school (Markham, 1990; Wright, 1994: 12; Dean, 1995: 24, 102). Significantly, Markham also suggests that their flexibility allows bursars to adopt a public relations role in the local community yet this is an aspect of leadership most associated with headship.

The contentious issue is that of bursars becoming involved in matters regarded as directly 'educational' and within the sphere of the professional educators. In the 1994 Wallace and Hall studies and in those of Mortimore *et al.* (1995), one finds bursars still largely confined to financial matters. In one school, a restricted role is signalled in its title – Personnel Controller – and in the restriction of the remit of that role to support staff only (Harris, 1996). There is, therefore, ambiguity in the place of bursars in strategic leadership. This is signalled by the senior administrative officer at one school who stated, 'I am not sure how I fit into this whole set up. I don't feel I make the contribution I should' (Wallace and Hall, 1994: 152).

Ambiguity over bursars' contributions is noted in other studies too:

> [*the*] *previous rigid distinctions between teaching and non-teaching staff have been replaced in many institutions by a more flexible approach. Associate staff, are assuming some of the tasks, inside and outside the classroom, previously regarded as the preserve of the teachers.* (Bush and Middlewood, 1997: ix)

In the 1994 Ribbins and Marland study, this flexibility was found to be already reality. The Director of Administration and Finance of a city technology college was noted by the headteacher for challenging 'our fixed assumptions and [putting] in ideas very different from the rest of us, which can be beneficial' (*ibid.*: 27).

The reactions of professional educators to the challenging flexibility of bursars is not always as appreciative as in the example quoted above. Support staff are seen as having different, lower status circumstances to those of teachers. Support staff have *jobs*, rather than the *careers* of their teacher colleagues. They are not generally paid on the same levels as teachers (Wallace and Hall, 1994: 54; Bush and Middlewood, 1997: 9). They are not perceived as motivated by a desire to support children's learning as are teachers (Hall, 1997a: 147). Teachers and support staff are noted as having 'almost total lack of respect … for the other's professional expertise' (Nathan, 1996: 222). This was evidenced by a deputy head who took over the financial and resources remit in the early years of financial devolution to schools. He was worried that thereby he would become seen 'as a bursar in the school and that's what I don't want' (Bowe *et al.*, 1992: 158).

Dean (1993) recommends the appointment of a bursar to manage the school office but notes that the headteacher would still have prime responsibility for it. One wonders if similar comments would be made about prime responsibility if the appointment were that of a curriculum manager or a deputy head. Of course a headteacher retains ultimate responsibility for all aspects of school life but it is scarcely necessary to state this explicitly unless, perhaps, it signals concerns about the advancement of 'non-teaching' staff. These concerns may have affected the headteacher in the Mortimore study who found it hard to 'let go' budget responsibilities to a bursar (Mortimore et al., 1995: 69). A similar reaction was reported by a headteacher who did not want a bursar because responsibility for non-teaching staff and premises meant power over a great deal of money (Ribbins and Marland, 1994: 138). In a school in which a deputy had been replaced by a bursar, other deputies objected because they found their academic and pastoral workload increased. There were tensions when teaching staff saw support staff employed as senior staff at higher pay levels instead of paying teachers to do the administrative tasks (Mortimore et al., 1992). In another school, teachers felt threatened by support staff making decisions and there was some resentment of pay levels equivalent to that of a deputy head (Mortimore et al., 1995: 110–12). Nathan cites an example of a situation in which there was conflict between the views of teachers and those of the bursar, arising largely because the bursar, it was felt, did not understand the education system. It was not suggested that teachers might not understand the financial system (Nathan, 1996: 222–5). Teachers were not happy at money being spent on appointing support staff which might previously have been used for teachers (Bullock and Thomas, 1997: 93) and were concerned about non-teachers taking roles which affected children's education (Knight, 1993: 49). Governors, too, have shown concern at bursarship becoming too influential; to avoid this, one governing body chose the term 'financial manager' rather than 'bursar' (Thomas and Martin, 1994: 25).

This conflict can be seen as symbolic of what has been portrayed as a total culture change in education from concern for values about 'learning, skills, knowledge and nurturing to a preoccupation with finance, competition, marketing and customer service' (Deem, 1996: 57). The developing role of bursars can be seen as enhancing this or it could be viewed as facilitating a return to centring on educational issues. Headteachers can be freed from managerial perspectives and given time to concentrate on educational issues because their schools have bursars (Markham, 1990: 17; Mortimore et al., 1995: 97–9). Most of the managerial tasks listed in Evetts (1996: 119, 124), for example, could appropriately be transferred to bursars, including negotiations with industrial and commercial organisations and finance management. At the same time, support staff could be seen as contributors to teaching as in the Kingshurst City Technology College reported in Ribbins and Marland (1994) or, at least, to the educational experiences of the children (Wright, 1994: 11).

The educated bursar

The notion that there should be education or training for bursarship is very recent. Riches (1981) recognised that the lack of education and training for support staff was partly the cause of their low status but there has been scant commentary on the professional development needs of support staff since then (Emerson and Goddard, 1993: 119), and little on bursar education *per se*. In-service training would improve their career prospects (Riches, 1981). The issues raised in the relationships section above, however, might explain why professional development for bursars has been considered to have been neglected. The evidence for neglect, however, is not entirely clear.

At the first level of training, i.e. induction, 1993 advice demonstrates how little recognised were the development needs of support staff. They could be more helpful if 'they are made aware of the educational intentions of the school' (Dean, 1993: 171). This seems such an undeniable truth that it is surprising that it has to be mentioned. Support staff training needs were recognised but staff development was seen as almost exclusively reserved for teachers (Dean, 1995). Stronger support for professionally educated support staff is given by Stevens (1991), and by Emerson and Goddard (1993), who recognised how poor this provision was. The development of quality assurance schemes, such as Investors in People 'reinforced the importance of staff other than academic employees and therefore the need for [their] training and improvement' (Middlewood, 1997: 176). The need appears not to have been recognised since there 'is little evidence that [the] increase in [support] staffing is being matched by an increase in training for support staff' (Raddan, 1995: 8). Support staff reported problems due to lack of training available (Mortimore *et al.*, 1992). A 1994 Understanding British Industry (UBI) report noted that training for school staff was interpreted as *not* including support staff. One special school, described in this report, spent their entire training budget on teachers thus leaving over half the staff without professional development (AZTEC, 1994).

None the less, training gains have been recorded. Teaching and non-teaching staff received the same professional development review process in 69 per cent of 63 schools surveyed in Northamptonshire in 1994–5 (Raddan, 1995: 62). Significant numbers of support staff acquired some training; 1993–4, 70 per cent of Raddan's sample attended in-house courses and 92 per cent went on external courses; by 1994–5, almost 100 per cent were attending the latter (*ibid.*: 38). Courses offered for associate staff by Northamptonshire's largest training provider between 1992 and 1996, increased by 304 per cent (Raddan, 1995). Informal education was also noted; most support staff developed an understanding of their role through working closely with, and under the guidance of, teachers (HMI, 1992). Bursars were, however, the exception to this.

Training for bursars and administrative staff has centred around what are seen as their most important functions – financial management and budgeting, computing and spreadsheet skills, time management, recruiting techniques, information management systems, computer training and clerking governing bodies. The LEAs have largely provided the training (Mortimore *et al.*, 1995: 27, 67, 150; Raddan, 1995). Bursars in Mortimore *et al.*'s 1995 study would have liked training in other functional areas, notably presentation skills, interviewing techniques and advanced accounting procedures (*ibid.*: 151). In Raddan's study (1995) bursars were taking advantage of courses for pre-Ofsted, team building, first aid, values and aims of the school and appraisal, issues relating to external audit, desktop publishing and management skills with the SMT. One 1993 study of independent schools recognised that bursars' development would need to extend to include 'the educational thinking which underlies the work he [*sic*] has in hand' (Smith, 1993: 22). Accredited courses for bursars were launched in the early 1990s; Leicester University established certificate and diploma courses for school administrators in 1993; Leeds Metropolitan University set up Postgraduate Diplomas for School Bursars; the first MBA for School Bursars was set up in 1996 by the University of Lincolnshire and Humberside.

While seeking their own training, bursars also acquired responsibility for educating their support staff (Warrington, 1992). 'Team training led by the bursar or senior administrative officer' is recommended (Raddan, 1995: 39). Bursars would also be needed to advise headteachers on how to establish training for teachers to show them how to make the most effective use of support staff (Harris, 1996).

So where are bursars now?

The elusiveness and scarcity of literature on the management of educational resourcing indicates that bursarship is still at an early stage of development. As yet there is no agreement on a common title for bursarship and although everyone agrees that bursarship is important especially with the development of self-managing schools, there is uncertainty about how this importance should be recognised in the tasks, role and status of the post. This uncertainty could be related to the potentially destabilising effect of elevating a '*non-teacher*' to senior management with commensurate salary and status to that of professional educators. Middle, and senior, managers who rose through the teaching route, feel threatened.

Like many innovations, the value of the 'technical' development of centring administrative management tasks on a bursar is not in doubt but the human development to accept the change is more problematic. Training can assist that development for both bursars and other support staff. Evidence on the extent of training, however, is unclear with some feeling that it has grown significantly and others reporting that it is still neglected.

From these beginnings, we set out to investigate what was happening to the position of bursarship in schools of the late 1990s. Our findings are in the following four chapters.

3
■ ■ ■

What Is the School Business Manager Expected to Do?

Introduction

To find out what bursars are expected to do, we analysed their job descriptions as a readily available indicator of governors' and headteachers' expectation of the whole bursarship role. From these, it was possible to determine the frequency of activities and responsibilities, skills and the position of the bursar in the hierarchy of the school. The methodology used to analyse the job descriptions is in Appendix I.

These job descriptions were certainly varied, ranging from several pages to the non-existent. The lack of a job description was usually attributed to a shortage of time but its absence could also be seen as an interesting comment on the bursars' status:

> *The only person in this school who does not have a written job description is ME!*
> (Bursar, GM secondary school, London, 1998)

The succinct did not necessarily indicate a low taskload. Six bullet points and an introductory paragraph on one sheet of A4 paper, for example, drew the comment:

> *Funny that 6 bullet points constitutes 100 hours a week!!!*
> (Bursar, GM secondary school, London)

The longest job description ran to seven sides and included a separate clerk to the governors job description and a person specification. Interestingly, two of the person specifications were identical, although emanating from schools in different areas of the country.

This chapter first discusses the responsibilities and major activities of bursars derived from the job descriptions before exploring their levels of responsibility, status and skills.

Bursars' expected roles: an overview

Figure 3.1 illustrates the six major responsibilities of bursars found in the job descriptions. The areas of responsibility referred to most often were financial, personnel and premises management as evidenced by the number of headings. The less often cited represent the more recent responsibilities of ICT, direct pupil services and marketing. Within each area of responsibility, the activities most frequently carried out by bursars are nearest to the centre of the chart and include budget setting and analysis, providing financial advice, accountancy and managing support staff. Those areas mentioned least often are at the edge of the chart. Some activities, such as health and safety, negotiating contracts and advising staff and governors occurred within more than one area of responsibility. This chart can be used to compare expectations of bursarship within your own school with those recorded here.

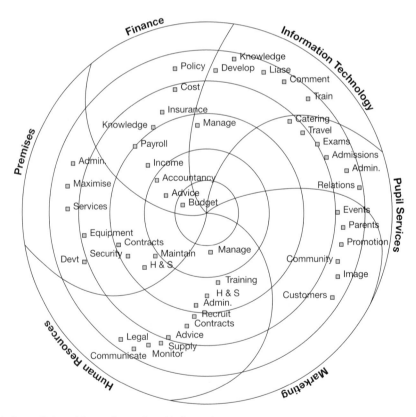

Note: Items cited most frequently are closest to the centre.

Figure 3.1 Bursars' responsibilities and activities

Finance

Financial responsibilities were included in every job description analysed and were referred to in most detail. These responsibilities included elements of money management and cost management. Almost three-quarters of the financial activities and responsibilities of bursars focused on money management and entailed planning and balancing the budget. Of the money management responsibilities, approximately three-quarters were accountancy based. Bursars were expected to perform or supervise essential accountancy duties such as preparing and maintaining school income and expenditure accounts and balance sheets. Approximately 40 per cent of bursars were responsible for such basic activities as the supervision of payroll and responsibility for insurance. Much of money management required a technician approach of operating control systems and keeping meticulous accounts as evidenced in the following job description.

> Oversee all aspects of the school accounting, bookkeeping and ordering systems and on a monthly basis reconcile all school accounting systems and complete A/7 returns using all available IT systems.
>
> (Bursar, locally maintained secondary school, London)

Budget management is a higher order activity and almost all the bursars surveyed were expected to monitor and report on the budget. Three-quarters were involved in preparing the budget but only 25 per cent were involved in managing the budget to inform the wider budgetary cycle process of consultation, decision making, monitoring and evaluation. Just 12 per cent of bursars were involved in policy-making decisions as this example from one of the job descriptions clearly indicated.

> Preparation for approval by the Governors of annual estimates of income and expenditure. Agreement of budgets with the headteacher and governors and monitoring of accounts against budgets. Preparation of regular financial reports for budget holders and on the financial state of the accounts for the Governors.
>
> (Bursar, GM secondary school, Wales)

Only 25 per cent of bursars were involved in the more important activity of cost management, which required the matching of resources to needs in the most cost-effective way. This activity requires a higher order approach of costing the operation, balancing the outcomes and looking for alternatives. Bursars were expected to keep cost analyses, ensure the effective use of resources and prepare information for capital projects. In summary,

> To manage the various resources made available with the object of providing the most effective services for the efficient management of the school.
>
> (Bursar, locally maintained secondary school, Wales)

Although bursarship is often seen as synonymous with financial responsibilities, the job descriptions generally failed to recognise bursars' contribution to management accounting. Most bursars were still expected to operate at an administrative level, keeping the books and providing information to the SMT for budget-making decisions. This level of operation was appropriate when LEAs set the budgets and allocated resources, but under GM status and latterly Fair Funding, many bursars have effectively become the principal finance officer at site level and have amassed a broad understanding and knowledge of the finances of their schools. As such they could be used more effectively at a strategic level if they were involved in the discussions of the SMT about the educational repercussions of resource allocation decisions.

Human resource responsibilities

All the bursars' job descriptions included some element of human resource management as Fig. 3.2 illustrates. The bursars' prime responsibility was for support staff, but there were also activities related to aspects of the management of teaching staff. Figure 3.2 indicates that of the 31 activities listed, all involved interaction with support staff and 65 per cent also included teaching staff.

When recruiting staff, bursars were involved in the administration of both teaching and support staff appointments and issued contracts to all staff. Perhaps surprisingly, not all bursars had responsibility for support staff. A third of bursars recruited their support staff, others only assisted in their appointment. Three-quarters of bursars managed and deployed support staff and 60 per cent were responsible for their training and development. A typical example of responsibilities purely for support staff would be:

> *Manage administrative and premises staff, including recruitment, training, supporting individuals' development and managing issues of conduct.*
>
> (Bursar, locally maintained secondary school, London)

A minority of bursars was responsible for organising daily cover for teachers and employing supply staff. Almost half the bursars maintained confidential school records. The involvement with teacher employment could be seen as an important indicator of the development of the bursarship role since this accountability can take the bursar into indirect influence of pedagogy and curriculum.

A responsibility linked to both human resource and site management, which featured in half the job descriptions was health and safety, with a further 25 per cent devising and implementing a health and safety policy in conjunction with the governing body. Most bursars held operational responsibility as health and safety officers.

> *Formulating, monitoring and implementing the School's safety policy with the requirements of the Health & Safety At Work Act and other legislation. Acting as School's Health & Safety Officer.*
>
> (Bursar, GM secondary school, Wales)

	Job description item	% of Job descriptions citing this item	
		Teaching staff	Support staff
1	Manage staff	0	75
2	Responsibility for training and development of staff	0	60
3	Responsibility for health and safety of staff	50	50
4	Maintain confidential staff records	45	45
5	Responsibility for administration of staff appointments	41	33
6	Recruit and select staff	0	33
7	Responsibility for issue of contracts for staff	25	29
8	Devise and implement health and safety policy with governing body	25	25
9	Assist in recruitment and selection of staff	0	20
10	Responsibility for appraisal of staff	0	20
11	Advise governors on personnel matters and legislation	20	20
12	Oversee staff leave and cover	17	20
13	Make appropriate returns	17	17
14	Responsibility for welfare and working conditions of staff	8	12
15	Monitor employment terms, services and duties of staff	0	12
16	Advise senior management team on personnel matters and legislation	12	12
17	Control and monitor service level agreements	0	8
18	Maintain sound employee relations	8	8
19	Maintain staff absence records	8	8
20	Responsibility for personnel matters	8	8
21	Answer staff questions on pay and conditions	8	8
22	Act as adviser and administrator on health and safety issues	8	8
23	Implement personnel regulations	4	4
24	Ensure supervision of staff through faculty heads	0	4
25	Provide efficient staff service	0	4
26	Evaluate and implement the administrative faculty policy	0	4
27	Develop work instructions for repetitive tasks	0	4
28	Represent governors at industrial tribunals	4	4
29	Manage communications with staff	4	4
30	Maintain good relations with all staff	4	4
31	Advise headteacher on personnel matters and legislation	4	4

n job descriptions = 23

Figure 3.2 Human resource responsibilities of bursars

Within the job descriptions studied in this research, bursars' responsibilities ranged across all the different levels of administration officer, support services manager and school business manager. Thus there were instances of record keeping and payroll activities as well as active involvement in recruitment and selection processes. There were also higher-level activities such as the development of a health and safety or support staff development policy.

Site and premises

Responsibilities for site management featured in 80 per cent of job descriptions. This site management involved:

- the maintenance of buildings;
- the maintenance of the site;
- implementing the school's health and safety policy;
- supervision of contracts.

Other areas linked with site management included responsibility for the maintenance and replacement of furniture and equipment. Fifteen per cent of bursars maintained school services and properties records. Security of the site became a major issue in the 1990s and featured in approximately half the job descriptions. An example of the requirements for site management would be:

> *Responsibility, through the caretaker, for the overall security, cleanliness and tidiness of the buildings and premises. Invite tenders for insurance, maintenance and services to ensure contractors perform duties according to contract and to review contracts and recommend termination/renewal to the Headteacher and Governors as required.* (Bursar, GM secondary school, South-west)

There was also a major role in the management of capital projects since half the schools from which the data was gathered were then GM schools and thus able to develop their sites with the extra finance available. The following range of activities in relation to capital work would be typical.

> *To arrange building development projects, inviting tenders for maintenance and services. To ensure that contractors perform duties according to the contract. To renew contracts and recommend termination or renewal to the Headteacher.* (Bursar, locally maintained secondary school, South-west)

Bursars were charged with 'ensuring the full utilisation of premises' in 12.5 per cent of job descriptions, examples included timetabling rooms and promoting the use of the school to outside agencies in order to obtain lettings income. Teaching staff were usually responsible for timetabling so it was interesting to find that some schools had transferred it to bursars.

Within the area of site management the role of the bursar was to provide pupils and staff with a safe, clean and well-maintained learning environment. This responsibility might conflict with the imperative of increasing income from lettings, for example the safety of pupils could be compromised and wear and tear on the site increased. The management of sites and premises, however, is an area where bursars can take the initiative in providing an optimum service for the school. As financial and premises managers they are well placed to assess the costs and benefits of contracting out services such as cleaning and grounds maintenance as opposed to appointing a dedicated team led by a site manager who will maintain, clean and provide security for the site and buildings.

Information and communications technology

Bursars were expected to promote and develop the use of computers for administration but only half of the job descriptions analysed expected them to manage the administrative computer system. This area of responsibility required bursars to train staff, apply data protection legislation and liase with computer technicians within and outside the school.

> *Responsibility for the systems and general management of the school's administrative computer network, the implementation of Word Processing and the computerisation of the administration accounting and record system. Acting as Computer System Manager.* (Bursar, GM secondary school, London)

In most schools the use and development of ICT was taken forward on two fronts. The administrative staff were the first to use computers regularly for generating and retrieving information and they are usually more comfortable using ICT for this purpose than many teachers. In contrast, the use of ICT for teaching purposes has a tradition of gifted amateurs in curriculum areas such as business studies, computer studies, music, art and design technology. The issue at the turn of the century has been to bring these two strands together through the effective utilisation of the power of networked computers supplied by central servers used both by support staff and teachers. The maintenance and development of such computer systems involve aspects of line management that need to be considered and resolved by senior managers in schools.

Pupils

All the responsibilities previously listed ensure that resources are provided and maintained for the effective education of pupils. Site and human resource management, mentioned above, are clearly a major but indirect part of this. General clerking such as providing photocopying of teaching materials was also under the supervisory remit of bursars. There was however, some direct service provision and 25 per cent of job descriptions required bursars to supervise catering and pupils' travel arrangements. Very few of the job descriptions included administration of admissions, examinations and pupil records, jobs more usually assigned to teachers.

*Responsible for the establishment and maintenance of student records and corres-
pondence files. Assistance with arrangements for examinations including collection
of examination fees where appropriate examination entries, security of examination
papers and notification of results. Responsible for arrangements for student enrol-
ments.* (Bursar, locally maintained secondary school, Midlands)

Direct responsibility for student learning was an aspect of four of the job
descriptions. In these bursars were asked to foster and maintain good relations with pupils and mentor students. The circumstances of this mentoring
were not elaborated.

The core business of the school is teaching and learning. Bursars therefore provide a service in resourcing pupils' education. Traditionally, most of their
responsibilities relate to the out-of-classroom support with teachers providing
many of the duties linked directly to learning, such as administration of examinations and the supply of teaching materials. Now, however, the design and
production of learning resources and the management of pupils assessment
information has become an important responsibility of the office team.
Catering, however, is an example of a service which impacts indirectly on the
pupils and staff of the school as a good quality and responsive operation can
increase the numbers who take meals and thus contribute to the development
of community spirit within the school. Although very few job descriptions
mention direct interaction between pupils and bursars, the development of
good relations with pupils should be an important aspect for providing a
responsive support service.

Marketing

In the light of the business and commercial imperatives that schools faced in
the late 1990s, it was not surprising to find that bursars were involved in marketing the school in the widest sense. Marketing is about providing a service
that meets customer requirements better than the competition and communicating the ethos, values and mission within and outside the organisation. An
analysis of the job descriptions in Fig. 3.3 indicates that bursars are mainly
involved in promoting the school, but they are also charged with improving
relations with the school's stakeholders.

It was not surprising that 75 per cent of bursars' job descriptions charged them
with income generation through lettings or other means (*see* above section on site
and premises). On the other hand 40 per cent of job descriptions address marketing of the school to external interest groups. These groups included parents, the
community, businesses and other schools, particularly through the maintenance
and development of good relationships, but also through publicity related to the
media and published material such as the school calendar of events.

It was surprising to note how few job descriptions either included marketing
or had a limited range of marketing functions mentioned. This may be because

marketing is considered the responsibility of deputy heads and headteachers who are regarded as the people at the interface with the community. However, bursars lead those support staff who maintain the site and who are often the first to communicate with callers to the school. Additionally, support staff often live in the neighbourhood and are frequently related to pupils in the school, and are thus powerful opinion formers in the school's immediate community. Bursars are therefore directly responsible for those staff who influence the first impressions of visitors and this is an area of accountability that should be addressed directly in their job descriptions.

Job description item	No. of citations
Events	
Arrange college functions	4
Publication of the school calendar of events	2
Parents	
Maintain good relations with parents	3
Close liaison with PTA	1
Marketing	
Contribute to marketing and promotion of the school to other educational establishments	2
Promote the college's facilities	2
Arrange promotional visits to college	1
Prepare printing and distribution of prospectuses and other promotional material	1
Administer publicity of school	1
Maintain good relations with press/media	1
Community	
Maintain good relations with the local community	2
Manage good relations with local businesses	1
Organise and report on community steering groups meetings	1
Assist headteacher in formation of community management group	1
Implement ideas generated by community management group	1
Oversee commercial activities with business partners and joint venture community	1
Image	
Help create and promote an image of the school consistent with its aims	2
Represent the college at functions	1
Customers	
Manage customer services ensuring enhanced standards of delivery	1
Create and maintain a complaints procedure and policy	1
n bursars with marketing responsibilities = 9	

Figure 3.3 Marketing responsibilities of bursars

Levels of responsibility

From the accountabilities described above, we could see different levels of responsibilities emerging. Assessing what these levels were involved some interesting linguistic analysis. The verbs in the job descriptions were analysed to discover how they were used to describe what bursars were expected to do and how they should work. In addition the levels of responsibility for each task were defined by assigning the verbs to administrative, management and leadership levels, combining ideas from Sawatzki (1997), West-Burnham (1997), the Teacher Training Agency (1998) and Surrey County Council (Curriculum and Management Consultancy, undated). Administration was defined as routine work such as organising and filing, management includes decision making and supervision of others while leadership is characterised by strategic thinking and policy formulation. It should be noted that in the UK, administration is regarded as the operational level and management as the tactical level. Outside the UK, the meanings of the verbs are reversed and administration is regarded as the higher order activity. Leadership is generally accepted as the strategic level. We thus had a hierarchy of verbs ranging through operational, tactical and strategic management. The outcome of this analysis is in Fig. 3.4.

Administration	Management		Leadership
Operational/clerical	*Tactical/decision making/supervision*		*Strategy/policy*
Administer	Advise	Handle	Create
Assist	Allocate	Inform	Develop
Circulate	Approve	Liase	Devise
Clerk	Arrange	Manage	Encourage
Comply	Authorise	Monitor	Evaluate
Distribute	Check	Organise	Initiate
Implement	Contribute	Present	Lead
Issue	Convene	Promote	Negotiate
Keep	Co-ordinate	Report	Plan
Order	Control	Responsibility	
Maintain	Decide	Supervise	
Prepare	Ensure	Support	
Provide			

Figure 3.4 Levels of responsibility of bursars

An analysis of the administration, management, and leadership activities of bursars indicates that they were working at the three levels across all areas of responsibility. The number of verbs found in the job descriptions in each category indicated that leadership is, as yet, still the minority activity but that administration already occupied considerably less time for bursars than management. This indicated a movement in the role from tasks that are standardised with rules that must be followed and no need for individual initiative (administration), through to areas in which bursars are expected to be proactive and creative (leadership).

Examples of administration included:

- provide necessary documentation and assistance to the school's auditors;
- assist with administrative arrangements in connection with the appointment of teaching staff;
- keep and maintain all school accounts and prepare income and expenditure accounts and balance sheets;
- issue cycle permits.

The largest number of activities fell into the management category. They are exemplified as follows:

- monitor employment terms;
- supervise the site manager and allocate areas of responsibility;
- liase with designated governors' committees;
- manage and promote a range of personnel services to customers ensuring service delivery standards;
- responsibility for health and safety procedures.

Figure 3.4 indicated that a major managerial activity was to 'advise'. Approximately 80 per cent of bursars were expected to provide specialist advice to governors, the headteacher and staff particularly within the areas of finance and personnel. The majority of job descriptions also explicitly stated that bursars should understand and provide advice and information on an astonishingly wide variety of issues.

> *The Bursar needs a working knowledge of all documents, articles and instruments affecting the School and its charitable status, including relevant contents of Education Acts and statutory instruments. The Bursar should be familiar with current legislation as it affects health, welfare and safety of all who enter the School, current good accountancy practice as it relates to the School, Employment Protection, Equal Pay, Sex, Age and Race Discrimination etc. and should always seek professional advice on these matters to protect the Governors' interests.*
>
> (Bursar, GM secondary school, Home Counties)

Almost half of the job descriptions analysed required bursars to be conversant with government regulations. A small proportion also required an understanding of taxation, employment and health and safety laws, local authority financial delegation, the education system and building construction and maintenance. Other areas of expertise included marketing, information technology, administration and management.

These administrative and managerial activities contrasted with leadership responsibilities such as:

- evaluate the administration faculty policy;
- create and implement a school journey's policy;
- devise and develop effective management policies.

Despite the general spread of the three levels of work, approximately 12 per cent of bursars' job descriptions did not involve them in any policy-making decisions. Thus, despite bursars being responsible for crucial management information and making resource decisions within the school, as evidenced in the job description of a London bursar, many were not expected to contribute to major policy decisions.

> *Advise and work with the Premises Committee and manage staff to develop the school premises and associated building ensuring all accommodation is systematically maintained and utilised to their fullest potential.*
>
> (Bursar, locally maintained secondary school, London)

Status

Responsibility levels were assessed by analysing the status accorded to bursars in the job descriptions. Indications were that the bursar's position is unclear within the hierarchy of the school. Half of the bursars surveyed were designated members of the senior management team, with a further 25 per cent advising or attending meetings when appropriate. Only two job descriptions included line management drawings and one job description articulated that '*the post carries a crucial leadership role in the school*'(Bursar, GM secondary school, London). The headteacher was designated as responsible for line managing bursars in half the job descriptions. Bursars themselves were accountable for a range of support staff including secretaries, caretakers, finance staff, administration staff, technicians, cleaners and lunchtime supervisors.

A quarter of bursars were also expected to be members of appropriate governing body subcommittees and half were responsible for providing advice and information when required. The link with the governing body was reinforced by 55 per cent of bursars acting as, or assisting the clerk to governors, and one bursar was expected to represent the governing body at appeals procedures.

Personal skills and qualities

The skills and qualities required of bursars were reflected in the diversity of their responsibilities. Apart from requiring expertise in, and knowledge of financial, site and human resource management (HRM), an understanding of information technology and marketing was also required and as they work in schools, they were required to have an understanding of the educational system and a commitment to education. Administration, management and leadership skills were highlighted and management training was considered to be particularly important. In keeping with administrative requirements and the advisory role bursars' skills also included systems management and an ability to present information and compile statistics. Two job descriptions expected bursars to demonstrate 'empathy with teachers'.

Personal skills and qualities can be seen in Fig. 3.5. In the light of the variety of bursarial responsibilities and relationships, strong organisational and inter-personal skills were a principal requirement and personal attributes such as flexibility, energy and a sense of humour were seen as valuable. One school expected the bursar to emerge almost as the 'hero-innovator' of Weberian leadership studies.

> *Well presented/public-speaking experience/charisma on order to be able to adequately represent the School to external bodies and organisations. Determined (but sensitive to the needs of others) and hardworking. Some extra-curricular interest would be preferred, ideally in the field of sport or music which could relate to the life of the School.* (Bursar, independent secondary school, South-east)

Job description Item	No. of citations
High level of personal organisation and efficiency	3
Excellent interpersonal skills	3
Articulate	3
Sense of humour	2
Ability to remain calm	2
Hard working	2
Effective communication	1
Flexible	1
Energy	1
Willingness to share in school community life	1
Commitment to ethos of institution	1
n bursars with personal attributes listed = 7	

Figure 3.5 Bursars' personal skills and qualities

Reviewing expectations

An analysis of the job descriptions indicated that bursars' roles and responsibilities were diverse and included the management or administration of all resources in schools as well as opportunities for leadership. They had direct and major responsibilities for financial, human resource and site management as well as providing marketing, ICT and pupil services. Some activities, such as contract negotiation, health and safety, and the provision of information, were required within more than one of these responsibility areas. They were also responsible for promoting the school to parents, businesses and the local community. There were areas where bursars were assuming responsibilities previously held by teachers, these included providing daily cover for teachers and supply staff, timetabling and administering pupil records, admissions and examinations.

Bursars were required to provide advice and information to staff, pupils and governors. They were expected to have knowledge of a wide variety of legal areas including taxation, government regulations, employment and health and safety. They also had to have an understanding of education systems, building construction and maintenance, marketing, information technology, administration and management. The skills and qualities expected of bursars reflected the diversity of their role and included such elements as interpersonal and organisational ability, flexibility, a sense of humour and commitment to education.

Relationships with other stakeholders in schools were complex and the line management of bursars was often unclear. Most bursars were expected to report to the headteacher, senior management team and governors but line management was explicit in only 50 per cent of the job descriptions. An indication of their leadership status was their inclusion in the senior management team and governing body committees. Our analysis of bursars' job descriptions showed that their responsibilities were mainly at a managerial level. There were also many administrative tasks, which they were expected to complete involving office services for teaching staff and pupils in the school. However, this was in marked contrast to their role as managers and leaders of support staff who they were responsible for appointing, deploying, training and developing.

This chapter has reviewed the formal expectations of bursars in our sample. The next chapter investigates how bursars operate in practice on a day-to-day level in discharging their duties.

4
■ ■ ■
What Do School Business Managers Actually Do?

Introduction

This chapter reports on observations of six bursars at work. Their daily life was recorded and analysed and this formed a basis for comparison with the job expectations of Chapter 3. The observations were carried out shortly before and after Easter 1998 when a non-participant observer spent a day with each of six bursars from different phases and types of schools. The overwhelming impression was of the bursar as a 'fixer' in a turbulent sea of problems and issues from which the bursar emerged as a well-known, respected and approachable colleague with considerable technical and managerial expertise.

Those bursars observed had the titles of Bursar (3), Administrator (2) and Registrar (1). They occupied varying positions in the management structure of their schools and had different lengths of experience in their posts. It is not claimed that this sample was typical of all bursars, or that six days told us everything we needed to know about what bursars did, but the range of experience represented that likely to be found in the profession. There had been no other observations of bursars using this technique and this enabled us to add the observer's view of bursars to those of the bursars themselves, their headteachers and governors as outlined in other chapters. Details of the methodology of the observations can be found in Appendix I.

The chapter draws a picture of the bursar's working environment, describes the structure of the six bursars' days, analyses what they do, who they interact with and their overall level of operation. From these observations a composite day in the life of a bursar in the late 1990s is created and then a forecast of what the post might look like in the twenty-first century is made. When this research was undertaken, the term for the school business manager was commonly 'bursar'. However, elements of the emerging school business manager and educational resource manager roles were observed in practice and these have been used to develop the future scenarios.

Bursars' offices

Offices convey messages of status, role, efficiency, personality and welcome (Lawton and Scane, 1991; Thody, 1997).

1   *Status*: There was a wide variety of work-spaces ranging from a desk in the corner of the school secretary's office to a purpose built manager's office. In all cases efforts had been made recently to upgrade the bursar's accommodation to reflect their changing status, particularly in terms of the office furniture, though there was still evidence of 'make do and mend' in finding office space which was both suitably situated and of an appropriate quality. In most cases the bursar's accommodation was close to the headteacher and the administrative office and/or near to the school entrance, thus symbolising the bursar's place in the school. The office was not always quite so prominently marked, nor as obvious to locate as the headteacher's office, but was usually less hidden away than the deputy heads' offices. Furniture varied, the office could be either specially refurbished or furnished with a motley assortment ranging from 'antique' fitments to the 'best of the rest' left over from refurbishment elsewhere. In one school, the furnishings were all antique school headteacher's style conveying an impression of the longevity of the school, while the headteacher had been recently equipped with more modern versions of the same. The general status message conveyed was that of a developing importance that was not clearly recognised.

2   *Role*: There were clearer messages about the administration management role of the bursars. The offices contained a range of ICT equipment such as computers and printers, filing cupboards, security cameras and telecommunications that were prominently placed for ease of use. The desks contained piles of paperwork. The bulk of the office equipment, however, was situated in the administration office, which was always busy with teachers coming in and out to ask questions and use the photocopier. The bursars' offices contained only the equipment that was the symbol of their trade that enabled them to work independently of the administration office when necessary.

3   *Efficiency*: Even in the most unpromising positions and with the least equipment, all the offices conveyed the message of an efficient organisation with a highly active role. Information was neatly stored and prepared for action. All surfaces were well covered with paper or desk accoutrements such as 'in and out' trays but it was under control. Given that most of the offices

were not custom built nor equipped, the bursars all displayed considerable ingenuity in arranging what there was to enable work flow. One bursar's desk, for example, was situated so that the school entrance security camera monitor can be seen in a mirror since there was no other way the room could be arranged to make it directly visible.

4   *Personality*: There were few pictures and ornaments as these rooms were primarily for efficiency and anyway lacked space. What space there was, needed to be devoted to essential notices and site maps. The noticeboards were usually up to date and tidily displayed. The artefacts chosen centred on family photographs, hobby interests or travel scenes. They lacked the *sine qua non* of headteachers' offices, examples of pupils' artwork. A visitor could easily have guessed that this was not the office of one primarily concerned with curriculum and pupils.

5   *Welcome*: Bursars came into contact with a range of the school's stakeholders during the day and everyone was warmly welcomed. Where the size of the room made it possible, the bursars' desks and chairs were situated so that bursars could emerge easily from behind the desk to greet visitors, and the desk did not form a barrier. Lack of space precluded there being what every self-respecting executive office must have: a coffee table and easy chairs in addition to the desk.

The bursar's day

There were differences in the detail among the six bursars' days but there were also similarities. Figure 4.1 shows the start/finish times of the bursars, the length of the day worked, the time spent working alone and at lunch, and the total number of activities and average time spent on each. Generally the bursar started before the teaching staff arrived and finished an hour or so after the end of the teaching day.

Bursar	1	2	3	4	5	6
Start time	8.00	8.00	8.20	9.00	8.00	8.10
Finish time	16.00	18.20	16.45	21.00	16.40	17.07
Time at work	8h	10h20	9h	12h	8h40	9h
Time alone	1h25	2h37	3h29	1h35	53m	3h3
% of the day spent alone	18%	25%	39%	13%	10%	34%
Time at lunch	4m	22m	27m		35m	
Number of activities	141	122	88	78	73	186
Average length of activity	5m	5m	6m	8m	6m	3m
h = hours, m = minutes						

Figure 4.1 The structure of the bursar's working day

The start time of bursars was in most cases around 0800 though the finish time varied between 1600 and 2100. The average length of the working day for the six bursars was nine and a half hours, though one bursar worked 12 hours, staying at school to run a trial financial year close down. All bursars spent a significant proportion of their day working alone and tended to take their breaks and lunch as a part of the working day.

The total number of activities done by each bursar was recorded, each activity being 'an identifiable single event with an observable beginning and ending' (Duignan, 1980: 10). The average number of activities for all bursars was 115, though this arose from recording every change of activity and hides the fact that some activities were returned to a number of times during the day. For example, one of the bursars worked on the end of year accounts over a very busy day for a total of 34 minutes on nine separate occasions. The longest period within this was for ten minutes, the shortest three periods each lasted for only one minute.

This fragmentation of the working day into a large number of individual activities has commonly been observed in the working life of senior managers (Mintzberg, 1973; Austin, 1975; Clerkin, 1985; Coulson, 1986; Hall, Mackay and Morgan, 1986; Hickcox, 1992; Thody, 1997). The observer might perceive this fragmentation as being interruptions to the 'real work', in practice many of the activities are 'joined up' over the day into a sustained piece of work or are themselves short periods of interaction which 'keep the plates spinning' on an ongoing issue (using the analogy of senior management as a juggler spinning plates on canes). Bursars, like other senior managers, were also responsive to the needs of their other colleagues, fitting in around their arrangements where necessary.

The bursars' activities

In some contrast to the expectations of the bursars' job descriptions, the most frequent of their activities was observed to be routine clerical work (e.g. filing, drafting letters and reports). Finance and HRM claimed the next major part of their work as their job descriptions had led us to expect. Premises/estates work came next and marketing/promotion took up the smallest amount of time. There were a few instances of bursars beginning to work with pupils on aspects of curriculum and learning (particularly test/exam results and visits/trips) but this did not take sufficient time to be aggregated in Fig. 4.2 which summarises all the bursars' activities observed.

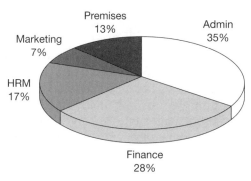

Figure 4.2 Bursars' activities

Who did bursars meet?

Bursars came into contact with a wide variety of people in the course of their days but they spent around a third of their time working alone (Fig. 4.3). In the remainder of the day observed they worked most commonly with other support staff, followed by external agencies (though this was to some extent exaggerated by audit and the end of year procedures at this time of year). The headteacher, SMT and teachers, with governors, community/business, pupils and parents were the least commonly encountered persons in the days observed.

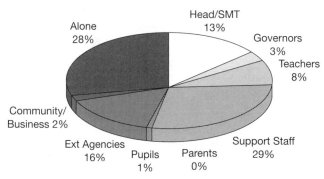

Figure 4.3 Bursars' interactions

At what level did bursars operate?

Using the definitions of administration, management and leadership developed in Chapter 3, the activities observed were categorised into three levels of work (Fig. 4.4). The job descriptions had indicated that administration might be expected to take less time than management and it is interesting that, although administration and management were by far the largest categories, opportunities for bursars to engage in leadership activities have become more common. Indeed the time spent on leadership varied from none at all to over a quarter of the day.

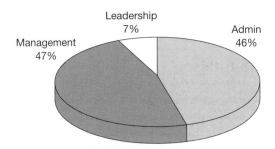

Figure 4.4 Bursars' levels of operation

Although the quantitative analysis above shows the average time spent on leadership aspects is only 7 per cent of bursars' days, there were some features in their days which point towards a more strategic and holistic approach to the role. Management and administration were often underlain by the leadership imperative of ensuring support for developments and challenges were used to steer and optimise work output relative to the priorities of the school. Examples were: liaison with the town/community councils over environmental/community systemic reform projects, working with governing body committees on curriculum as well as finance or HRM issues, organising teaching cover and job succession plans.

Bursars today and tomorrow

We used our observations of the bursars to produce a combined and condensed version of what might be expected to happen in a 'typical' day for the bursar at the beginning of the twenty-first century and an educational resource manager of the future (Fig. 4.5). It reflects the fragmentation of the working day noted above and the constant interactions with almost every client group in the school as well as external agencies. Oases of relative calm are at the beginning of the day and included, 'warming up' (Thody, 1997) activities such

Time	The bursar of 2000	The educational resource manager of tomorrow
8.00	Arrive at work, check cleaning staff, consult calendar for the day, switch on and check ICT system.	Arrive at work, check calendar for today and Internet page, meet with ICT system supervisor, office and site managers.
8.15	Staff begin to arrive, collect, sort and distribute mail, socialise with support staff, teachers, SMT.	Management by walking about, checking teaching and support staff cover and start up of teaching day.
8.30	Organise support staff duties for the day, assist teaching staff to start the teaching day (e.g. minor problems with premises, reprographics etc.), field incoming calls and queries from parents.	Site walk, checking operation of traffic management scheme, greeting pupils, parents and support staff (if wet, brief outdoor walk, then in lobby).
9.00	School in session, security system on (bursar covers this during the day to answer callers, receive deliveries), supervision of office staff on duties for the day.	Site issues: meeting with Site manager and senior premises staff to discuss implications of new build and effect on working patterns and site supervision/maintenance schedules. Staff asked to draw up scheme for supervisory cover.
9.15	Meeting with caretaker(s) over site maintenance/decoration schedule/cover for community sports club in evening. Interruptions for: invoice signing, phone calls from prospective interviewees for teaching post, pupils to be entered in the late book, LEA/FAS (Funding Agency for Schools) enquiries, stock order/supply queries.	SMT (internal) meeting planning major site improvements: budget, funding, community/ business/curriculum links (includes chair of governing body and development committee). [Refreshments brought in by leisure and tourism learning group.]
10.30	Coffee taken 'on the fly', fielding staff queries, accepting reprographics requests, dealing with pupils returning/issuing administration forms.	Continuation of meeting to 12.00. Meeting with chair of governing body to plan calendar for headteacher replacement for next academic year.
12.30	Many interactions during lunch, e.g. teachers chasing travel/INSET claims, pupils purchasing items or returning administration forms, checking canteen operation with support staff, supervising any emergency premises work.	Civic lunch (provided and served by catering staff and Leisure and Tourism learning group) for SMT, senior site staff and community/business partners. Civic tour of site (if wet in coach).
1.30	Work for the afternoon begins – external auditor arrives for preliminary meeting about year end audit. During the two-hour meeting encounters asthmatic pupils for inhalers, support staff for job-sheets or minor queries, SMT for references for upcoming staff interviews and requests to fix the ICT system.	Site Liaison Group meeting: to discuss learning needs of new business park and sports/leisure/adult education of local community (includes planning authority, business, leisure and local news media representatives).
3.30	Brief period of intense activity. Teaching staff with range of urgent queries for tomorrow, parents with requests for information or administrative returns, supervision of office staff progress before the part-time staff leave, gathering papers for SMT meeting.	Appraisal meeting with budget manager for science faculty area discussing out-turn finance and development plan/budget for next period.
4.00	SMT meeting, organising future staff appointments, reviewing term/annual calendar, update on budget tabs, discussion on promotional literature for next year's intake.	Planning and reporting on finance, HRM or premises issues usually related to governing body curriculum development committee.

Figure 4.5 A day in the life of a bursar – a composite illustration

Time	The bursar of 2000	The educational resource manager of tomorrow
5.15	Tidy office, complete filing and prepare desk for next day.	Check Internet page daily hits, calendar for tomorrow.
5.30	Check calendar for tomorrow, close down ICT system, collect any urgent mail for posting, check cleaning staff/caretaker for evening, depart home.	Meet with evening site supervisor and handover, collect professional journals to read in evening, make confirmatory call to professional association about final assessment of candidate for chartered status.

Figure 4.5 A day in the life of a bursar – a composite illustration *continued*

as collecting the mail and switching on the ICT system. Other calm periods are those devoted to meetings such as those of the SMT or at end of the day when the majority of the teaching and support staff had left.

This 'typical' day in 2000 on the left-hand side of Fig. 4.5 is set against a 'factional' illustration of a day in the life of an educational resource manager later in the twenty-first century shown on the right. (Factional or fictuality entails developing archival materials with imaginary or fictional elements added.) This arose from our identification of the more strategic and 'futures thinking' aspects of the work which we might expect to see develop as a day in the life of the education resource manager of the future.

How was it for real?

We observed the initiation of change in the role of bursars and a potential increase in the opportunity to show strategic leadership at the bursar level which can be viewed alongside the emerging professionalisation of the role. Bursars still occupy a wide range of job titles and positions in the management hierarchy but the observations demonstrated that they were becoming involved in strategic aspects of school leadership as well as the more functional management and administrative roles. They remained more involved with administration than their job descriptions indicated that they would be. However, the school business management role is certainly expanding and the trends towards a greater leadership role, identified in the previous chapter, were also observed in practice. As site-based management develops, we can expect more emphasis on the wider school business management role and the emergence of the strategic overview implicit in the role of the educational resource manager. This potential change in the role of the bursar will have significant implications for the roles of senior leaders in schools as well as the future training and development of bursars themselves. This is a concern for the next chapter.

5

■ ■ ■

Coming from ... Going to? The Career of the School Business Manager

Introduction: the identikit bursar

The retired military person, the ex-businessperson, the accountant, the secretary; these are the stereotypes often associated with bursarship in both the public and private sectors of schooling. The other conventional identikit bursar is that of a female, returning to work after a career break, with few formal qualifications and a variegated career background. We set out to find the characteristics of school bursars in the late twentieth century. Did they confirm or deny the stereotypes?

In Section I of this chapter, we outline the qualifications and previous careers of bursars, including both where they worked and at what levels, with a brief digression into gender issues. In Section II, we consider the career aspirations of bursars and how current and future training and professional development can contribute to these. Information on how we obtained the data is explained in Appendix I on research methodology.

I Career origins ... coming from?

Qualifications

The striking features of the qualifications were the extent and variety which some bursars held, their virtual absence for others and their incompleteness.

However, the entire group had some preparation for aspects of bursarship from the subjects they had previously studied as Fig. 5.1 shows.

Qualifications	%
Secretarial	33
Business management	21
Accountancy/banking	13
University degrees	10
Teaching	10
IT	4
Miscellaneous	4
Health and safety	3
Engineering	2
n bursars = 36, n qualifications = 103	

Figure 5.1 Bursars' post-school qualifications

Mainstream qualifications and NVQs

At school level, 75 per cent of bursars had achieved GCSE level, or its earlier equivalent of O-levels, and 50 per cent had Advanced level or Advanced/ Ordinary level General Certificate of Education (A- or AO-levels). The areas of post-school certification are shown in Figure 5.1. The levels of these ranged from NVQ Level 2, or its predecessors, to masters degrees (the latter held by two of the sample of 36). Six held first degrees and there were two still completing degrees through the Open University. Two bursars had Masters' degrees though not in subjects related directly to management.

Professional qualifications

Professional qualifications could generally be grouped into four main areas of secretarial, accountancy, business management and teaching. There were other miscellaneous qualifications relevant to aspects of bursarship including catering, librarianship, engineering, health and safety. Few bursars had ICT certification but it appeared that many had attended non-certificated short courses in this.

1 *Secretarial qualifications* were mainly generalist, centring around shorthand, typing and word processing. A few bursars had specialised in either private or medical secretaryship.

2 Among those with *accountancy qualifications*, there was a slight preponderance of certified accountants but generally the scatter ranged widely including accountancy technicians, a chartered accountant and one from public finance.

3 *Business management certification* was more disparate. Several bursars had Higher National Certificates/Higher National Diplomas (HNC/HNDs) but beyond that there was a large number of individuals with generalist certification such as NVQs Levels 4 and 5 or their forerunners, Diplomas in Management and Ordinary National Certificates (ONCs). There was one specialist business management qualification and that was in personnel studies. Significantly, those with management qualifications included three of the first holders of the Advanced Diploma in Management for School Bursars, thus indicating the beginnings of a recognised career route to bursarship.

4 The group with *teaching qualifications* was largely part-time certificated through City and Guilds in further education (including teaching of business subjects) and special needs. One held a BEd.

Levels of qualification

Despite this range, there was a lack of what might be seen as appropriate level qualifications for the responsibilities being handled. One bursar of a secondary school, who has five GCSEs and a Business and Technical Education Council National Diploma (BTEC National), described the job's responsibilities as:

> £2.5 million budget ... budget management, preparation and monitoring, presentations to Governors' subcommittees, management of buildings (maintenance and cleaning), grounds maintenance, resource generation (hiring of school facilities for outside agencies), administration, personnel, line management of support staff.

Those promoted to bursarship had apparently coped with the responsibilities despite the lack of appropriate qualifications but as one remarked:

> six years ago I started work. The speed I have progressed from secretary to senior manager without some basis of training apart from common sense is down to opportunity. One person plucks you from the typing pool and plonks you down on the SMT.

(Secondary school bursar, 1997)

Finally, of the qualifications listed by this group, there were a significant number which were 'in progress' or did not appear to have been completed (notably among accountancy qualifications). This may have been due to the wide range of environments in which members of the group had worked where preparations may have been made for careers and then made obsolete by a forced or selected change of career direction.

Career experiences

In the independent sector, jobs are given to the old boys network – high ranking ex-servicemen. (Secondary school assistant bursar, 1997)

Schools have been employing ex-military personnel with management skills but a lot haven't. (Secondary school bursar, 1997).

The military stereotype is reflected in these two quotations but Fig. 5.2 provides an impression of the wider range of previous responsibilities which influenced bursars' appointments in addition to the 'old boys' network' and military experiences.

Many, especially the female bursars, had previous careers in schools which is contrary to suggestions that schools may be better served by bursars from commercial or administrative backgrounds (Knight, 1993: 49). Significantly for the development of career routes to bursarship, 21 of the group of 36 studied obtained their present bursarship positions after serving in other in-school or

Environment	Nos of organisations	F%	M%
Education: Schools, pre-school, adult education, exam. board, LEAs	39	51	19
Commerce: Clothing, defence, engineering, leisure, salvage, manufacturing, retail, security	34	16	38
Government: Central, local	7	8.5	5
Health care: Administration hospitals/health centres	7	8.5	5
Armed forces: Air force, army	6		16
Financial services: Accountancy, banks, building societies	6	5	8
Libraries/publishing	4	6	
Charities/church	2	3	
Consultancy – management	2		5
Utilities: water/transport	2	1	2
Farming	1	1	
Total	110		

n bursars = 36, F = female, M = male

Figure 5.2 Pre-bursarship career environments

bursar-related posts in schools (not necessarily in the same schools in which they were employed at the time of the survey). Some of their present positions appeared to have evolved as their earlier posts had gained responsibilities, a finding also of the Mortimore *et al.* (1995) study. Thirteen came directly to bursarship from outside education. Before obtaining their bursarship posts, the holders averaged seven years, four months in bursar-related posts in schools (the range was between one year and twenty-five years) and held one or two posts during that period (the range was from one to six posts).

LEVELS/RESPONSIBILITIES	% of nos. of posts	F%	M%
Armed services: Regimental sergeant major; flight lieutenant; group captain	4		12
Company secretary	2	2	3
Inspector – quality control	1		3
Manager/director: Bursars; contracts; curriculum; facilities; general; marketing; personnel; office; supervisory	42	26	73
Assistant manager: Lower administration grades in local government; accountancy; libraries; bursarship	14	20.5	
Secretarial: – Clerical	6	9.5	
– Medical	4	5	
– Personal	10	16	
– School	4	5	
Self-employed: Building; farming	7	8	6
Teachers – full and part time: including adult education tutors, playgroup leader	6	8	3
n bursars = 36, n posts = 107, F = female, M = male			

Figure 5.3 Bursars' career levels and responsibilities prior to current appointments

Many bursars had worked in commerce during some stage in their careers in a wide range of manufacturing and retail organisations. There were few with previous career experiences in financial institutions, perhaps not surprising in the light of the views of one of the sample group researched who highlighted the difference between accountancy and bursarship.

I found the work in a Chartered Accountancy practice ... terribly boring ... I met bursars who I found had very interesting jobs. I then set about finding a job as a bursar and was pleased to be appointed to my current position.

(Secondary school bursar, 1997)

The sample researched came almost equally from bursarship posts in locally maintained and GM schools. Commercial experiences figured more extensively in the career histories of bursars in GM schools but otherwise there were no significant differences in the proportions from any of the other environments. The size of schools in which the bursars worked did not seem to have any relationship to their previous careers.

It was difficult to estimate and compare levels of seniority in posts held prior to bursarship without detailed job descriptions of every post but managerial abilities would have been evidenced in many of them. Figure 5.3, however, demonstrates the diversity of job titles and levels of operation that ranged from clerical to company secretary and group captain. For men, previous experience as managers was likely; for women, previous experience as assistant managers was more common. Within the sample there were no significant differences in previous posts held by bursars in the locally maintained schools compared with those in GM schools.

A job for the little woman? Gender issues

For too long the bursarial function has been carved out by housewives' choice ... it is no longer women working in schools just so they can have the school holidays off ... they are suddenly expected to carry out a broader function with little or no training.
(Secondary school bursar, 1997)

Bursarship can no longer be denigrated as 'housewives' choice' but the view above reflects its emergence from school secretaryship which is very much a female preserve. The movement to management of school bursarship could be one of the factors that attracted more men to administrative careers in schools at the end of the twentieth century but the female origins of the post were still evident. Men holding a bursarship role were more likely to have the title of 'bursar' than were women in similar posts (Figure 5.4).

Gender distribution			
Titles	% of sample	F%	M%
Bursar	50	36.5	72
Administrator	25	36.5	7
Manager	11	13.5	7
Financial	8	9	7
Registrar/director/deputy head	6	4.5	7

Note: Administrator titles included: Administrative Officers, Head of Administration or Administrative Team Leader. Managers were designated 'General', 'Business' or 'Facilities'.

n = bursars = 36, n female (F) = 22, n male (M) = 14

Figure 5.4 Bursarship titles

A larger percentage of women reached bursarship with secretarial qualifications than did men. Male bursars were more likely to have accountancy certification and university degrees than were women (Fig. 5.5). Female bursars were more likely than male bursars to have had previous experience in educational environments (Fig. 5.2). The numbers of women in bursarship might be reflected in a comparison of the genders attending similar courses for headteachers/bursars. On the University of Lincolnshire and Humberside's MBA for School Bursars, 1996–8, 61 per cent of those enrolled were female while, for the same period, 43 per cent of those enrolled on the MBA for school headteachers were female.

Qualifications	F%	M%
Secretarial	43	7
Business management	23	17
Accountancy/banking	11	21
University degrees	7	17
Teaching	8	14
IT	3	7
Miscellaneous	5	0
Health and safety	0	10
Engineering	0	7
n bursars = 36, n qualifications = 103, n female (F) = 22, n male (M) = 14		

Figure 5.5 Bursars' post school qualifications: gender distribution

II Career aspirations ... going to?

the job ... doesn't seem to have any career development ... I can't progress any further ... I could go to a bigger school and do the same job or stay in the school and develop in more education management areas than pure finance. (Primary school bursar, 1997)

The aspirations of this bursar and colleagues for career progression and for leadership in areas wider than finance pose challenging issues for appointments to senior school posts. Once having achieved bursarship, a next career step appears to be headship. Headship is traditionally accepted as reserved for those who have been teachers, and few headteachers will have had experience of non-education related occupations. To admit 'outsiders' to headship threatens the career routes for teachers who have usually followed career paths through qualifications and experiences focused on teaching and learning.

Governments, however, have tried and failed, to encourage business people to enter headship. In 1997, for example, courses for the National Professional Qualification for Headship (NPQH) were offered to those from outside schools but very few took up the offer and, it was rumoured, those that did so, chose not to complete the training.

The preceding analysis shows that those occupying bursarship roles have not followed career paths similar to those of teachers from whom school senior managers are usually recruited. Despite this,

> I really believe the role of the principal chief executive co-ordinator does not have to be a person who is a good classroom teacher. [It] needs a professional manager. Bursars who are simpatico with education and who are competent managers could do the job.

(Secondary school bursar)

Bursars are a way of bringing in business organisation to schools. The career aspirations of bursars then wanting to move from organising the business of education to its leadership raise what may be uncomfortable issues, e.g. the following.

1   Why are bursars generally paid less than their colleagues in senior management teams? Bursars acquire extensive knowledge of all aspects of school life. A majority from this sample had previous occupations related to education and some had not inconsiderable experience in schools.

2   How would the present situation in which education professionals become headteachers assisted by business advisers differ from one in which a business professional becomes a headteacher 'with an academic adviser', as one primary school bursar suggested?

The challenges to traditional patterns of authority and power in schools posed by these possibilities may be one of the reasons why bursars' status is not always readily accepted by teachers (Chapter 2). If a bursar 'could be a leader of the school with experience' (primary school bursar, 1997) then there is another competitor for senior management. However, it is not as simple as this as some teachers have moved into bursarship roles, either as designated 'deputy heads' or as school administrators, and there are examples of bursars acting as headteachers (either temporarily during the replacement of a headteacher or, in one case, as the chief executive of a charitable foundation who appoints the headteachers of the foundation's schools). If teachers can become bursars, why not vice versa? Indeed, we did see this happening in some instances with bursars taking evening classes, option or sixth form subjects or acting as form tutors.

If bursars are to attain a position of educational professionalism, what education and training is needed and how does their current education and training prepare them for their roles?

Patterns of education and training

One of the striking characteristics of the current education and training of bursars was the variety of qualifications and routes into the position. Prior to the mid-1990s, the main source of professional development for bursars has been the somewhat *ad hoc* training carried out by LEAs as part of the induction and support related to the delegation of funds through the local management of schools. As might be expected, such training was designed to enable the transfer of skills from LEA administrators to school bursars and their staff and tended to be narrowly focused on functional aspects such as budget management, personnel issues, sites and premises maintenance. Only in the last few years of the twentieth century, did a more coherent pattern of in-service education and training (INSET) and opportunities for pursuing courses leading to the award of recognised further qualifications arise (*see* Chapter 1).

This more coherent pattern began as some schools opted for significant autonomy as GM schools from 1989, when INSET relevant to school bursars became available, largely through the Grant Maintained Schools Centre. This was strengthened and more directly related to the roles and responsibilities of school bursars first with the establishment of the Grant Maintained School Bursars Association in 1991 which grew out of the bringing together of a number of regional GM Bursars Associations. The 'flagship' course was the annual School Administrators Conference which was first held in 1990. Of course, the Independent Schools Bursars Association had been in existence for some considerable time before this (since 1932 as an association and from the early 1950s as the ISBA) and had run a whole range of courses along with other commercial concerns for the private sector. Indeed, administrators from state schools did attend such courses from time to time where the topics were relevant to their specific circumstances.

After 1995 INSET opportunities for bursars and support staff began to grow in all schools, prompted by increased delegation. This was given a further boost by the transformation of the Grant Maintained Bursars Association into the National Bursars Association in 1996 as the national organisation for bursars in all schools. In this period a typical pattern of INSET was:

1 *periodic skill training* on functional aspects provided by LEAs and semi-commercial concerns. These tended to be day courses or one/two-day conferences;

2 *co-ordinated skill training* provided by LEAs, often linked to NVQ level 2/3 (Management Charter Initiative [MCI] level 1/2) through the local Training and Enterprise Council (TEC). From 1997 such courses also began to be provided by the NBA with support from the DfEE;

3 *higher professional training awards* run by Further Education (FE) and Higher Education (HE) institutions for administrators in public service manage-

ment. Typically these were Certificates and Diplomas in Management Studies (CMS, DMS) and were not exclusive to schools, though bursars were often able to carry out work-based assignments as part of their assessment. One university designed and runs an advanced professional diploma in management specifically for school bursars;

4 *Master of Business Administration*; one university adapted its educational leadership course for headteachers and deputies to the specific needs of bursars and has been successfully offering a two-year postgraduate professional programme since 1996.

As schools extended their autonomy and became more site based in their management there was an increase of interest in the role and qualifications of bursars, partly as a recognition of the valuable role they play in the leadership and management of schools but also as a possible way of responding to the perceived overload of headteachers. It was inevitable that headteachers would incur a much heavier burden of responsibilities under the increased delegation of funding to schools. The arrival of cash-limited budgets at the school level in a time of severe constraints on public sector funding also had the effect in many schools of reducing the number of deputy heads and other senior managers as a way of making the budget balance. Thus headteachers experienced the double pressure of increased duties and less support.

This problem was so severe that the House of Commons' Select Committee on Education and Employment held an enquiry into the workload and duties of headteachers in 1998 (HoC, 1998). One of the solutions proposed was to enhance the position of bursars and their staff to take on the major part of the legislative and administrative load (HoC, 1998: para. 77). Connected to this was an increased willingness of the DfEE and TTA to talk to bursars' representatives about the roles, responsibilities, training and qualifications of school bursars. In the former case, council members of the NBA had regular meetings with officials in the DfEE and the NBA was supported in the early years while it became established. There was great interest in the establishment of National Standards for Bursars modelled on those for headteachers (*see* Appendix II) and the Licentiate Registration Scheme which was piloted by the NBA in 1998/9 and accredited through the University of Lincolnshire and Humberside. These issues are explored further in Part Four.

As the role of bursarship grows we can expect to see a more coherent pattern of training and qualifications developing, for example:

1 *induction*: school-based preparation for educational administration, management and leadership including specific skills for clerks and a general introduction to educational administration for experienced managers;

2 *up-skilling*: short courses related to specific functions, possibly linked to NVQ accreditation;

3   *multi-skilling*: introductory and advanced courses in functional areas to enable support staff to broaden their expertise, linked to the National Standards for Bursars and the Licentiate Registration Scheme;

4   *professional development*: certificate, diploma and masters' level programmes in bursarship, leading to the achievement of chartered status;

5   *advanced programmes*: EdD, MPhil and PhD in education resource leadership.

Whither bursarship?

The stereotypes which opened this chapter existed as school bursars at the end of the twentieth century but so did a diversity of other characters. This variety in qualifications, career experiences and environments did not parallel the routes which teachers followed to reach senior management. Informal conversations with bursars and senior teaching staff indicated that this variety in experience was somewhat denigrated by teachers and could cause bursars some feelings of inferiority. One might conclude from this that variety should be celebrated and that education professionals should be made more aware of all that can be contributed from outside experience.

> *I've had the benefit of being a bursar in GM and independent schools, company secretary and finance director.*
>
> (Secondary school bursar, 1996)

There is no doubt that the role of the school bursar was entering a new era in 2000 with increasing opportunities for people from teaching and business backgrounds to transfer to the administration track in education at the school level and a range of professional and academic qualifications specifically for bursars becoming available. Together with their own professional association, there was thus clear evidence of the establishment of a profession. With the rise of professional recognition for school bursars and a coherent training and qualification pattern, a new breed of educational administrator was possible who was aware of pupils' needs and thus organised the provision of resources so as to effect the raising of achievement of pupils and of the whole staff in the school.

A well-established bursars' profession then has potential to alter the power balance. In the latter part of the twentieth century a number of government initiatives encouraged closer liaison and exchange between the industrial/commercial sector and education. This began to open up potentially different routes into school senior leadership positions. Teachers are often criticised for their narrow career experiences (school–university–school) yet still reach headship. If those with different career patterns to those of teachers and fewer traditional qualifications can, none the less, reach senior management posts in schools, does bursarship with its wider experience begin to offer a different route to headship?

6

■ ■ ■

Roles and Relationships

Introduction

So far, these chapters have outlined how others view bursars. This chapter shows how bursars view themselves. In Section I of this chapter, they talk about their roles and responsibilities and in Section II, their relationships with the others in their school communities, headteachers, senior staff, teachers and governors. In both sections of the chapter, the comments are collated to show how far bursarship is developing through the four types described at the end of Chapter 1: administration manager, support services manager, school business manager and educational resources manager.

The bursars' views presented in this chapter were gathered from interviews in 1996, 1997 and 1998, the methodology of which is explained in Appendix I.

I Roles and responsibilities

Administration manager

> *I'm just a bureaucratic administrator.* (Secondary school bursar)

> *I enjoy school administration, the diversity, complexity and sheer breathtaking lunacy of a busy school office mirrored the enjoyment of my children's early years and I have never wanted to seek an alternative, calmer or more ordered working life.* (Secondary school bursar)

The negative and the positive poles of bursars' views are encapsulated in these quotations. There were more negatives than positives with the adverse reactions arising largely over 'administrivia', or the *'quagmire of day-to-day administration'* as one independent secondary school bursar described it. More picturesque, was the bursar with her *'head stuck under 15 inches of paper'*. This model was recognised by other secondary school bursar colleagues who saw themselves as *'glorified administration clerks'*, *'bogged down with mechanics … a glorified clerical worker'*. Still, at least the use of the word 'glorified' ironically indicated that some status was being accorded to the role.

The administrative combined with the legal formalities such as *'ensuring compliance with accountancy laws, procedures and rules'* (secondary school bursar), acting as clerk to the governing body to which presentations had to be made and budget formulations prepared. Apart from preparing the figures, administration included also such features as setting up the systems for letting premises.

For some, this administration was as far as the post went: *'I have nothing to do with the development plan'*, was the uncompromising statement from a primary school bursar. Another was so incensed at being excluded from the senior management team as to contemplate leaving the post. It was generally accepted that these bursars had responsibility for the day-to-day running of the school but a common experience was that *'I am not involved in the senior management team meetings or planning'* (secondary school bursar).

All such administrative roles and responsibilities are the base of bursarship. These are its origins in the basic office functions that were the first requirements of site-based management which headteachers and senior teacher staff wanted to devolve from their own jobs. Now, the bursars are, in their turn, devolving such administrative tasks to other office staff, some having acquired a grade of assistant bursar. Such devolution makes possible the move to the role of support services manager.

Support services manager

Emerging from the type of administrative management were those who described themselves as *'blending the bursar's traditional role with that of a modern administration and systems manager'* (secondary school bursar), so they had *'an enabling function'* (secondary school bursar). This covered *'all non-core activities (i.e. not educating the kids)'* (secondary school bursar).

When you contemplate the non-core activities listed below by bursars as their roles and responsibilities, it is possible to see how

1 the traditional administrative position is moving imperceptibly to the more extended positions of manager and leader;
2 the expectations of the job descriptions in Chapter 3 have grown in the practice of bursarship;
3 the bursar becomes the 'catch-all' as more business-related functions are required of schools.

A facilitator who can provide those directly involved with teaching and learning with the resources ... to achieve and improve upon their objectives.

(Primary school bursar)

My role's all encompassing – to manage the school's financial resources effectively and productively. To advise the head and governors on the best practice for investment, marketing ... Daily administration work. Responsibility for cover, personnel responsibilities for all staff including teachers. Utilities management and contracts.

(Secondary school bursar)

Finance manager, budget controller, premises manager, contracts manager, information technology (IT) administrative manager, personnel manager (with the head), public relations liaison, marketing co-ordinator, industrial/business links co-ordinator, line manager for support staff.   (Secondary school bursar)

Manager of multi-disciplinary support staff ... financial management of charitable educational institution, preparation and control of budgets ... preparation of financial and administrative returns to the Funding Agency for Schools and to the Department of Education and Employment; collection of boarding fee income; preparation of management accounts and annual accounts; operation of payroll; preparation and management of capital bids; internal audit; financial, premises and legal advice to the governing body; management of trading company. Premises management of multi-site campus; building project management; letting of facilities; security; marketing operations; insurance matters; health and safety management; personnel management of support staff; contract management; management of computerised administration and accounting systems.

(Secondary school bursar)

Thus, the basics centred around managing staff and budget problem solving but *'there is no common title, no common job description, no-one does the same job ... there is a wide difference from one school to another'* (secondary school bursar). The *'nitty gritty of finance'* remained the irreducible minimum for all bursars but beyond this the only common denominator could be summarised as *'everything that is not to do with teaching'* (secondary school bursar) or just *'everything'* (secondary school bursar).

At the same time, this group were at pains to point out that they, as yet, felt they lacked essential *'educational grounding so it is difficult to make decisions'* (secondary school bursar). Without *'curriculum knowledge'* (primary school bursar) *'you can't know about education if you are not a teacher'* (secondary school bursar). Despite this, bursarship was *'increasingly the role of a deputy head'* (primary school bursar) or *'the same as a non-teaching deputy head role'* (secondary school bursar). The 'lift-off' point in this category appeared to be the responsibility for support staff which gave bursars the role for which they were most likely to accord themselves leadership status: *'I am responsible for everything that is non-teaching and lead a team of twenty-five people. I run my own INSET days for my team, and have instigated an appraisal system'* (secondary school bursar).

There was a need expressed to stress the importance of the role and to extend it, particularly its management aspects and to see the centrality of bursarship in developing links between schools and industry. This was particularly important in view of bursarship's perceived importance to the effective business management which applicants felt that schools lacked. Comments were made, for example, that showed dissatisfaction with schools' resource utilisation. *'Buildings are empty 60–70 per cent of the time'* (secondary school bursar). To these problems, the bursar should be able to bring *'a wide business perspective'* (independent secondary school bursar).

While some were critical of this mainly operational, support services manager role, others realised its importance: *'the bursar is responsible for building, maintenance, heating and lighting, provision of desks and chairs, purchasing of books, paying salary, collecting fees, flogging uniform, feeding children. If none of these happen, there is no learning. If even one doesn't happen, learning is damaged'* (secondary school bursar). None the less, there was hope expressed that the future role would be a *'bit above the mundane'* (secondary school bursar) and that bursars would be able to spend *'less time doing things others should be doing'* (secondary school bursar). The mechanics should no longer be done by bursars, *'our job is pulling it all together'* (primary school bursar). This was regarded as the means of change to enable the role to be enhanced and more respect paid to the bursar's views.

School business manager

To *'interpret dreams to reality'* (secondary school bursar) was a delightfully evocative description of how the realisation of practical responsibilities was seen as giving bursarship a wide remit and importance.

The bursars had their views on how this might happen in reality: *'I'd like to be more involved with the application of the finances – the way they impinge on education ... currently my role is anything with numbers in it ... It takes me into almost everything apart from curriculum issues'* (secondary school bursar). The starting point for this movement would be very practical, *'make sure on the financial front we use resources to provide value for money considering learning outcomes'* (secondary school bursar). There was a clear expectation that the bursar should be part of senior management with a very strong leadership role as a *'decision maker with input to whole school development at all levels'* (secondary school bursar). *'It is vital that I am not only able to manage on a day-to-day basis but also to plan effectively for the school to use its resources as efficiently as possible'* (secondary school bursar). Bursars were envisaged as an integral part of management and planning and to do this they wanted to *'widen [their] perspectives ... have a structure for thinking about strategic issues'* (secondary school bursar).

One of the ways to achieve this was not to attempt to breach the citadel of education directly but to move in through using bursars' particular expertise in business management. *'Someone with a good knowledge of traditional business skills ... not just financial and personnel'* (secondary school bursar) would enable bursars to lead in areas such as organising marketing, looking after premises and support staff, advising the headteacher on finance and on the finance for teacher training. *'Ensuring the school's image and ability sells itself and is a functioning successful organisation – these would be my responsibility'* (secondary school bursar).

To achieve this required personal, political skills ranging from the overt to the covert:

> *There's no formal administrative system – things are done the way they are done ... the college runs on gentlemen's agreements so it's important how I impose change ... sometimes one has to be hostile and autocratic.* (Secondary school bursar)

> *I have infiltrated into children's education, the skills, practices and reasons behind it.* (Secondary school bursar)

One bursar had felt that the deputy head was initially hostile to him but as the bursar learnt the political, collegiate and other processes of decision making, they became friends, able to work together effectively. This effective working was reflected in the whole SMT; as bursars gained confidence, they felt able to express their views more forcibly in meetings and to make recommendations on whole-school issues.

The bursars felt they had a role to play in improving the education offered, *'schools have to radically change and put students foremost'* (secondary school bursar). To participate in this, bursars wanted to be better informed, professional managers. Like other school managers, their role was to make teaching and learning effective, to become involved with the children and to understand what learning entailed. The bursar, therefore, had to be a *'person who can understand what teaching staff are trying to achieve sufficiently well to prioritise spending, someone sympathetic'* (secondary school bursar) and *'looking at the learning of children'* (secondary school bursar). This was not just expressed as woolly altruistic aims but as *'making sure that what we do as a team achieves pupil expectations ... attainments at GCSE'* (secondary school bursar).

The desire to become involved directly in education did not preclude a continuation of pre-existing functions but these were operated with an understanding beyond that of administrative efficiency.

> *To provide an excellent support to the school and to parents, pupils, staff, governors and any customer who will help the school to achieve its own objective of enabling pupils to learn effectively. Within that there's a lot of human resource issues – you have to make people feel important to the school. People who provide the service have to be well looked after ... they need to feel valued, not exploited – especially on the support side. Make sure on the financial front we use resources to provide value for money considering learning outcomes.* (Secondary school bursar)

The bursar's role ... is not one of just preparing accounts. It also encompasses ... development of the strategic plan, development of personnel policies for both academic and non-academic staff, development of a marketing strategy, development of an accommodation strategy, achieving Investors in People. (Primary school bursar)

There were indications of readiness to move on to the educational resource manager role. These included suggestions for renaming the role as Director of Resources, for seeing the role as adding value to education through allowing teachers to do what they were trained to do. Once these were achieved, a bursar *'could be a leader of the school with experience'* (primary school bursar), though for the moment the evolving bursarship role looked for active involvement in all school life but at *'a level of responsibility that's recognised and accepted'* (primary school bursar).

Education resource manager

This was the role to which almost all of the respondents aspired, perhaps most poignantly expressed as the desire to *'deal with visionary issues not petty cash or toilet smell'* (secondary school bursar). The aim was to be an active part of the SMT so enabled to understand and provide departments with the right resources at the right time, with responsibility for being in control of the total administration of the school. Their interest in strategic matters had been aroused, *'having been exposed to the education system, values are wonderful ... People should help with the great changes. Children are worth the effort – and I wouldn't have said that five years ago'* (secondary school bursar). This vision and its associated values translate into a bursarship which is a *'whole school person ... responsible for everything in the school'* (secondary school bursar) and going to the *'ultimate extreme – managing the direction of the school'* (secondary school bursar).

Few had yet reached this position but for some, it was a reality.

I was appointed instead of one of the four deputies and at the same level. I am now paid more than the deputy head. My position is second to/alongside the head because of the different responsibilities. I even had the head asking permission for things. I have had to stop the head doing things. (Secondary school bursar)

The general view was of three possible types of education resource manager.

1   Being involved with the curriculum as *'supportive of teaching and learning ... with a good understanding of educational issues'* (secondary school bursar). Having such an educational viewpoint, *'over the years ahead, deputies and senior teachers won't be able to ignore bursars. We'll contribute more than just office staff, accounts, premises and personnel'* (secondary school bursar).

2   Being *'in charge of everything except the learning interface'* (secondary school bursar).

3   Being in charge of everything, including teaching, by becoming the headteacher: *'Heads don't have to be teachers. [We] could in future become heads of*

schools ... leading the school forward. Providing the best education for children personally and academically, make the school a community belonging to the people' (secondary school bursar). One was not so optimistic: headship, could only be *'in the right context – maybe in another country, can't expect it here'* (secondary school bursar).

II Relationships

Who are you Miss? I've seen you around but I don't know who you are. (Question from a pupil recorded during a day's observation of a secondary school bursar at work, as the bursar paused outside the staff room)

The interviews did not include questions directly on relationships so it was interesting to notice how many of the bursars raised the issues without prompting and which of the relationships were most, and least mentioned. Relations with teachers received the most notice, closely followed by head-teachers and the SMTs. Contacts with governors were largely confined to the formal. There were no comments about interactions with parents, nor with pupils. This was not surprising in the light of what we had observed of the bursars' daily contacts and it perhaps explains the pupil's question above that opened this section.

Whatever the stage of bursarship outlined below, there was no apparent relationship between the title of a post, its status or its relationships. Those titled 'bursar' were no more likely to be full SMT members than those with designations such as 'Administrative Officer' or 'Business Manager'. One bursar felt that her status was complicated by her being the only woman in the team but no one else mentioned gender issues.

Administrative manager

Comments on relationships indicated much more of an administrative role than had the comments above on roles and responsibilities. The relationship with governors was formal, often legally so, as bursars could be clerks to governing bodies. Even where the bursars did not have the official relationship they attended governors' meetings and reported to them.

More controversially, teachers were regarded as finding it very difficult to come to terms with the idea of bursars as anything other than office clerks. All the bursars' views indicated an underlying tension and a sense of inferiority summed up in reports from secondary school bursars, such as *'I have a problem with colleagues. There is an "us and them" attitude'. 'Staff don't know what a bursar is.'* The bursars wanted to be taken seriously as professionals but, *'I don't think we're seen as professionals at all. [We're] very much looked down on by teaching staff. The attitude makes me quite angry sometimes'.* The relationship with teachers was clearly not perceived as a happy one by the bursars and this bears out the findings in Chapter 2. Teachers gave the impression that non-academics were there to serve them but the bursars wanted an equal say with the teachers. Bursars felt that teachers did not appreciate their problems. Teachers felt that bursars did not appreciate theirs.

Attitudes were in need of change at middle management level too. Middle managers were reported by the bursars as seeing anyone in administrative or non-teaching roles only as someone who had to stay later at school after the majority of teachers would have departed. This was translated by bursars into feeling that there was *'a lack of respect – the divide between the academic and support staff means we're viewed as lesser mortals ... that is caused by the difference in our academic backgrounds'* (secondary school bursar). Dissatisfaction was also felt with senior management. Bursars considered they should be part of the SMT instead of being regarded as *'the school secretary which demeans the role'* (primary school bursar). One was angry at not even having access to the SMT. Those not in the SMT were dissatisfied with their lack of status and resented being excluded from school planning processes for which they had to provide information, plaintively summarised in this comment:

> *I'm given so much responsibility but I don't sit on the SMT ... the school does value me but there is a view that non-academics should not come onto the SMT [it's] difficult to accept.* (Secondary school bursar)

On the other hand, bursars themselves did not always appear to value their teaching colleagues. Bursars felt that teachers were unable to cope efficiently with the managerial tasks to which they were assigned to the extent that *'my respect for teachers has lessened'* (secondary school bursar). Teachers might have superior academic qualifications but bursars felt they were not managers or good administrators. *'Teaching staff are not practical'* (secondary school bursar) and were very insular in their approach to businesslike issues within the school. Bursars regarded teachers as having no experience of worlds outside education unlike bursars who *'can bring alternative points of view or suggestions the teachers would not have thought of'* (primary school bursar). Interestingly, one of the most critical comments on teachers also included the view that educational values were exceptionally good.

Moving out of the administrative manager stage may be facilitated for the bursars by their professional development: *'Three years ago, before we did the ... course (MBA for Bursars) we were very different people, diffident, unsure, almost apologetic: 'I know I'm not a teacher but ...' I'm definitely far more confident now'* (secondary school bursar). The confidence was growing because bursars felt that their extending knowledge of education was making it possible to speak in the same language as their academic staff counterparts.

How teachers will react to this confidence remains to be seen but it will be an important indicator of the possibilities of bursarship moving on from its administrative origins.

Support services manager

For those at this stage, the bursars' position as line manager of the support staff was well established; with the governors, this stage involved an advisory relationship outside of the legalities of clerking and the other roles *'were as the head thought they should be – HRM, finance, site, premises manager'* (secondary school bursar). The roles were not, however, part of the SMT and the bursars wanted to be accepted into this.

Headteachers were not interested in running the support staff side or, at least, did not see it as a priority, as one bursar remarked, *'I got it by default. I have full rein with support staff. The head's only interested if there is a problem'* (secondary school bursar). Bursars were aware of the importance of having taken over the leadership of support staff. It could be a proving ground for progress to a wider role. Understanding of human resource management therefore was essential: *'people who provide the service have to be well looked after ... they need to feel valued, not exploited – especially on the support side'* (secondary school bursar). The bursar had to be the champion of support staff while also coping with their inadequacies: *'I've been at school ... until 11 p.m. helping Dynarod unblock drains because the site manager couldn't cope'* (secondary school bursar).

Relations with teachers were easier than at the administrative manager stage. Bursars and teachers recognised that support staff had to be integrated with teaching staff *'because of all the changes and ways of educating kids, there is a bigger role for support staff'* (secondary school bursar). Bursars realised the significance of their role to effective teaching:

> Without support services working effectively , there can be no teaching ... It's like enabling a driving instructor to run a car that works ... You can't go back to good teachers running the support systems ... Without support staff the classroom cannot exist. (Secondary school bursar)

Once through the administrative barrier, however, relationships with senior management team members became more problematic since bursars were now interacting with them more regularly. Bursars were dissatisfied with their current status, seeing their membership of the SMT as being a *'lip service appointment'* (primary school bursar). Almost all the bursars indicated a desire to upgrade to being regarded as *'a key member of the management team'* (secondary school bursar), or *'a full member of the SMT ... with a salary equivalent to a deputy'* (primary school bursar). There was some resentment of being given what bursars perceived as senior-level tasks without senior-level status.

> My own personal goal is to become a full member of the SMT ... I could help the school more and feel more involved in all areas ... I need less daily tasks and more time for planning and looking at the whole picture. (Secondary school bursar)

Status as a senior manager was wanted with recognition as a professional. Many complained about being devalued and treated like second-class citizens. They were aware that they lacked the paper qualifications which were something by which people, particularly in a school environment, were judged. Bursars were aware that to progress their roles, they had to earn the respect of the education professionals.

School business manager

Respect had been achieved where bursars had used professional development opportunities as one primary school bursar agreed, *'I meet regularly with Heads of Departments – my MBA course has allowed me to gain their respect because I knew about education'*. Such learning was also significant in relations with headteachers. At one school, both bursar and headteacher were studying for their MBAs (though at different universities). This had engendered the attitude that *'we are doing it together. I'm looking forward to reviewing School Development Planning together'* (secondary school bursar). At another school, the bursar reported that, *'My head is doing an EdD ... If I'm doing this, I can work better with her ... Helpful if you're both thinking current stuff'* (secondary school bursar).

But all was not sweetness and light. Once a bursar is moving into the school business manager stage, relationships with headteachers become crucial. In these circumstances, education could be dangerous:

> *I think my growth and development caused a problem in the school I was in. I had to learn to tone [my learning] down so that it wasn't so threatening. The head who allowed me to develop was beginning to feel I was more than she could cope with. I was always tempering my viewpoint.* (Primary school bursar)

> *He perceives me sometimes as a threat to undermine his authority ... he considers me a great manager and administrator but does not see me as a leader ... I want to support him.* (Secondary school bursar)

Some of the schools had managed to reach a happy working relationship between bursar and headteacher where, for example, the bursar saw him or herself as assisting the headteacher in achieving a positive learning environment. That type of relationship was described as a *'partnership between the headteacher and the bursar – the head can't lead without the support of key people or positions and one of these must be the bursar'* (secondary school bursar), with the bursar as *'the fulcrum between teaching and non-teaching staff'* (secondary school bursar). With governing bodies, bursars at this stage were either *ex officio* or co-opted members, often serving on several subcommittees. One bursar had become a governor-trainer (though not at her own school) but this indicates the level of expertise with which bursars could now match that of governors.

Whatever the style of relationships, bursars at the school business management stage were all full and accepted members of their SMTs as the following, typical, responses make clear.

> *I am a member of the School's Planning Team which creates all whole-school plans and manages the work of all members of staff. The team ensures coherence across all*

areas of the school and monitors all performance indicators ... The other members of the Planning Team are the Headteacher, two Deputy Headteachers and the three Senior Teachers. I am also a member of the Senior Management Team which consists of all members of the Planning team and all the Heads of Year and Heads of Cluster. (Secondary school bursar)

The bursar is very much a professional alongside other professionals in the SMT ... I wouldn't look at a bursarship that doesn't include membership of the SMT. (Secondary school bursar)

School business manager bursars felt equal to their colleagues and able to contribute strategically on all matters.

Within the school business manager stage were bursars occupying the position of deputy heads, although only one of this group of 34 bursars had the title of deputy head and he had been a teacher and previously a curriculum deputy. In another school, the bursar's post had been created by combining vacancies for a deputy and for a bursar. It was notable, however, that the title of deputy head had not been conferred and this led, it was felt, to the views of the post holder not being taken seriously. Another *de facto* bursar had fared better and was working very closely with the headteacher in running the school. For this bursar, this included networking with councillors and officers of the LEA though this was the only bursar who mentioned being an active part of managing a school's external relationships, a position generally taken by headteachers.

Education resource manager

In the roles and responsibilities described in Section I of this chapter, there were some signs that the final stage had been achieved but there seems to be a gap between the relationships and the technicalities. Bursars' progress threatens each group of professional educators in turn. Each has to be 're-educated' to accept a new role for bursars. Bursars have to learn how to operate with the education professionals. For some, this has clearly been accomplished, *'I'm in line with other members of the SMT – me and two deputies'* (secondary school bursar), integrating core and non-core activities. This provides,

an independent perspective ... to contribute positively ... [I've] gained their respect ... provided them with ideas they've taken away and thought about even if they disagree and they've come back and developed them. (Primary school bursar)

Summarising the reality

The best way to conclude a chapter recording bursars' voices is to end with this one which realistically recognises that the role development will be as much from the bursars themselves as from changes external to them:

I think bursarship is very much what a person makes of it. It can be a very mechanical job ... it should be a key role in the life of the school ... there are some people who will do just the mechanics and there are others who live the job ... you have to give your time – that's the attitude for this job. (Secondary school bursar)

What bursars have made of their posts follows in Part Three.

Part Three

■ ■ ■

Continuing Development: Case Studies of Effective Practice

These chapters review case studies of aspects of the work of the bursars whose activities and backgrounds were the subject of Part Two. The range of studies selected relates to major areas of bursars' responsibilities. The studies were chosen from a variety of schools and to show the different levels at which bursars operate. The projects with which the case studies are concerned took place in the last five years of the 1990s. The bursars who provided the information for these studies, and their schools, are gratefully acknowledged in the list at the beginning of the book.

7

■ ■ ■

Strategic Planning

Introduction

Following the Education Reform Act of 1988 the greater autonomy experienced by schools has exposed them to market forces and the need to move from tactical to strategic decision making as discussed in Part One. Schools became increasingly aware that, for strategic planning purposes, information should be site specific. They also recognised that if a culture of monitoring and evaluation were not created there could be a limited response to local community and school needs, which would result in a fall in the budget and a restriction in school development. Schools in England and Wales continue to operate within a climate of change and uncertainty, where considerations of teaching and learning must also incorporate responses to social and economic trends, competition from other schools and the provision of a wider service to pupils. In order to respond to these developments, schools needed to consider the appropriateness of their management structure and mode of strategic planning.

Alongside headteachers as leaders of the whole school, bursars as resource managers needed to develop a strategic overview of their own responsibility areas and they were particularly well placed to monitor information and trends relating to their own and competitor schools, analyse it and report to the senior management team for further evaluation. We, therefore, collected case studies to demonstrate how bursars have become involved in strategically analysing school issues. The first two studies show bursars considering strategies for dealing with falling or rising rolls and suggesting approaches to take to provide information for the senior management team to use in their deliberations. The next four case studies describe how bursars, using the school's strategic plan, ethos and culture, supported the teaching staff of the school by providing relevant information, motivated staff, and optimum office and classroom support. The final study examines how the use of strategic planning can lead to the provision of a better service for both pupils and staff on an ongoing basis.

The case studies

7.1 *Strategic analysis of resource deployment*. This describes the bursar's development of a method for analysing resource implications of proposed projects for school expansion.

7.2 *Introducing nursery provision*. In this study the bursar examines the consequences of the school introducing a nursery. Strategic planning tools and financial costing linked to survey results and the school development plan are used.

7.3 *Finance information for budget holders*. The bursar in this study explores the quality and relevance of information provided to budget holders.

7.4 *Reviewing administrative support for teachers*. In this study the bursar institutes an office support system, which is guided by the school's development plan, culture and ethos.

7.5 *Effective use of support staff*. The bursar in this study carries out a survey of support staff involvement in whole school activities, which coincides with the revision of the school development plan.

7.6 *Efficient catering for staff and pupils*. This examines the strategy used by the bursar to develop a better catering service for the school.

7.7 *Managing classroom support staff in an infant school*. An apparently successful infant school fails its Ofsted and is placed on special measures. The bursar identifies the classroom support staff as a potential but underutilised strength and conducts a detailed literature survey and series of stakeholder interviews to put together an improvement strategy as part of the recovery plan.

Case study 7.1: Strategic analysis of resource deployment

School

Midlands, GM, mixed school, 600+ pupils, secondary phase.
35 teachers, 17 support staff.
Bursar from accounting background.

Context

The school had a falling roll and very poor A*–C, GCSE passes. It was due to close at the beginning of the 1990s. In response to the threat of closure,

GM status was acquired and a new headteacher was appointed. The strategies introduced by the new headteacher increased pupil numbers and dramatically improved the A*–C, GCSE passes in the first three years. The pass rate was still improving at the time of the case study, but the percentage increases were appreciably smaller. The school had increased its pupil numbers to a point where it was very close to its maximum capacity and had to decide whether or not to limit numbers to its current capacity or make changes to accommodate more pupils, especially in the light of new housing development in the area.

The bursar's role in the project

The bursar took a strategic overview of the options available to the school to accommodate extra pupils. Options were explored that would allow the SMT to make an informed choice using a wide range of information and included:

1 continue with the present situation unchanged;

2 increase class sizes;

3 remodel existing accommodation and build a new learning resource centre;

4 extend the school day and operate a split lunchtime system.

These options were assessed on their suitability, acceptability and feasibility to determine whether they achieved an optimum solution for the school.

The bursar developed a technique for analysing resource deployment, which could be used to highlight disparities between the school's current capacity and its capacity to develop alternative strategies. The technique is illustrated in Figure 7.1.

Key financial, physical and human resources are listed, plus any other resource areas appropriate to the school. The present school situation was estimated against each resource area and assigned a number between 0 and 5, where 0 was a major weakness and 5 was a major strength. A glance down each column was then enough to ascertain the school's strengths and weaknesses in each resource area.

The resource implications were then assessed against each option and assigned numbers between 0 and 5, where 0 is unimportant and 5 was critical to the success of the strategy. Any option could then be chosen or discounted according to the resources it required and, whether those resources were or could be made available. For example in Option 2 where the availability of cash and the ability to raise funds were critical to the success of the strategy, if the funds could not be made available, then the option would have to be discounted. By totalling the resource implications and comparing them with the

Key resource areas	Resource implications			
	Present school situation	Option 1 Increase class size	Option 2 Remodel	Option 3 Extend school day
Financial				
Available cash	2	1	5	2
Ability to raise additional funds	1	1	5	1
Physical				
Well maintained premises	4	5	4	4
Up-to-date equipment	3	4	4	4
Human				
Skilled staff	4	5	4	5
Quality of leadership and management	3	5	3	5
Other				
Reputation for quality	2	5	3	5
Community/business contacts	4	1	4	3
Total	23	27	32	29
Mismatch		+4	+9	+6

Figure 7.1 Resource deployment analysis technique

total for the present school situation, a numerical figure was arrived at that indicated the level of extra commitment to resources there would be. For example in Option 3, financial and physical resources would not be a problem as long as the school maintained its current position. A strategy would need developing for up-skilling staff and the management team and this would be likely to improve the reputation of the school, which was also important if enough students were to be attracted to fill the extra places.

The bursar's contribution: discussion

The bursar made time to understand the strategic position of the school in relation to its competitors and planned scenarios for dealing with the envisaged increase in numbers. Consideration of resource implications was not limited to finance, but included physical, human and other pertinent resources. The presentation of the implications in a tabular form provided the SMT with an easily understood visual aid for debating the options. The bursar could then provide a detailed costing for the preferred option rather than for each option. This strategy therefore saved the bursar's time in relation to providing detailed costing and the SMT's time because the resource implications were presented in an accessible manner.

The bursar had also considered the school's position in relation to Handy's sigmoid curve (Handy, 1994: 41) and determined that it had reached the point where a new strategy should be determined to drive the school forward. The fact that GCSE results had plateaued and the school had reached full capacity were indications that this was the case. This information would also be useful to the SMT during their decision making as projected pupil numbers might be affected.

Case study 7.2: Introducing nursery provision

School

Home Counties, GM, mixed school, 200+ pupils, primary phase.
11 teachers, 14 support staff.
Bursar from teaching and local government background.

Context

The school was experiencing a period of sustained success and becoming increasingly popular. The development plan included an objective of extending provision for voucher bearing four-year-olds or establishing a nursery. To maintain its position, especially in the light of increased parental choice through the voucher system, the school reviewed its current strategy. Initially, infant admissions were extended by instituting a single intake in September for the reception class. In the mean time the school considered alternatives for further nursery provision including either building a nursery or refurbishing part of the school. The bursar was part of the team investigating the use of alternative space within the school. The school then carried out a survey determining the number of children in the current intake who had taken advantage of nursery playgroup/provision. Parents were also asked whether they would have used the school's nursery if one had been built. A further survey was carried out in the school's catchment area to determine future pupil numbers and the extent to which a nursery would be utilised if one were built.

The bursar's role in the project

The bursar made use of a range of techniques in order to understand the strategic position of the school in relation to its plan to develop nursery provision. Porter's 'Five Forces' approach cited in Johnson and Scholes (1993) was adapted for the school and the following areas examined.

1 Potential barriers to the provision of nursery education such as local and national government policy.

2 The implications of resource allocation and funding opportunities.

3 The needs of the parents as 'buyers' of nursery education.

4 The options available to parents as alternatives to mainstream education.

5 The variety of institutions offering the same service in direct competition.

An analysis was then carried out by the bursar to identify the school's strengths, weaknesses, opportunities and threats (SWOT) in relation to providing nursery education (Figure 7.2). The analysis revealed that the nursery voucher system was both a threat and an opportunity and emphasised the position of other local schools in competition for limited public funds.

The results of the analyses were then used to determine whether or not a capital outlay was viable and whether the voucher system would cover running costs. The bursar provided information on the Private Funding Initiative and the implications of servicing a bank loan. Examination of the school's budget requirements and any deviation from the development plan's driving force on the current budget was undertaken to ensure that the school's plan remained educationally rather than resource orientated. A priority list was established by the governing body and the senior management team, of whom the bursar was a member. The bursar provided calculations over a year of funding available from the voucher system and the extra costs involved in equipping and

Strengths	Weaknesses
• Rising roll	• Some members of staff unable to cope
• GM status	with change
• Well maintained buildings	• Lack of funding
• Active members of governing body	• Lack of internal space
• Large area of land available for possible development	

Opportunities	Threats
• GM status	• Competition from local schools
• Area available for development	• Competition from nurseries and
• Investment in IT an attraction to parents	playgroups
• Nursery voucher scheme	• Current catchment areas
• Alternative sources of funding available	• Local and national government influences on LEA

Figure 7.2 SWOT analysis of the school's strategic position for introducing a nursery

running a nursery. The costing included the salaries and on-costs of the teacher and ancillary staff, maintenance, materials, other premises and miscellaneous costs. The costing exercise revealed that expenditure would outweigh income and resulted in a revised plan being agreed using staff more cost-effectively.

The bursar's contribution: discussion

The bursar was able to plan for the link between the school's development plan, its educational priorities and their resource implications as a member of the senior management team. By analysing survey results, as well as investigating the costs and implications of nursery provision strategic planning, information was provided which was based on:

- a strategic analysis of the school's position in relation to the community and other local schools;
- a detailed costing pertinent to the school's specific situation;
- a costing which was based on an understanding of the school's values and educational priorities.

The overall information presented to the SMT would therefore facilitate strategic decision making based on sound educational criteria and thoroughly researched data.

Case study 7.3: Finance information for budget holders

School

Urban, GM, mixed school with sixth form, 800+ pupils.
57 teachers, 40 support staff.
Bursar from military background.

Context

The bursar was concerned about the quality of financial information provided by the finance department to its budget holders and how much it would help them assess their spending strategies. Monthly reports were provided, but there was uncertainty as to whether the information was understandable, up to date, accurate, complete and consistent. The bursar was preparing to introduce changes in the reporting procedure for the new financial year and particularly wanted to meet the information requirements of the budget holders.

The bursar's role in the project

The bursar distributed a questionnaire to the budget holders, which asked them to rate how understandable, up to date, accurate, complete and consistent the information they received was. The questionnaire design is illustrated in Figure 7.3. The questionnaires were followed up with interviews to determine specific needs in terms of financial information required.

The results of the enquiry indicated that the information provided did not meet the budget holders' needs and provided the bursar with an overall view of the changes that would need to be made to supply them with a report that they could use more effectively. The changes identified were that:

1   line entries should be clearer and understandable to the budget holder without consultation with the finance officer;

2   there should be an audit trail for part orders, which linked the original to each part;

3   photocopying charges should be renegotiated;

4   photocopying charges should be up to date.

The bursar initiated the changes necessary to enable budget holders to make more effective decisions.

It is interesting to note that after completing an analysis of the questionnaires and interviews, the bursar discovered that budget holders believed that the format of the reports could not be changed and for that reason had not discussed their requirements with the finance officer. On the other hand, the finance officer considered that the format of the report was perfectly clear and had therefore not seen the necessity of asking budget holders if they understood the information they were receiving. The bursar concluded that more effective communication in both directions would have led to a better use of time for both parties and was looking at strategies to improve communication in the future.

Do you receive financial information from your monthly reports that is:	Poor quality 1	2	Moderate quality 3	4	High quality 5
Comprehensible to you?					
Published soon after the end of the month?					
Accurate, free from error and valid?					
Free from omissions or false data?					
Capable of being compared with different time periods?					

Figure 7.3   Questionnaire for establishing relevance of financial information to budget holders

The bursar's contribution: discussion

Improved monitoring and evaluation, which the bursar investigated here, are important aspects of the planning cycle. Without accurate data and a considered response to that data, it is not possible to make informed decisions on which strategic plans are formulated. Teachers and the senior management team receive large amounts of information and data every week that they use in decision making not all of which may be easily understood or accurate. Many teachers, even Heads of Section do not have a background in finance or administration and there is often a need for more than a little training for them on these aspects. Similarly, support staff are not always completely aware of the specifics of teaching and learning. If support staff can provide the relevant information required by the decision makers, then not only is there an understanding of the issues both by support staff and teachers, but the teacher's time is not wasted in trying to convert the information into a more comprehensible form. This type of understanding can only be achieved through regular communication between both parties.

Case study 7.4: Reviewing administrative support for teachers

School

South-east, GM, mixed school with sixth form, 1500+ pupils, secondary phase.
100 teachers, 10 administrative staff.
Bursar from secretarial background.

Context

Due to changes in the senior management of the school, the post of deputy head was abolished in the mid-1990s and a new team constructed consisting of the headteacher, senior teachers and the bursar. Responsibilities were allocated in the areas of curriculum development, post-16 education, curriculum delivery, curriculum support, pastoral care and the development of financial, administration and premises management systems. The school had adopted a policy of cost-effectiveness linked to the school development plan, which encompassed its aims, culture and ethos. It was a prime concern of the school's strategic planning that as far as possible, teachers were not involved in administrative tasks and that the bursar's task was to facilitate this.

The bursar's role in the project

The bursar took a strategic overview of office systems and teacher support in relation to the school development plan and the need for cost-effectiveness. Changes were implemented that included providing value-for-money services, restructuring the office staff to reflect the needs of the school and setting up a training programme for office staff to provide support in specific areas.

Office systems

Cost-effectiveness was achieved through a series of measures, which encompassed:

- the implementation of a computerised package providing good financial reporting information;
- using a purchasing system that balanced quality against low prices;
- providing good quality equipment;
- setting up financial procedures to monitor income and expenditure for school trips in order to prevent them operating at a loss.

Teacher support

A decision was taken to employ several part-time support staff instead of a few full-time staff to provide a prompt level of service. All the support staff were trained to be multi-skilled and handbooks were written detailing the jobs to enable staff to cover for one another. The bursar believed that this situation created a good teamwork ethos. In addition, two critical posts were created to provide support for teachers in the areas.

1 *Management information systems.* The post holder administers examinations, produces pupil performance statistics, assists the Head of Curriculum Development with timetabling and updates pupils' teaching groups. Duties were extended to include monitoring attendance, registering pupils with special needs and assisting the Head of Curriculum Development with assessment and reporting procedures.

2 *Admission and appeals procedures.* As the school was oversubscribed, the post holder was able to concentrate on providing a sympathetic and informed service to parents of children applying for a place.

The bursar's contribution: discussion

Apart from a very small core team, support staff in schools are commonly part time, task related and on short-term contracts. The first task of the bursar in this context was to consider resource provision in terms of cost-effectiveness and the coherence of a support staff team while retaining personal contact, involvement of individual support staff and the teaching and learning activities they support.

In this case study, the bursar put systems in place to provide both financial and statistical management information and identified key support areas as critical part-time dedicated posts. Bearing in mind that cost-effectiveness was important, value for money was achieved by purchasing the best possible equipment within an allocated budget rather than at the lowest cost and through the setting up of additional systems for monitoring extraordinary spending. A flexible team of committed, part-time, multi-skilled staff was assembled to provide a personal clerical and administration service and hand-books developed to provide backup information.

Case study 7.5: Effective use of support staff

School

South-west, GM, mixed school with sixth form, 900+ pupils.
Bursar from service industry background.

Context

The school is located on a split site, part of which is shared with a neigh-bouring school and leisure centre. The playing fields are off-site and the leisure centre provides the school's PE facilities. One site has been substan-tially extended and enhanced by additional accommodation built in the 1990s. The other site consists of several independent buildings of varying ages that have benefited only minimally from capital projects. As a conse-quence of the difference in the two sites, staff based on the second site perceived themselves as segregated and lower in the school's hierarchy. They felt neither ownership nor involvement in the goals and policy making of the school.

In addition, the school had also suffered a decline in its reputation and pupil roll followed by a rapid upturn on the appointment of a new head. The absence of a period of consolidation after the appointment, com-pounded by the changing demands of the National Curriculum created a stressful environment for the staff. The school was, however, at the time of the case study, in a strengthened market position, offering excellent science, technology and ICT facilities, improved accommodation and a range of vocational courses. Exam results had improved.

There was a structure in place, which involved teaching staff in discussing policy issues and strategic decisions. Support staff were not included in this process and felt that their contribution to the school was not recognised. Consequently, they felt marginalised. A SWOT analysis carried out by the teaching staff identified priority issues, which included staff morale and self-esteem, communication, school vision and values, site development and the consequences of working on a split site with unequal accommodation, but the support staff were not involved in this.

The bursar's role in the project

As there was no framework in place for consulting with support staff, the bursar undertook a survey to determine whether they were familiar with the school's purpose, saw themselves as working in a team and considered that their contribution to the school was recognised. The survey was timed to coincide with the revision of the school's development plan and staff development framework. The results indicated that although staff were clear about the purpose, strategies and goals of the school and their individual roles, they felt a low personal and collective sense of power and did not feel that their contribution was recognised. As the survey was timed to coincide with the revised development plan, the findings were taken into account during the development of the new plan. Steps were then taken to promote greater participation of support staff by restructuring the staff development framework to include both teaching and support staff and to involve support staff in INSET days. Appraisal was also due to be set up for support staff as the school intended applying for Investors in People. Support staff were then involved in the SWOT analysis process.

The bursar's contribution: discussion

Motivating staff in a school can be a problem for any of its leaders. In particular it is important that they understand the school's aims and subscribe to its culture. As leaders of the support staff, bursars are responsible for integrating them into the life of the school and helping teachers to understand their value. In this particular situation, the bursar suggested that by raising an awareness of the support staff's case and their possible contribution the school benefited from:

- improved communication between all staff and between staff and governors;
- an understanding by the support staff of what the school was trying to achieve and how it proposed to reach its targets;
- enhanced motivation of support staff generated through valued individual contribution and teamwork.

Case study 7.6: Efficient catering for staff and pupils

School

Welsh, GM, mixed school with sixth form, 700+ pupils.
39 teachers, 13 support staff.
Bursar from retail and local government backgrounds.

Context

The school's mission statement explicitly values the pastoral care of pupils and subscribes to building a school community based on religious values. The provision of a well run, well used catering service in pleasant surroundings is seen as a reflection of this aspect of the mission. The governing body was also keen to provide a self-supporting service, which provided the best value for money. Improving the catering facilities also formed part of the school development plan.

The catering service had been run by the County's Direct Services Organisation. After the school became grant maintained, a three-year contract was awarded to a new catering provider. The school then made an initial investment into the service by providing new catering tables and small equipment for the kitchen. Initially, the service was well received by the staff and pupils but it did not improve in line with expectations and use of the service fell while costs rose.

The bursar's role in the project

The bursar's strategic intent was to enhance the catering service in order to improve the pupils' pastoral care. To achieve this a business plan for bringing the service in-house was produced by the bursar and a consultant was commissioned to carry out a diagnostic review. The main findings suggested that the quality of food was average while costs were high and that the service was slow due to an inadequate layout of the servery and lack of suitable tills. The bursar then met with the catering company and some changes were implemented. Continual monitoring of the catering invoices enabled the bursar to determine that costs to the school had fallen but only due to the reduced quality and quantity of food served.

The bursar developed a strategic plan, which determined that the critical success factors for the catering service would be that it became a self-supporting service within two years and that there would be increased uptake of the service through responsiveness to the customers' needs. The customers were identified as the staff and pupils of the school and a 30 per cent sample of these was issued a questionnaire to determine their needs. A comprehensive SWOT analysis was also carried out to determine the service's strengths, weaknesses, opportunities and threats, paying particular attention to external and internal management, staff, the kitchen area and equipment, catering provision, customers, finance, the governors' wishes and possible future scenarios. The analysis suggested that the external contractors should give more support to the kitchen manager and show more understanding of the school's needs. Investment would be required to alter the servery arrangements and provide new equipment. Menus would also need to be changed to reflect customers' needs and a review system should be put in place to regularly monitor the use of the service.

When the catering contract became due for renewal the governing body invited tenders and, after short-listing, visited schools in which the companies were operating. The SWOT analysis, questionnaires and costing provided by the bursar enabled the governors to make informed decisions about the level and type of service required and they authorised spending on the servery and kitchen to coincide with the uptake of the new contract in order to make the greatest impact. An implementation plan was then drawn up by the bursar which articulated the school's, caterer's and builder's agreement on what they were doing and the date of completion.

The bursar's contribution: discussion

Much of the learning environment with which a pupil comes into contact is not in the classroom. 'Corridor life' is an important part of the ethos, climate and culture of the school. The way in which a school makes provision for non-teaching functions is readily evident after visiting toilets and canteens. This case study examines how the bursar reviewed the existing catering provision, established what was needed in both cost and service terms, and implemented and evaluated a customer responsive approach to school meals provision.

Dissatisfaction with the catering provision had prompted the bursar to critically examine all aspects of the service. The budget was analysed, customers surveyed and the staff in the school interviewed about the service they were able to provide. The information collected was then used to carry out an analysis of the catering provision and develop a plan for improving the service. The bursar was then able to provide specific information to those involved in setting up the new contract and organise a swift transfer.

The lessons learned from the decline in the service offered by the previous contract were also used to develop a procedure of monitoring and review in order to avoid replacing the previous provision with something similar. Thus a service was developed, which was responsive to the customer and built on an understanding and positive relationship between the contractor and the school. Figure 7.4 illustrates how the strategic techniques used by the bursar resulted in these outcomes.

Strategic technique	Outcomes
Implementation plan	1 A swift transfer was possible.
	2 All work has been completed on time.
New procedures resulting from SWOT analysis	1 The area manager gives constant support to the kitchen manager.
	2 The area manager has regular meetings with the bursar.
	3 The area manager has arranged training and support for all catering staff.
	4 Trading figures are reviewed regularly by the bursar and the area manager and reported to the governing body.
Regular review	1 A procedure has been agreed for evaluating the service, which includes an annual customer survey, a monthly financial review and a termly SWOT analysis.
	2 The bursar has weekly meetings with the kitchen manager, visits the kitchen daily to use the service and has informal meetings with the kitchen staff.
	3 Customer surveys are carried out and an action plan drawn up to respond to comments.

Figure 7.4 Outcomes resulting from the use of particular strategic techniques

Case study 7.7: Managing classroom support staff in an infant school

School

Home Counties, GM, mixed school, 200+ pupils, primary phase.
11 teachers, 14 support staff.
Bursar: part time, local government background.

Context

The school gained GM status in 1994 and was close to full capacity at the time of this study. There was a maximum of nine classes in operation though the school had recently opened a further extension of provision for four-year-olds, originally through the nursery voucher scheme. The school shares its site with an LEA controlled junior school. The school was perceived as a successful school having a rising roll, a waiting list for the reception class and a belief at school level that the quality of education offered met the needs of the pupils. The school saw its primary objective as providing a caring and protective learning environment. In late 1997 the school was inspected by Ofsted and was judged as giving 'unsatisfactory value for money' and placed on special measures. The headteacher had been in post since 1970 and was due to take early retirement in summer 1998 but in practice had been on long-term sick leave from early 1998. Governors had also left unfilled the deputy headteacher post until the new headteacher had been appointed.

A key focus in the inspection had been the use and deployment of the seven classroom support staff. The inspectors found they were well trained and supported in their work, were effectively deployed, provided sensitive support for small groups and pupils with special educational needs, gave valuable support to their teachers and were usually well briefed on day-to-day tasks. A criticism was made that there were occasions when they were not used to best effect, for example, looking on while lengthy explanations were given to the whole class. The bursar determined that the foundations for developing this valuable resource of support staff had been laid and a fuller analysis of the role and management of classroom support staff would be a key weapon in the armoury of school improvement techniques as part of the recovery plan to take the school out of special measures.

The bursar's role in the project

The bursar's first task was to analyse the current group of classroom support staff. They were all female between 35 and 45 years old and had been employed by the school for an average of three years. Four had NVQ level 2 certificates in non-teaching duties, one had a BTEC in art and the remaining two had no specific qualification related to their support role. The number of hours allocated to the seven staff was 160 per week in term time which compared well with the national average of 120 hours a week for all education support (including technicians, special educational needs [SEN] and nursery nurses). The turnover of staff in the support staff group generally was low and the school had been able to maintain the level of support over the past five years. Thus the base level of experience and expertise was high, which had been confirmed by the Ofsted inspection.

Individual classroom support staff were timetabled to different classrooms but there was no whole school policy for the deployment of individuals, the class teacher determining their use of time. There was no monitoring of performance although the school was considering introducing performance development reviews but this had been put on hold awaiting the appointment of the new senior leadership. The job descriptions were still those provided by the LEA before the school became GM and had not been updated, though a number of tasks had been changed. None of the classroom support staff posts had person specifications. The development opportunities for individuals had been limited in the past few years but individuals had been able to study for work-related qualifications.

Having analysed the situation, the bursar identified that the issue was to ensure *'the potential link between the effective utilisation of classroom support staff and the contribution this can make to the school improvement process'*. Two main strategies were adopted by the bursar to gain further data about how this group of staff could be better utilised: a survey of key studies in the field of classroom support staff utilisation and an analysis of the perception of a sample of school staff through interviews. The final outcome was a report to the governing body giving the findings of the investigation and recommendations for changes to be included in the action plan to take the school out of special measures.

Although there was not a great deal of literature on the effective utilisation of support staff, the bursar identified some key studies (*see* Chapter 2). Ofsted reports also contain reference to the use of associate staff and the bursar examined a number of these from local schools and reviewed some texts in the fields of resource management and change, coming to the conclusion that *'effective resource management can thus be seen as an approach that maximises the available resources to the fullest, success being measured by the learning outcomes achieved'*. The analysis of these studies helped the bursar identify four characteristics of effective utilisation of classroom support staff.

1 The roles were perceived as enhancing curriculum provision.

2 Skills of support staff complemented the skills of classroom teachers.

3 Support staff freed teachers from routine classroom tasks.

4 Their presence improved pupil/adult ratios which allowed a more flexible approach to classroom organisation.

Grounds had therefore been established for the bursar to proceed with the next stage of the investigation – the interviews. These were conducted over a three-week period. The sample included the major stakeholder, the classroom support staff themselves (all seven), two teachers (from the 11 in the school) and two governors (from the seven left on the governing body after the Ofsted report) both of whom were parent governors. The interviews covered such areas as the contribution to learning, the classroom support role, relationships with the class teacher, their contribution to planning, communication, professional 'boundary management', and the overall utilisation of the classroom assistants.

The general findings were that classroom support staff showed a clear awareness of the school as a learning environment and the contribution they could make to this, but there was criticism of the ineffective use of their individual time. There were instances of teachers who were able to fully utilise any support staff that they were given, whereas other teachers found it difficult to respond positively to the presence of another adult in the room. In producing the report for the governors the bursar made the following recommendations.

1   Regular planned meetings to facilitate communication between classroom support staff and teachers would enhance the improvement process by allowing regulation of classroom practices.

2   The school should be the first school to inspire new innovations in the use of classroom assistants building on the example of the art and design technology co-ordinator.

3   Careful consideration should be given to identifying suitable benchmarks for effective performance by support staff drawing on Ofsted reports and literature on the characteristics of effective schools.

4   Establish monitoring and review procedures for classroom support staff to ensure their equitable distribution and its positive contribution to the improvement process.

5   Develop a clear policy for the training and development of classroom support staff in line with their role as paraprofessionals.

6   Establish a period of induction for support staff to introduce them to the ethos and procedures of the school learning environment.

The bursar's contribution: discussion

This case study is an important exemplar of the potential role of a professional experienced in organisational development and sympathetic to the learning priorities of the school. Although the topic seems to impinge on the organisation of the classroom and, as such, may be considered to be outside the purview of an administrator, it is clearly a legitimate area in which the bursar should be engaged. In this case, each classroom teacher had been left to organise their own relationships with the classroom support assistant and thus policies on their use varied. Despite this, the group of support staff, had developed a good sense of cohesion and empathy with the learning objectives of the school. The school was not, however, using this team in the most effective way and this may help to explain why an apparently successful school came to be the subject of special measures. The bursar's detailed analysis of the situation and painstaking review of relevant external sources and the perceptions of the stakeholders offered both specific ways forward for the school and a model for approaching future issues in school improvement alongside the teaching staff. Finally, the school was effectively leaderless during most of the time when this case study was carried out (although the Funding Agency did engage a recently retired local head to act as a consultant) and the positive and sensitive role played by the bursar in tackling one aspect identified by Ofsted as needing improvement shows the leadership potential of such a post.

Final thoughts

By 2000, the effective bursar was at the heart of the business function of the school and providing a range of services responsive to teaching and learning requirements and to the school's position in the external community. These services include:

1 *Data handling and the provision of information.* If regularly analysed, pupil roll numbers, Standard Assessment Tasks (SATs) and examination results and budget figures will provide the SMT and middle managers with data to inform their decision making. In addition, because bursars or their staff are regularly in contact with the community, parents and agencies outside the school, they also have an understanding of the school's relationship with these groups. On the whole, the teacher's main task is pupils' learning and, although they do have some contact with the wider community, the bursar's position is more appropriate for examining the status of the school within its community and organising, analysing and reporting on surveys and interviews with relevant stakeholders and collecting information on competitor schools.

2 *Management of outsourced contracts.* This was achieved in the case study through the bursar contemplating the service supplied and applying strategic thinking to develop a more cost-effective and client-responsive provision based on consultation, communication and review.

3 *Leadership of support staff.* The bursar is usually the leader of the support staff and case studies in this chapter have demonstrated how school services can improve by appraising, assessing and analysing the role of the support staff in the school and adapting provision to respond to requirements.

4 *Scenario planning to enable rapid response to unfolding futures.* The bursar, as manager of the school's office and records is in a prime position to monitor the school's situation in relation to its current strategy.

5 *Membership of the strategic leadership team.* Comprehension of basic educational issues and current trends is crucial in assisting the bursar to understand the relevance of the information being collected, particularly when presenting it to the SMT.

The next chapter will explore the bursar's contribution to developing the service offered by support staff in particular.

8

■ ■ ■

Support Staff

Introduction

This chapter describes case studies in which the roles of support staff were changing in the 1990s and how bursars led these changes. Responsibility for the leadership of school support staff is one of the two major areas which virtually all bursars had as part of their jobs (the other was finance), as shown in Part Two. The number of support staff to be managed in any school at the end of the twentieth century was approaching equality with, or even exceeding, the number of teaching staff; this made their contribution to a school's success more visible and, with it, the importance of their being effectively managed and led as these case studies illustrate. The relationship of bursars to support staff is important in the twenty-first century; it is their main role in school human resource management and their success in this could indicate the extent to which their HRM authority might later extend over teaching staff. In this chapter, support staff are identified as anyone not directly delivering, nor managing, teaching.

The case studies

8.1 *Increasing support staff numbers to achieve cost and teacher effectiveness.* This illustrates how support staff were seen as teacher replacements especially when cost reductions were sought. The school investigated the value of a possible increase in support staff; the bursars' plans and rationale for this are presented here.

8.2 *Reorganising the support staff for team effectiveness.* This describes how support staff numbers had to be reduced to achieve economies but how a team approach was developed to use the remaining staff more effectively and economically.

The third and fourth studies relate to the comparisons between support and teaching staff in their remuneration and rewards and their appraisal, and how bursars have helped support staff to come to terms with this.

8.3 *Teacher equivalence? The bursar reviews support staff benefits.* In this example, the bursar investigated the extent to which support staff felt that their rewards were fair and suggested how these might be altered.

8.4 *Teacher equivalence? Introducing support staff appraisal.* This outlines how an appraisal system was introduced for support staff to parallel that of the teachers.

8.5 *Investigating a sites and premises team.* In the last case study, the bursar relates problems in one particular team of support staff. To solve these, the possibility of using external contractors rather than the in-house team was considered and various ways of restructuring were tried. The bursar did not claim to have the definitive solution but the investigations were wide.

Case study 8.1: Increasing support staff numbers to achieve cost and teacher effectiveness

School

London, Catholic, GM, mixed school, 700+ pupils, secondary phase with sixth form.
45 teachers, 8.8 support staff.
Bursar from accountancy and consultancy background.

Context

The bursar believed that the support staff in the school were employed on an historical rather than a needs basis and that the teaching staff might be better assisted than was currently the case. The bursar therefore surveyed teachers to ascertain the support that they felt they required. From this, a report was produced for the governors. This took the teachers' needs and teaching and learning in the school into account.

The bursar's role in the project

The bursar's report demonstrated that an increase in support staff was needed to release teachers from non-teaching tasks. What was needed initially, as the bursar's plan demonstrated, was to prove that employing support staff would be cost effective in comparison with paying teachers' salaries. The bursar's rationale went much further than this. Support staff would replace tasks provided by teacher 'goodwill' with obvious reductions in teacher stress and time. Of course, the bursar's justification for the changes also picked up on the assistance afforded to learning and to whole-school aims. The proposals were set within the school's action plan as contributory to a whole rather than to an immediate, short-term problem in a particular area. Finally, in selling the idea, the bursar showed a clear understanding of both the formal and informal needs of teachers and of their insecurities. Extracts from the report follow, showing the justification and costing for increased support roles,

---

Proposal for increased support staff

School librarian

The School Action Plan recognises the need to prioritise the Library's resources to create an area with a range of resources that support and encourage our students to maximise their learning experiences. The existing library is to be upgraded and a multi-media computer based resource centre accessible from the library is to be created.

The new facility must be appropriately staffed. A Chartered Librarian should be employed.

We have attempted to use our existing staff particularly from the adjoining English Department. This has not proved successful with their main teaching and departmental duties clashing and taking priority over the librarian duties. We have not, however, fully explored the possibility of part time voluntary help from our parents and it would be desirable that any appointment that is agreed is only filled after the School has tried to obtain such help.

The perceived benefits of this appointment are:

For teaching staff:

- *expert help with obtaining resources*
- *knowing that students using the library will not be wasting their time*
- *not having to take responsibility for the area at lunch time*
- *access to centralised resource facilities*

Students will benefit from:

- *more open access to the library*
- *having an experienced professional to give them library and resource searching skills*
- *greater access to computers*

Annual Cost estimate (1998 figures)

Employed week days, 0930–1530, thirty hours weekly, term time only @ £10 per hour
£11,400 + 20% on-costs = £13,800.

IT Technician

The School Action Plan includes the expansion of our Computer based information technology with computers in each department, a sixth form resource centre and facilities in the GNVQ [General National Vocational Qualification] teaching base. The IT specialist staff has reduced to one with the redundancy of the Head of Technology. Much of the expansion in equipment will occur quickly by utilising leasing contracts, a grant received under the National Grid for Learning and funds for us as a school in 'special measures'.

NB: Schools deemed to be failing by the Office for Standards in Education (Ofsted) are given additional funds and other support to correct their faults This is referred to as being in 'special measures'. The school will be inspected again after an interval of time and may then be removed from this category if it has met the requirements of Ofsted.

At present, the technical support has been obtained from the goodwill of the Science Department allowing one of their laboratory technicians to spend time in the IT area. Demands on technicians' time will increase in the Science area as we commence formal staff training in preparation for the introduction of Cognitive Acceleration through Science Education ... This requires specialised activity equipment that the technicians will construct ... as directed by the teaching staff.

These pressures emphasise the need to employ an additional technician who would be an IT specialist ... It is proposed that part-time only is required to allow the existing Science Laboratory Technician the continued job satisfaction obtained by involvement in both duties.

The perceived benefits for teaching staff:

- *computer expertise*
- *not having to worry in front of students about minor problems with the IT equipment that appear insurmountable*
- *time to concentrate on their professional duties*

Students will benefit from:

- *having another person to answer their computer questions*
- *more teacher contact time*
- *less equipment downtime so that they can maximise their learning opportunities in lesson time*

Annual Cost estimate (1998 figures)

Employed week days, 0830–1230, twenty hours weekly, term time only @ £8 per hour
£6,080 + 20% on-costs = £7,296.

Classroom Support (Art and Food Technology)

In each of the Art and Food Technology Departments, there may be the greatest misuse of trained teacher time. The teaching week is divided into twenty-five one hour teaching periods. The teachers try to ensure that all materials are available so that those students can quickly start working ... There is no Technician support in either Department. The teachers obtain the materials and prepare them for the students. At the end of the lessons, the same teachers will be found tidying-up, washing tables, bottles, ovens, sorting-out equipment. These are all jobs that could be done by classroom support staff.

The perceived benefits for teaching staff:

- *being freed from mundane tasks*
- *less stress so they are enabled to concentrate on students and their learning*
- *assistance available when needed*

Students will benefit from:

- *another interested adult freeing the teacher to give them more teaching time*
- *improved learning experience when they become aware of greater expectations of preparedness.*

Annual Cost estimate (1998 figures)

Employed week days, 1200–1700, twenty-five hours weekly, term time only @ £5 per hour
£4,750 + 20% on-costs = £5,700.

Probably, most teaching and support staff were convinced that teachers did jobs that could be just as easily done by support staff, thus releasing valuable teaching time, but such generalised statements were not likely to precipitate changes when governors and senior managers were considering financial costs of changes. Thus, this bursar also reviewed the non-teaching tasks of seven of the teaching staff through a questionnaire. The bursar asked which daily tasks the teachers felt did not need their professional expertise and how much time they spent on these. On average, it was found that 43 hours weekly of the time of these seven teachers were being used in non-teaching duties which others could have carried out for them. For the entire 47 teaching staff, the total would thus be approximately 290 hours per week. As the bursar noted, there were 'a myriad of mundane jobs' with which support staff might help as indicated in Figure 8.1.

Non-teaching tasks	Hours
Photocopying	6
Typing and letters	6
Registration	8
Invigilation	9
Equipment checking	5
Equipment cleaning	3
Others	6
n = teachers	

Figure 8.1 Non-teaching tasks of teachers in one week

The bursar's contribution: discussion

The bursar's rationale for the changes showed that the bursar had moved beyond the brief of merely costing increased support staff. In doing this, not only could the process enhance the bursarship role but the type of staff to be employed could also do so. The bursar could become the leader of a team of highly qualified experts just as the head leads the highly qualified teachers. Note, however, the realism that creeps into the plans above when the bursar recognises that it might be possible to fill a post with volunteers. A bursar managing a team of unpaid volunteers, however, would likely be less highly regarded than one leading full-time professional. The example above also illustrates the disparate 'ownership' of support staff; they do not all come under the remit of the bursar. Some are responsible to teaching staff with consequent diminution of the bursarship role and complications of line management.

This illustration demonstrates what may be a major hindrance to employing additional support staff; currently, teaching or other staff provide the support services free in addition to their normal workloads. Relieving teaching staff of such additional duties may make them less tired and stressed but that will not appear in the budget: the costs of additional staff will. The costs of not providing teachers with adequate support services had already appeared, however, for this school. It was in special measures following a second, poor Ofsted report. The bursar's plan was part of the whole-school initiative to remove the school from special measures. The bursar concluded that:

> The Senior Management Team must create more valuable 'thinking and planning time' by empowering and allowing others to act. In preparation for this we will review with the staff what help they consider that existing or additional support staff could give. It is hoped we can remove some of the tasks presently completed by our teachers which do not require the pedagogic skills of their training. The time released may allow our staff to properly assist in the leadership and management of the school.

Case study 8.2: Reorganising the support staff for team effectiveness

School

Provincial, locally managed (LM), co-educational school, 1100+ students, secondary phase with sixth form provision.
Bursar from financial and school services background

Context

The school was having difficulty keeping within its budget. To contribute to solving the problems, the bursar considered how support staff might be more effectively utilised. There was overstaffing in office administration, restrictive job descriptions preventing flexible working, disputes over school holiday work and confused team structures. The bursar's aim was to save money by making changes to solve these problems.

The bursar's role in the project

The changes instigated involved both extensive reductions in numbers of support staff and reorganisation of their roles. This would be a difficult enough change to lead but there was also the major development of teamworking for which acceptance had to be won. The extent of the structural changes planned by the bursar and the senior management team can be seen in Fig. 8.2. The major change in the teams came in the area of the bursar's own main responsibilities, those of finance and administration. This offered the opportunity for the bursar to demonstrate how a team attitude could be built. The change of attitudes from staff working as individuals to staff accepting notions of what is best described as 'extended job sharing' or communal working, is discussed below.

Once the plan was accepted, the bursar commenced the task of developing effective teamworking. The bursar first did a needs' audit, assessing the knowledge, motivation, confidence and experience of the original groups. This strongly influenced the ensuing redundancies and job redefinitions, a process which took approximately one year. To create teamworking from this less than promising start required extensive and continuing communication and consultation within the team, facilitated and led by the bursar. Second, the senior teaching staff created a Code of Conduct explaining what was expected of the support staff. This helped to avoid senior teachers continuing with old practices and enabled junior teachers to feel confident in pressing for the use of the new formats of support staffing. Third, the mutual retraining necessary to make teamworking possible proved to be a bonding experience. Communal working meant communal learning. Job skills had to be transferred and members of the team inducted each other into skills previously guarded rather jealously by individuals. The result was a move from a working group to teamworking.

Leader and service → 1997	Leader and service 1997 →	Staff → 1997	Staff 1997→	Service changes 1997→
Bursar: Finance and administration	Bursar: Finance and administration	Finance and administration officer F/T Finance assistant P/T 3 Secretaries P/T Head's secretary P/T 2 Receptionists P/T	Finance and administration officer F/T Secretary F/T 2 Clerical officers P/T Careers adviser from LEA P/T Clerical first aider (term time, school hours)	Reduction of 9 posts to 6 All posts have changed responsibilities Dedicated support for SMT discontinued Head's secretary post combined with secretary for SENCO and SMT Clerical officers became multi-functional and split shift; careers and first aid moved to the team
Bursar: Premises	Bursar: Premises	2 Full-time caretakers on shifts, 0600–1400; 1400–2200	2 Full-time caretakers on shifts, 0600–1400; 1400–2200	Finance from lettings to meet costs of evening caretaking
Bursar: Technicians	Bursar: Technicians	1 Senior technician F/T 1 Science technician F/T 2 Science technicians P/T 1 Art/PE technician P/T 1 Food technician P/T	1 Senior technician F/T 3 Science technicians P/T 1 DT/Art technician P/T 1 PSHE technician P/T (food)	All science technicians to term time only; No PE technician Rationalised service to DT and art
Headteacher Care and guidance	Team leader: Pupil counselling and support	Counsellor F/T Careers adviser from LEA SENCO 3 Support assistants P/T 1 Behaviour support P/T 5 Midday supervisors P/T Nurse P/T Volunteer counsellors	Counsellor term time Nurse P/T Volunteer counsellors	Rationalisation to smaller specialised teams Reductions in hours – term time only Redefined jobs to cover Child Protection
N/A	Head/ registrar: midday supervision	N/A P/T	8 Midday supervisors	Increase to ensure effective lunchtime cover Separation from pre-1997 counselling and guidance group
N/A	SENCO: learning support team	N/A P/T	4 Support assistants	Reduction Team organisation Separation from pre-1997 counselling and guidance group
Deputy head: Examinations	Deputy head: Examinations	Examination officer P/T also as Clerk to Governors; Assistant examination officer and invigilators – casual	Exam. officer P/T also as Clerk to Governors; Assistant examination officer and invigilators – casual	Increased workload with modular exams No alteration in hours or pay
Deputy head: Library	Deputy head: Library	Librarian – term time Assistant librarian P/T Term time volunteers	Librarian – term time Volunteers term time	Reduction of library assistance

P/T = part time, F/T = full time

Figure 8.2 Reorganisation of support staff

The bursar's contribution: discussion

In this case, the changes directly within the remit of the bursar were inextricably intertwined with changes in the organisation of support staff whose line management was not directly to the bursar. The changes made had to accord with much that the bursar could only influence indirectly. There was some opportunity for this indirect influence since the bursar's team was the one most affected by the development of teamwork and thus these might serve as a role model for both the process and outcome. The restructuring offered an interesting insight into how responsibilities for support staff are divided and which staff are deemed to be more directly in support of teaching than others.

Case study 8.3: Teacher equivalence?
The bursar reviews support staff benefits

School

Home counties, GM, co-educational school, 870+ students, secondary phase with sixth form provision.
Bursar from a military background.

Context

The bursar had been concentrating on integrating the support staff into the school community as a whole and believed that it was important to ascertain whether they felt they were treated fairly in comparison with other staff. The results of the survey would be used to determine a strategy for their integration into the school.

The bursar's role in the project

The bursar decided to investigate how support staff perceived the differences in treatment of themselves and of teaching staff. Would they see the system as unfair? If so, did this make them feel undervalued team members? If so, was there anything that could provide some alleviation (accepting that increased salaries were not going to materialise)? The bursar surveyed 16 of the school's 40 support staff including administrators, technicians, classroom assistants and cleaners. They averaged just over 46 years of age, just over six years' service at that school, a 32.75-hour week and salaries of £11 437.50, including on-costs.

In general, the support staff perceived some teachers as overpaid for their levels of commitment and competence compared with that of support staff. Job security, working conditions and retirement provision were not perceived as inequitable but the support staff felt that teacher unions had much greater recognition than their own unions. Support staff considered that they missed out on mentoring and counselling available to the teaching staff but that appraisal provision was equitable. Despite differences in pay and conditions among support staff, they tended not to perceive themselves as unequal and although they saw some obvious differences with teachers, the response was not grudging except in one area, that of training. Support staff held strong views that their professional development was the 'Cinderella' provision after teaching staff needs had been met. Training was considered vital in view of the changed expectations of support staff, the recognition of support work as a career and the impact of new technology on support roles. In all areas, some of the perceptions were found to be based on inadequate information. More training, for example, was available but not everyone knew about it.

From this, the bursar identified long-term needs to be met. These were: more training related to the needs of the whole school, union recognition and personal counselling. In the short term, an information booklet for support staff was needed explaining salary progression and career routes for associate staff together with information on opportunities for personal growth and development, and how to upgrade skills. A coaching and mentoring service was offered for all staff. Retirement provisions, grievance and discipline procedure, and performance management also were to be outlined.

The bursar's contribution: discussion

There is a growing gap between teacher and support staff remuneration, increased further by inducement payments for teachers of shortage subjects. When extra support staff are employed, it is often to replace teachers' roles. The 'replacement' support staff do not, however, receive the same salaries as the teachers they replace and, however much the importance of support staff is recognised, that recognition is unlikely to have the effect of awarding them comparable salaries to those of most of the teachers. While the majority of support staff were of 'part-time, term-time, working parent' origin, perhaps the differences seemed acceptable. Now that support staff are seeing their jobs as careers, there are possibilities that support staff might feel aggrieved. This study revealed, though, that most support staff did feel reasonably satisfied and that there were rewards other than pay which can help support staff feel valued. It is within the bursar's power to improve these so that all staff benefit from the same development and guidance opportunities so enhancing the chances of support staff feeling more a part of the schools they serve.

Case study 8.4: Teacher equivalence? Introducing support staff appraisal

School

Welsh, GM, co-educational school, 1300 students, secondary phase with sixth form provision.
Bursar from a teaching background.

Context

Continuous improvement of teaching staff performance was a priority for the headteacher of the school and appraisal procedures had been in place for some time. The newly appointed bursar had been given the priority of developing financial and budget systems and developing support staff to service the technology and accounting aspects of the school. As these projects neared completion, the bursar decided to set up an appraisal system for the support staff to bring them in line with the teaching staff of the school.

The bursar's role in the project

Noting how much stress was placed on teacher appraisal to raise performance, it seemed important to the bursar that the same expectations and appraisal system should be in place for support staff. To achieve this, the bursar had first to work on the attitudes of support staff. The bursar commented that:

When appraisal was first introduced it was viewed by many of the support staff with suspicion although it had been thoroughly discussed with them. It was seen as a tool for imposing change upon them and there was some fear of being assessed.

To encourage acceptance, the appraisal system adopted took on some elements of the teachers' scheme; support staff had an interview, completed a form in advance of the discussions and documentary records were kept of the concerns and desired professional development for staff. Only observation was excluded as this was not considered appropriate for support staff who are seen regularly about their work, whereas teachers still largely operate solo behind the classroom door. At this school, the bursar realised that adequate time had to be given for both appraiser and appraisee to prepare for the interview. The interview itself was regarded as a job review in which there was discussion of past achievements against targets and the setting of new targets. Those being appraised were asked to rate themselves against agreed criteria and these ratings were compared with those decided by the appraiser. Appraisal for the support staff stressed that targets were needed, first, for whole-school improvement, second for the needs of the individual and, third, for the needs of the whole support staff. The emphasis was firmly on the school at the centre with its core business of teaching and learning.

While no appraisal system can entirely allay fears of performance review, the identification of support staff requirements with that of teaching staff was important to the system's acceptance. Its outcome was also to be the same as that for teachers in terms of professional development activities planned to meet the needs noted in appraisal interviews, as the bursar described:

> Because of the style of the interviews and because employees were encouraged to participate in goal-setting, after their first appraisal interviews, the suspicion and fear were much reduced. Most recognised appraisal as an opportunity to become involved in reflecting and reviewing their own responsibilities. Even where there was a need for significant improvement in performance, the appraisees found the process less threatening than they feared. The transparency of the process and the emphasis on improvement rather than negative criticism eroded the appraisee's inclination to conceal known weaknesses.

The bursar's contribution: discussion

The support staff initially needed convincing of the value of appraisal and it is possible that its equivalence to that of the teachers helped with its acceptance. There remained the challenge of convincing the teaching staff that it was desirable for all staff to be treated in a similar way. At the moment, changes of attitude seem to be occurring within the support staff but less so within whole staffs. Bursars have a pivotal role in helping to bring about changes in approach by both support and teaching staff, though it is clearly more difficult for them to influence the latter. In helping with this, bursars are at the interface of the two groups and can see both points of view especially if they are part of their schools' senior management teams. It thus becomes possible for a bursar to 'sell' an innovation such as support staff appraisal to both groups of staff in the school as this bursar clarified:

> All members of the support staff team should be aware of the difficulties and extra demands being experienced by the Senior Management Team. The support staff can 'go that extra mile' and look for ways to help, often the offer of help is much appreciated by those under pressure, even if they do not immediately take up the offer. If the Support Staff Leader is a member of the SMT then many opportunities will arise to illustrate support to other SMT members.

The membership is not just important for facilitating communication but is also important as a symbol of the status of bursarship and of support staff. Similarities of treatment for both teaching and support staff are also important symbolically as this study indicated.

Case study 8.5: Investigating a sites and premises team

School

South-east, GM, co-educational, 1500+ students, secondary phase with sixth form provision.
100 teaching and 25 support staff.
Bursar from a secretarial background.

Context

The school has a mixture of buildings from a listed, eighteenth-century house to 1993 purpose-built blocks. It overlooks open countryside and has its own lake and woodlands. This idyllic setting is important to the school's image, conducive to teaching and learning (though not always ideally so) but expensive and complex to maintain. Rising pupil rolls put pressure on facilities. Both minor alterations (such as new offices) and major works (a new technology building) were under way. In making these site developments, the bursar aimed to increase cost-effectiveness, to minimise disruption during the school day and to improve the comfort and appearance of the school so that the environment itself became an educational experience. An additional short-term objective was that better kept premises would be more easily let to outsiders thus enhancing school income.

The bursar's role in the project

The staffing implications of the site developments raised two major questions. First, should all premises management be provided by outside agencies? Second, if it were to be provided in-house, then how should the team be structured?

In answering the first question, there were the obvious cost factors to be taken into account and the control and monitoring of the work done. Less obviously, there were the intangible benefits of loyalty and attachment to the school of an in-house team and of the status of support staff. If a major element of support work were to be outsourced, would it downgrade the notion of support work as integral to teaching and learning? Outside contractors might be less likely to be committed to the core school business than were those directly employed by that school.

The review by the bursar found that outsourcing would provide specialist expertise and that it would leave internal staff with more time for day-to-day management. The challenge was to set the standards that external contractors had to achieve and to monitor those standards. The review also brought the realisation that much of the work was not regularly needed and could be contracted out to small, local businesses on an *ad hoc* basis. Local cabling engineers and electricians were found to provide services at much more modest charges than those of a 'catch-all' contract. There were also problems in finding a firm willing to provide total facilities management for just one school. It would only become economic for a company able to contract to a group of schools.

In assessing outsourcing, the bursar used a proficiency plan (Figure 8.3), which analysed the effectiveness of the alternative routes.

	In-house	External
Financial	• Salaries + on-costs = 1.5 salary	• Salaries + profits = 3.25 salary
	• Overheads to be added	• Overheads included
	• Paid monthly by school	• Expense incurred only when needed
	• Increases with annual pay rises	• Peaks and troughs are levelled
	• Paid regardless of workload	• No costs of staff appointments
	• Cash outlay is lower than with outsourcing	• Large contractor can make economies in purchasing
	• Time needed for contract negotiation	
Non-financial	• Flexible/quick to meet school need	• Could use more than one firm to permit flexible response
	• Not subject to contractor's other workloads	• Workers only employed when needed
	• Direct supervision	• No time needed for appraisals
	• Workloads can be balanced	• No sick pay or holiday pay
	• No contracts, no invoices	• No problems finding skilled workers
	• Not reliant on external labour market	• Contractors maintain quality control
	• Understanding of, and commitment to, the school	• Specialist knowledge, e.g. In health and safety, visual display units, lighting schemes, disability provision
	• Pride and job satisfaction	

Figure 8.3 Comparative effectiveness of in-house and contracted-out provision

Working on the decision to proceed with in-house provision, the bursar then assessed the possibilities for improvement by internal restructuring. Figure 8.4 illustrates the various approaches that had been tried by the school.

The bursar then investigated staff attitudes into changing the site team structure and concluded that any change needed to change the mindsets as well as the structures. The premises and site staff wanted much more co-operation from teachers. This ranged from teachers ensuring that support staff had information about school events in plenty of time for action to be organised, to teachers being berated for failing to close windows at the end of the day's classes. Support staff felt frustrated by the constant interruptions to their work

Pre-1991	1991 → (GM status)	1992 →	1995 →	1996 →
Caretaker	Premise and site manager £13 257	Premise and site manager £14 000	Premise and site manager £18 400	Premise and site manager £20 000
LEA central provision services	Assistant £10 000	Assistant £11 500	Assistant £12 000	Assistant – opening and closing school, swimming pool duties, litter clearance, spot washing, toilet checks and cleaning, light cleaning, furniture moving, banking and porterage, maintaining minibuses; shift 0700–1500 £10 5000–£11 400
	Assistant £10 000	Assistant £11 500	Assistant £12 000	Assistant – as above; shift 0800–1700
		General hand litter picking £21.50 per day	Assistant £12,000	Assistant – as above; shift 1500–2300
		Casual carpenter £24 per day	Carpenter £13 000	Maintenance – multi-skilled – responsible for boilers and heating, carpentry, building. Plumbing £13 00–£14 000
			Plumber £13 000	Maintenance – as above

Figure 8.4 Restructuring approaches

by teaching staff and students. To these views one can certainly be sympathetic but should students and staff be regarded as interruptions in an organisation dedicated to teaching and learning?

These changes clearly demonstrate how the work of leading support services has altered and shows how much leadership abilities have become as vital as having practical knowledge of the specialism of cleaning floors. The restructuring arose partly from increased specialist expertise needs, partly from teaching and premises staff discontent with the service and partly because it proved difficult to find a team leader who had both practical and leadership skills. The role of the bursar in all this was to work to maintain good relations between teachers and premises staff, to redesign the structures and to attempt to find the right appointments for the restructured roles.

The bursar's contribution: discussion

Costs associated with site management absorb the second largest part of the school budget after teachers' salaries. Usually, the search for greater cost-effectiveness centres on finding cheaper suppliers of materials but the bursar here decided on a much more extensive initiative, reviewing the staffing structure for the delivery of sites and premises management. Here was the bursarship role being developed as strategic facilities' management rather than as tactical operative.

The bursar, as the strategic leader of all support staff, and the formal link between support and teaching staff, is the linchpin for the changing of mind-sets. In this case study, the issue was as much changing people's attitudes as changing operations. This attitude change had to take place while schools were acquiring responsibility for their own premises. This not only gave rise to demands for more support staff and more specialised staff, but also for better quality staff. Expectations of the standards for school appearance rose and with it the need for more direction, control and leadership. The bursar thus became less of an operations tactician and more of a managerial motivator.

Final thoughts

These case studies have several linking themes which underpin bursarship development. All demonstrate the growing recognition of the importance of support staff. This recognition has arisen initially from their cost-effectiveness because of their specialist knowledge combined with their relatively low salaries. These are major inducements to the employment of support staff in place of 'multi-functional' expensive teachers trying to perform associated tasks while also leading learning. In most schools, over 70 per cent of expenditure will be on teaching staff salaries, 20 per cent on non-staff costs and only 10 per cent for support staff salaries. It can be the bursar's role to demonstrate the financial and other values of making the change from using teachers on non-teaching tasks to operating support services with non-teachers. In so doing, bursarship itself can be enhanced through the prospect of an increased personnel empire with experts whose knowledge is outside the sphere of the teacher.

The bursar is both a principal actor in the development of support staff and the playwright of the script. Bursars are reacting to opportunities as support staff themselves but also are changing the direction proactively. The overall impression from these case studies puts the bursar between an administrator and a manager. Support staff are still not, however, regarded as being as important as are teachers. Therefore, the leader of the support staff will not have the same standing as the teachers' leader. The constraints of costs and of the availability of good support staff also currently restrict the bursar's emergence as a leader but the plans are there.

9

■　■　■

Sites and Equipment

Introduction

The case studies selected here illustrate a range of site management activities in which bursars have been involved. They indicate how bursars have offered services which were not only directed to implementing operational targets but were also concerned with suggesting and deciding strategic directions in site management. The bursars in these case studies move from implementation activities, to development planning, through strategic planning to visioning the future.

Site-based management was one of the first euphemisms for the devolution of financial responsibilities to schools in the mid-1980s. For many headteachers, site management was felt to distract them from educational leadership. A system which relieved them of some of this responsibility, therefore, would enable headteachers to concentrate on those areas of their professional expertise which are directly related to teaching and learning. A bursarship role could be central in achieving this.

The case studies

9.1 *Implementing a plan for establishing self-study areas.* This concerned the implementation of a plan to establish self-study areas. It discusses the technical and human implications of a major change in teaching methods.

9.2 *Development planning through investigating funding for new sports facilities.* This illustrated the planning for the funding of a sports centre through a lottery grant and how curriculum needs had to be balanced with the requirements of external, funding agencies.

9.3 *Development 'unplanning' through investigating what to do when funding for new sports facilities did not materialise.* Should lottery funding fail to materialise, this case study may provide guidance on alternatives but the case also sheds light on the bursar's role in a school's responsibility to the community.

9.4 *Strategic planning for a reprographics service to free teachers from non-teaching tasks.* The bursar, in this case, became proactive in investigating how to save teacher time with better reprographics services.

9.5 *From strategic planning to futures thinking through developing more cost-effective utilities.* A cost reduction exercise for utilities in the short term but with a long-term vision for the future.

9.6 *Futures thinking from a whole-school approach to making better use of sites and facilities.* A consideration of the contribution of the school's site and facilities to the quality of schooling as pupil numbers increased.

Case study 9.1: Implementing a plan for establishing self-study areas

School

Provincial, locally managed, co-educational school, 1100+ students. secondary phase.
Bursar from financial and school services background.

Context

The school's vision in its two-year School Improvement Plan, was to extend its students' learning opportunities through supported self study. This was to be realised by installing information communications technology in self-study facilities attached to each teaching area. An IT development group considered the options and selected one which the governing body and senior management team approved. The bursar was appointed as the project manager to oversee the implementation. The school had good IT provision throughout the school and with the school's plan to apply for specialist school status, these facilities were considered a priority. The school is increasingly popular causing great pressure on available space. The process from inception of the idea to the inauguration of the new facilities took 12 months.

The bursar's role in the project

Stage I: pre-project audit

The bursar focused on the practicalities of room space available, the curriculum issues in relation to Design/Technology and the human resource issues of morale, motivation and training. Led by the bursar, the project team investigated every room, every corridor and every cupboard. Space was found but to ensure its redesignation required the movement of some teaching staff from established bases, a reduction in the numbers of curriculum options, an increase in class sizes and the possibility of introducing twilight classes. The likely impact of this on a staff already demoralised by a redundancy programme arising from financial constraints can be imagined.

The bursar's plans could offset this to some extent by the projected room changes facilitating clearer demarcation of curriculum areas, facilitating more readily available IT staff, providing for more cross-curricular activities through subjects sharing adjacent self-study areas and by beginning the improvement of the Design/Technology provision and teaching criticised in a recent Ofsted report. The bursar also planned that the actual physical movement to the newly equipped and redesignated areas would take place during the summer months to minimise staff discomfort and learning disruption.

During this stage, various options had to be investigated. Each had to be presented with its technical and financial advantages and disadvantages but also with its closeness of fit to the school's aims, ethos and culture. What was chosen had to meet the teaching and learning objectives of providing independence for students, of improving special needs features and of facilitating a variety of teaching and learning styles.

Stage II: project management

Once governors' approval had been obtained for the final plan, the bursar assumed the role of project manager. This involved identifying teacher movement and alteration of room use and when it would take place. The head and deputies then saw individually each member of staff who was personally affected to explain what would happen and why, in order to ensure that the process was open and personalised. The bursar then initiated talks with each of them to identify the practical implications of moving. Hardware and software options and costs were investigated and orders placed. There were extra workers to be found for the removals, and students were happy to provide this, together with additional hours from the part-time caretaker. Keeping the critical timelines straight was a logistics challenge for the bursar who had to accommodate staff holidays, the arrival of the hardware, staff sickness and contingency plans if staff or equipment did not arrive as scheduled.

Stage III: project review

The project was completed ahead of schedule with few difficulties and its last stage was reviewing this accomplishment. The senior management team considered that the success was attributable to:

- the planning which had emphasised that the aim was to enhance student achievements;
- the thorough research into the issues of rooms, staff motivation and relationship to curriculum needs;
- the detailed scheduling;
- the wide communication with staff throughout the project;
- good liaison with the contractors.

The bursar's contribution: discussion

The objectives for the bursar included determining the optimum use of space, negotiating the movement of staff and facilitating the move with the least disruption to the school. These aims were achieved and in advance of schedule. The bursar was aware from the start that this was not just a case of implementing a technical development. The change would reduce teacher time in front of classes, introduce more peer supported study, lengthen the school day and offer greatly enhanced learning opportunities both in the actual technology and in the access it offered to widen student sources of information. While teachers acknowledged the value of all this, it also represented a challenge to traditional patterns of teachers as sole providers of knowledge; teachers had to accept this cultural change. In making the change, these human reactions have to be accommodated as well as the accommodation itself being changed. This project addressed these issues but the bursar acknowledged that not all staff fears could be allayed, especially of those who felt inadequate in dealing with information technology. Money and time was devoted to staff training in the new technology but learning takes time to internalise. The second, strong feature of this case study was the focus on the teaching and learning objectives of the school as the driving force for both the initial decision and for how its implementation would be managed.

Case study 9.2: Development planning through investigating funding for new sports facilities

School

London, Catholic, GM, comprehensive, co-educational, 700+ pupils with an expected increase to 850 by 2002. Secondary phase.
100 in Years 12 and 13.
45 teachers, 8.8 support staff.
Bursar from accountancy and management consultancy background.

Context

The school had a rising roll and had had to expand to five-form entry to meet demand, with further increases planned. The last new building work on the site had been in 1977 with little money for repairs and maintenance since then. There were several, unsuccessful bids for government grants to relocate and upgrade buildings. From acquiring GM status in 1993, the small, formula-based capital allocation each year was used for investment in information technology and for converting surplus changing-room space into urgently needed teaching areas. In addition to this, the school needed laboratories refurbishing, other minor works, significantly improved and extended sports' facilities, better IT provision and developments to meet the needs of performing and expressive arts. The popularity of the school put pressure on accommodation already regarded as inadequate to meet Health and Safety requirements. Ofsted were critical of the lack of football facilities. The school obtained a Basic Needs Grant which corrected some of the immediate shortfall and it was then decided to concentrate on the needs for sports and performing arts facilities.

The bursar's role in the project

The initial decisions in the senior management team, of which the bursar was a member, finalised the targets for sports facilities. These were to enlarge the sports hall to at least two courts' size, create triathlon facilities for swimming, cycling and running, and provide adequate football areas and all-weather hockey pitches and tennis courts. These were to be for both school and community use and this would involve liaison with partnership groups in the local council and hospital trust, various local sports clubs, businesses and associations. The bursar's task, then, was to consider alternative sources of funding and to advise the SMT on the preferred options.

The suggested options were to put a bid through the Sports Council to the National Lottery, which would involve the school in finding substantial matching funding, or to set up a partnership with a commercial enterprise which would require minimum investment from the school. Despite the apparent evidence that the first option was the least financially sensible, the bursar needed to consider far more than merely the financial imperatives.

The bursar's report first considered the requirements for National Lottery funding. A major focus of this was to be facilities made available to local community sports' groups who would work with the school on the bid and fund raising, and would need to be involved in management once the centre was established. Identifying those interested was not difficult; there were men's and women's hockey clubs and a tennis training school. The British Triathlon Association was willing to be involved and the facilities would provide a Regional Centre of Excellence for this sport just as it had been recognised for the 2000 Olympics. These bodies might collectively reach the lottery funding target of using the facilities for more than 40 hours per week though, as the report showed, some general public usage would also be needed. Revenue costs are rarely eligible for lottery funding except for a strictly limited time period. Thus the school would have to bear the risks of becoming financially viable from the inception of the project, in addition to having to find between 10 and 50 per cent of the capital costs (in deprived areas lottery expectations of self-financing are the lower figure).

The bursar ascertained that the Funding Agency for Schools (FAS, terminated in 1999 when GM status ended) would provide seed-corn funds and the bursar also investigated the possibilities of advance block booking fees to support traditional fund-raising efforts. None the less, the bursar's report illustrated the effort that would be needed by the school to fund raise for a project of this size, to maintain a complex management group of interested associations and to provide the items not covered by the lottery funding, such as equipment, that was not an integral part of the building itself. A holistic view had also to be presented; the absorption of fund-raising efforts into this project could deflect Parent-Teacher Association (PTA) and other funds from areas with at least the same priority as sport; the bursar noted that the function of a lottery funded project could not be primarily for curriculum delivery but had to be for community sports.

To report on the proposal that the sports facilities might be provided in conjunction with a private company, the bursar and the headteacher visited other schools' facilities currently run by the company to discover their experiences and successes. The commercial director of the private company visited the school for negotiations with the bursar and for discussions with PE staff. Again, there were other agencies and sports groups to consult but there was no ongoing commitment to them for future management. In assessing the value of the commercial proposal, the bursar centred on the financial considerations; the company would be the financial risk taker, not the school; the school's contribution could be met by the school conceding an initial rent-free period to the developers; there would be no need to fund raise; curriculum objectives could take primacy; all-weather pitches would be provided, together with a four-court sports hall (even larger than originally proposed) with changing facilities, weights training room, store and bar, and an access road and upgraded car park. Of course, the 'downside' also had to be presented; the school lost the freedom to change the use of one of its fields for 50 years.

The bursar's contribution: discussion

One of the basic tasks of bursarship is that of providing financial information to guide management decisions for *'the maximum benefit of our curriculum delivery'*(bursar of the school). Here the bursar was facilitating a governors' decision to offer the maximum range of sports facilities by investigating the options for funding. This took the bursar beyond financial considerations and into the wider issues of the capability of the school to raise funds for, and manage, new sports facilities, into making contact with external agencies and reporting on how they might be involved, into considerations of demand for the new service from outsiders and the need to assess the viability of a company making a bid to provide services. In the end, the commercial company, as the bursar stressed in the report, would provide all that the curriculum needed without the school taking a financial risk or committing itself to fund raising that would deflect energies from the educational aims of the school.

Case study 9.3: Development 'unplanning' through investigating what to do when funding for new sports facilities did not materialise

School

Provincial, independent day school, single sex, 680 students, multi-phase with sixth form provision.
49.5 teachers, 14 support staff.
Bursar from service and industry background.

Context

The school, on the outskirts of a market town, has a village site, to which it moved six years before this study, leaving behind its swimming pool but gaining more accommodation, a theatre and a sports hall. A bid for National

Lottery funding failed. This was to build a new sports complex, including a pool but the Trust running the school had promised at least a pool should the bid fail. This promise had now to be realised.

The bursar's role in the project

The bursar's task was to *'forward the thinking of the senior management team in order to develop a strategy for the project'* (bursar at the school). The bursar's starting point was to analyse the teaching and learning needs of the school through discussions with teaching staff; from these discussions, it emerged that:

- swimming is encouraged for Key Stage I and is a requirement for Key Stage II;
- swimming would extend the sports education offered;
- there were opportunities to adopt a whole-school approach to pool use rather than considering its use as restricted to being relevant to physical education only;
- community access to the pool would offer the students the chance to participate in a wider learning experience through, for example, assisting with swimming for the disabled or with acquiring life-guard skills.

Despite these advantages, the pool was not deemed central to curriculum needs so, more significantly, the bursar reflected on the external implications of the planned pool. The marketing of school activities was one of the bursar's responsibilities, hence the interest in both the community use of the pool and its possible impact on student recruitment. The bursar assessed the pool as critical for the long-term credibility and success of the school. The bursar felt that the costs might be offset by outside lettings and that encouraging parental use of the pool would enhance the attractiveness of the school. On the other hand, the bursar was less sanguine about the high capital and running costs of a pool and was aware that teachers were ambivalent about allowing community access to the pool.

The bursar adopted scenario planning as the first stage for the strategy, presenting the possible alternatives for community use to the senior team. The scenarios arose from the possible range of involvement according to what might be senior management views on the extent of community use inside and outside school hours, weekend and holiday use, security and financial implications. The scenario options were identified.

1 *No community involvement.* This would relieve staff of concerns about the disruption and security problems of opening the pool and would mean there would never be a clash with school needs. The bursar felt, however, that this option would waste the opportunity of projecting the school to its community and of helping to meet the running costs.

2   *Use by parents, staff and school clubs.* This would be a controlled community use with few opportunities of a clash with school needs or worries over security. There was the possibility that the Parents' Association might be one of the funders with this type of access encouraged. It still represented a loss for marketing and finance.

3   *A members' only club, with either an annual or per usage charge.* This scenario solved some of the financial and security problems and resolved possible conflict with school use. Such a club, however, might reinforce the exclusive image of the school, possibly good for marketing but less so for relations with the community.

4   *Open public access for a usage charge.* Such a scenario presented a clear statement to the public about the school being accessible and had potential to generate significant income. It raised major issues about security and about continuous staffing of the pool

Underpinning all the scenarios were the 'technicalities' of finance, marketing and management. Once consensus had been reached on the preferred scenario, then other decisions followed. The pool design, for example, would need different changing facilities if intended for school use only and there would be no need for a reception area or for considering the possibility of developing gym facilities suited to adult use. Operating costs would differ according to the scenario particularly concerning staffing; additional staff would be needed if community use were adopted but costs would be offset by fees. Current maintenance staff would need additional training.

The planning had to be done against a background of the inevitable disappointment of students, parents and the community that the original bid had failed. Part of the bursar's initial planning included consideration of the way the 'marketing' of the bad news should be announced and the 'damage limitation' that could ensue from having ready the alternative plans as it was suspected that the National Lottery bid would fail. All those who had been interested in the original bid had to be contacted and a draft letter and press releases prepared. These needed to state when an alternative might be ready and what level of community use would be allowed so that those who had participated in the community bid would not feel that their support had been rejected. Internal public relations were also an important responsibility highlighted by the bursar. Staff had initially resented the idea of community involvement and it was important that their hard won support should be maintained.

The bursar's contribution: discussion

Curriculum needs were the starting point identified by the bursar for making the decisions here. In this case, however, the public relations of the school provided the stronger imperative. Bursars, as shown in the research reported in Part Two, interact with the community frequently, probably more than teachers do, and are thus likely to put the external point of view strongly as happened in this case. The teachers were somewhat unhappy about community use of the pool but the bursar intimated its importance for the school's image and for its recruitment of pupils.

Case study 9.4: Strategic planning for a reprographics service to free teachers from non-teaching tasks

School

London, GM, co-educational, 1100+ students, secondary phase with sixth form provision.
Bursar from a school office background.

Context

In 1980, this school was the proud possessor of a photocopier and a duplicating machine. The thermal-type photocopier needed special paper, three processes and had an image that faded after about three weeks. The Roneo duplicator with its inked, wax sheets was supplemented by spirit duplicators, the Banda, beloved of so many schools. Later, two electric Gestetners joined the school, uncomfortably housed in a corridor and the staff room. The quality of reproduction was poor. Teaching staff did much of their own duplicating but often needed technical assistance from the support staff. By 1987, with no extra money or staff, the bursar had set up a specialist reprographics room, serviced by support staff on a rota basis. Demand grew quantitatively and qualitatively as computers and software facilitated top-quality printing. New offices for administrators had space for reprographics and there was both a specialist reprographics officer and a desktop publisher, albeit part time. None the less, there was still a need for a better quality service.

The bursar's role in the project

Despite the reprographics service meeting the demand efficiently, the bursar considered that the service was not good enough. There had been no strategic planning of the service nor any consultation with users about their needs. The service had grown *ad hoc* with machinery purchased often at the end of financial years when money had to be 'spent up'. At the same time, the standard of externally produced graphics had risen and school information produced to a lower standard made a poor impression on students and parents. The bursar set as priorities the production of *'good quality documents – lesson notes, worksheets, diagrams, work books etc. for the use of students to enhance their learning and for top-quality communications with parents'* to ensure their satisfaction with the school.

The first need was to obtain the views of users and consumers. A questionnaire was therefore sent to teachers, open discussions held with reprographics staff and a SWOT analysis conducted with all heads of departments. Teaching staff were asked to state what services they required and which services they currently did or did not use and why.

Once consumer views had been collated, the bursar's next task was investigating the machines and services to meet the needs and then to find the resources to finance the requested development. The bursar realised that *'either a substantial portion of the school's grant must be ear-marked (which is undesirable as this ... would mean less funding for other necessities) or finance must be found from elsewhere'*. The bursar's idea for 'elsewhere' was to offer a commercial service to feeder primary schools unable to afford such high-quality services, and to shops and small businesses in the area which had no printing shop business locally. That too was viewed by the bursar as having double value: *'it would ... give the school the added bonus of serving the community which would provide good publicity for the school'*.

The questionnaires and discussions revealed a satisfied majority of teaching staff but a lack of awareness of cost differentials between photocopying and digital printing. Staff wanted a much faster service with particular availability after teaching hours and during school holidays when staff were preparing lessons. Teaching staff also disliked having to spend time discussing their graphics requirements before desktop publishing could begin. There was insufficient support staff time to meet teachers' demands for the work and there was no scheduling of urgencies. Colour photocopying and production of transparencies and more typing support were all new requirements.

Interestingly, while revealing needs, the enquiries also demonstrated misunderstandings between teaching and non-teaching staff. Duplicating machines were available after school hours and in school holidays as were reprographics staff but teaching staff did not seem to be aware of this. The discussions also showed how the bursar has to balance the needs of different groups of staff. The dedicated reprographics technician did school office reception duties each day between 1530 and 1630. This enabled her to gain wider experience and to have a social element in a working day otherwise spent alone, whereas teachers wanted the technician accessible to them between those hours.

Responding to these needs, the bursar planned to purchase a digital printing machine selecting the machine that was the most versatile, easy to use, low maintenance, with good after-sales service and the lowest cost per copy for excellent standard of mass reproduction. A new photocopier was also purchased providing cheap runs of any size together with an assortment of laminators, binders and perforating machines. A colour photocopier awaited a future time of greater financial ease. Assessing how best to deploy staff was the bursar's next task. Here both copying and other duties had to be accounted for including non-related tasks of, for example, distributing locker keys and recording videos, jobs which had 'drifted' into the ambit of reprographics. *'How much more can one person be expected to do?'* enquired the bursar in addressing the problem. The solution was to remove the non-related tasks and institute improved administration for the desktop publisher such as establishing a prioritising system for work required. Lastly, there was the financial planning. To make the service viable, departments would have to be charged for its use and its services sold to outsiders, each group requiring differential pricing. The bursar, mindful of the educational implications, reported that:

> *it is ... a service we want staff to use. If we 'charge' Departments too much, they will not buy the product and this will have a detrimental effect on the teaching and learning of the students which will, probably, have a detrimental effect on examination results which, in turn, could have an effect on the number and type of applications to the school. However, there must be some 'charge' ... in order to make teachers use the service responsibly.*

The bursar's contribution: discussion

Here was an issue on which the bursar took the initiative to consider how to make a good service better. It illustrates extremely well the meaning of 'support' service and shows that support staff are aware of the implications of their activities for standards in the school. Throughout, the interests of the school as a teaching and learning business were seen by the bursar as paramount. There was also the subsidiary theme of making the new service financially viable without increasing costs to the school. The bursar's decision to develop a reprographics business for the local community, demonstrates the external awareness of bursarship.

Case study 9.5: From strategic planning to futures thinking through developing more cost-effective utilities

School

Welsh, independent mixed school, 300 pupils, sixth form only.
36 teachers, 99 support staff.
Bursar from military background.

Context

The school's costs had to be reduced. Fees are according to parental means so substantial sums have to be raised to support scholarships. Curriculum-related staffing had to be maintained and building costs were little amenable to change because of the fixed, and expensive, nature of available plant. The options were to raise fees (but risk lowering recruitment and not meeting the school's ethos of access on merit) or make teaching or support staff redundant (but risk not providing a full education and of lowering staff morale). Both of these would impact directly and badly on the core business of teaching and learning. One alternative was to consider reductions in spending on heating, lighting, water and sewage disposal. Was this worth doing? Could it be done without lowering the quality of life for staff and students?

The bursar's role in the project

The first consideration was to maintain educational provision. Projections indicated a potential saving on energy costs of around a maximum of £50 000 (1998 figures) per annum which would fund the entire academic consumables' costs for the school each year and the bursar's task was to assess how this could be achieved. The second consideration was community responsibility with the school keen to demonstrate global awareness of 'green' issues. This also had a curriculum spin-off with students becoming involved in the 'futures' research for this project through a study of how to make future utilities provision more environmentally friendly. Thus, investigating and implementing a strategic plan to save money became stages I and II of the project; moving into futures thinking became stage III.

Stage I: review

This began, as might be expected, with a review of utilities usage. Electricity was found to be the most costly energy item in the budget though its use was confined to lighting, heavy duty catering and secondary heating. Principal heating was from gas-oil and liquid propane gas, from a central boilerhouse to the whole site. Much was carried in above-ground pipes without insulation, requiring two pumps to get it around the large site with many buildings. In common, no doubt, with many schools, electricity was wasted with lights, computers and appliances left on unnecessarily. There had been no tariff management or competitive tendering. The bursar's research showed that average water usage per person per day at the school was about 80 litres more than the domestic average. Were the users exceptionally keen on cleanliness or were there other causes of a potential 'wastage' of around £13000 per annum?

Stage II: options investigation

This investigated possible options for improvement, including the technicalities of radiator or room thermostats, temperature sensors, insulation, metered tanks and motorised valves as well as competitive tendering for fuel supply. Detailed costings of fuel units and cost benefit analyses were included of course. Changing just an electricity tariff saved £18000 per annum. The next ideas moved into people management; meters were needed so that the origin of usage could be more accurately allocated. It was hoped that cost and usage awareness would enhance an energy-saving campaign concerning such issues as turning out lights or managing with lower temperatures and more blankets.

Stage III: futures thinking

This concentrated particularly on finding alternative sources of fuel. Mains gas would be cheap and the pipework to install it would be paid off by savings within two years. Given the cliff-top position of the school, wind turbines to generate electricity were researched by students, revealing a pay-off within five years of installation. The bursar had to be the 'devil's advocate' for this plan, pointing out that the costing statistics were over-optimistic and planning permission was unlikely to permit wind generators in the heritage area in which the school is situated. Solar panels were a much more likely option with the bursar noting that various European Union (EU) grants might help with capital costs. The bursar also researched the new combined heat and power units but reported that they were still too experimental to guarantee savings in less than around 12 years, much too long a time for a school needing some savings now. There was investigation of a more ecologically and organically responsible method of sewage disposal which would have the 'spin-off' of creating a wildlife area.

The bursar's contribution: discussion

One of the bursar's central roles relates to financial management and this is a clear example of the exercise of that responsibility within a strategic framework. The school was seeking savings and this one area was particularly within the bursar's remit. Here was the scope for the ideas. In this case, the ideas went beyond the immediate and into the long term, even if somewhat speculatively. Practical solutions emerged to reduce costs and the bursar also involved the students in research which considered suggestions for future savings and developed the students' project management skills.

Case study No 9.6: Futures thinking from a whole-school approach to making better use of sites and facilities

School

Welsh, comprehensive, GM, co-educational, 1300 students, secondary phase with sixth form provision,
Bursar from a teaching background.

Context

The school's popularity was growing and it was expected that this would continue. The site is relatively compact with a mix of age and construction for its buildings. It has its own sports provision but also has access to athletics, swimming and other facilities at the adjacent leisure centre and park. The school's main building houses most of the classrooms and specialist teaching areas in craft, design and technology (CDT), music and art and also contains the library, hall and dining room. Recently built were the centres for Years 12 and 13 and for information technology, which included business studies teaching. In 1997, work had begun to remodel the library, extend the dining room and add more classrooms.

The bursar's role in the project

The bursar decided to consider the extent to which the school's site and facilities could continue to contribute to the growing popularity of the school, how they might make more effective use of its extensive plant and ensure the continuation of high-quality schooling as the numbers of students grew. To glean ideas, a comparative study was made of other secondary schools but with a very different provenance to the school in the case study: one was in the USA and one was an independent school. The bursar felt it was important to consider other models so as not to be constrained by expectations limited to the state sector. The bursar's recommendations had ramifications which went beyond tinkering with room use and illustrated the significance of a bursarial role in strategic planning to improve teaching and learning. Many of the proposals would involve major changes in teachers' contracting, the school day and the school year.

The bursar first undertook a site audit of the school before the comparative study began. It was found that the computer suites were all fully utilised all day and extra, after-school, classes had to be set up to meet demand. All sixth form work could be accommodated in the Year 12 and 13 Centre except for subjects requiring specialist provision. Private study areas in the Centre were fully utilised. The Resource Centre and Library provided after-school homework and revision clubs. All sports facilities were fully utilised all day. Extra-curricular activities ran every afternoon after school. Teaching staff rooms and administrative areas had been refurbished and upgraded. Classrooms were hired out for community evening sessions. There was no obvious underuse of site or facilities during the school day but that left much of the day and the holidays when the buildings were virtually empty and little flexibility for facilities already stretched to their limits during the day.

From the studies of the other schools, the bursar developed far-reaching suggestions. The first was for an extended school day, with start times more akin to those in the working environments to which students would progress on leaving. The concomitant, earlier finish time would then allow for many more targeted after-school activities, particularly to meet the needs of the most and least able, two groups on whom the school needed to focus. A split day was recommended. Classes for the younger students would be taught from morning until early afternoon; classes for older students would commence in the afternoon, finishing in the evening. This would enable community participation in the evening sessions. Additional revenue from this might facilitate extended curriculum provision.

Community involvement was envisaged as very important. Summer and Easter Schools were seen as family provision as much as for students' revision. Activities for pre-secondary school children and for the elderly would be a major part of these. The main source of revenue could, however, be revision courses for students in addition to those from the case study school. As the bursar pointed out, *'private tuition is a booming business'*, largely privately run and in seaside locations. This school could develop its own business in this field. The wider community might also be better served if languages were offered through the school as an International Centre, integrating its audio language laboratory with video, satellite television and IT facilities. The teaching undertaken by the school in child care could develop into crèche and nursery provision for the community.

Within the IT arrangements, there was felt to be a need for computer-linked display screens as bulletin boards and for all students to be equipped with laptops. More readily implemented was the idea of extending the networks around the school so that staff could access student data as needed. Every teacher should have a mobile phone.

Proposals which went outside what is usually seen as a bursar's brief, included the establishment of a staff exchange scheme and greater flexibility in staff timetables. There would be Saturday and evening teaching and days off for teachers working unsocial evening hours. Tasks previously associated with teaching staff could be devolved to administrative staff, such as lost property, book purchase, relaying parent and staff messages, student attendances and absences, and examination entries and administration. Electronic swipe cards were needed for registration so that administrative staff could more readily check room use and student movements, and save teaching staff the time needed to take registration. Sports activities would be concentrated only in the mornings or afternoons for each split shift group rather than being interleaved with other provision during the school day. On a grander scale, consideration of a merger with less popular schools was suggested so that a wider curriculum might be offered with larger groups making extended provision viable and schools not expending energy on competition.

The bursar's contribution: discussion

While in this 1997 case study, it might have seemed difficult for an individual state school to implement such wide-ranging proposals, it appears clear that they will become much more likely in the new millennium. The first locally maintained state school instituting a five-term year occurred in 1999; many schools had altered their start and finish times and lunch hours, even if only marginally; summer literacy schools began in 1997 in state schools; plans for Life Long Learning through the Adult Education Service in 1999–2000 will impact on community provision in schools; Education Action Zones from 1998, the Private Finance Initiative from 1999, commercial companies taking over state schools, all offer the prospect of facilitating changes such as those outlined above. Finally, more flexible teachers' contracts were indicated in the 1998 Green Paper (DfEE, 1998c) proposing a national, mobile force of young teachers and of advanced skills teachers.

Final thoughts

In these case studies, bursars fulfilled their administrative tasks of implementing projects, of managing that implementation and its preceding strategic planning, and of demonstrating leadership roles in the futures' planning examples. Bursars were aware that in all of these roles, they were to be management information systems for headteachers, senior management teams and governors. They reacted to plans originating from those groups but also began to be proactive in the proposal of ideas to those senior groups. Whether in reactive or proactive mode, the bursars in these studies took the rationale of their decisions to be curriculum needs and their outcomes to be contributing to improved teaching and learning. They were aware of both human and financial costs. The examples also illustrated the position that bursars have in relation to the external groups with whom schools must liase in these times of accountability. How bursars approach these groups impacts on the image of the school, a theme which is taken up in the following chapter.

10

■ ■ ■

School Image

Introduction

This chapter discusses roles that bursars can adopt in marketing their schools by considering five case studies, two from independent and three from state schools. For bursars, income generation is one aspect of marketing, which features in most job descriptions but other marketing responsibilities are articulated less strongly (Chapter 3). Their roles concentrate on developing public relations outside the school through personal interaction, media publicity, development of the school prospectus or facilitating public events. Bursars' abilities to promote the school's image through their staff are also important to their role, as these staff are often the first to be encountered by visitors to the school.

Since parents have been given the choice of which state school their child will attend, the marketing of the school's image has become an important aspect of school management at the site level. Schools are now competing against each other in order to attract pupils and presenting a positive image to the community has become an integral part of school strategy. In the independent sector a marketing policy has always been a necessity but now schools in both sectors must become equally adept in this field.

The case studies

10.1 *Promoting increased community use to the school's staff.* This describes how a bursar ascertained staff attitudes to increased community use of the school and the recommendations proposed for involving them in the changes.

10.2 *Determining the reasons for a falling school roll.* The bursar makes suggestions for assessing and communicating the school's mission statement and for gathering and disseminating marketing data after the school's roll started to fall.

10.3 *Developing a marketing plan after consultation with the school's stakeholders.* The school studied had been improving the resources and facilities offered to its pupils and was considering a further radical change. Its Ofsted inspection report, however, highlighted a potential problem in its communication with stakeholders. The bursar examined the school's marketing strategy and used outside help to gather data. This was used to determine how changes could be achieved with the consent of the stakeholders. From this a marketing plan was developed for consideration by the senior management team.

10.4 *Recommendations for a school marketing plan linked to the operational budget.* The bursar analysed the operational budget before making recommendations for a school marketing plan. This would accommodate the school's mission statement and policy and would allow for a growth in student numbers.

10.5 *Market research and the sixth form centre.* This reviews part of the planning resulting from the resiting and recruitment into the sixth form centre of a mixed comprehensive school. The bursar conducted a detailed market research survey to investigate the potential for developing the reputation of the college.

Case study 10.1: Promoting increased community use to the school's staff

School

Provincial, independent, single-sex school, 600+ pupils, multi-phase with sixth form.
49.5 teachers, 14 support staff.
Bursar from service industry background.

Context

In 1992, the school moved from a town centre site to a Grade One listed building in open parkland. New facilities included a purpose built sports hall and theatre but the new site had outbuildings, which required renovation. The senior management team was hoping to attract a National Lottery grant to build a sports complex, which included a 25-metre swimming pool.

Key objectives in the school's development plan involved fostering community links and increasing income from lettings. In particular, the senior management team hoped that increased lettings would promote community awareness of the school and increase recruitment and revenue in a highly competitive area. The school had made the decision to develop the outbuildings and build a swimming pool even if the National Lottery bid for the sports complex was unsuccessful. These developments would only be successful if community use could be encouraged.

The school facilities were used for weddings, family celebrations, conferences and exhibitions, rallies, fairs and sports tournaments, but these had only been promoted by word of mouth. Despite this, income from lettings had increased threefold between 1995/6 and 1996/7 and a further increase of 50 per cent had been projected for 1997/8. An analysis of the use of the facilities suggested that a tenfold increase on the original income was achievable.

The bursar's role in the project

Increased use of the school by the local community would require the support and contribution of all staff; however, there was a general impression in the school that they did not appreciate the benefits of community involvement. In order to ascertain the views of the staff a questionnaire was devised by the bursar, to determine their perceptions of:

- the school's relationship with the community;
- whether or not the school should encourage community use;
- the parents' view of community school use;
- benefits the school would derive from increased community use;
- concerns arising from increased school use by the community;
- whether community use would increase, decrease or remain stable in the future;
- the school's need to increase community usage;
- areas where community involvement could be increased in the future.

An analysis of the results of the questionnaire, by the bursar, indicated that the majority of the staff were not ready to embrace increased community involvement with the school and, therefore, that relationships were in need of development. Staff believed that community use of facilities would increase income, improve relationships and aid recruitment, but they were concerned about security, loss or damage to school property and a conflict with school use. Most were unaware of the school's need to increase its income and felt that community use would remain fairly stable or increase marginally.

The bursar had already determined that the staff in the school had the experience and capability to contribute to increased community use. By administering the questionnaire, however, there was clear evidence that awareness of the community relationship aspect of the school's development plan would need promoting before staff were ready to contribute. The bursar concluded that:

1 the acceptance of this change would take time and so the process should be started as early as possible;

2 a staff training day should be arranged to concentrate on benefits of community involvement to address staff concerns and to plan developments;

3 it was important to make the staff aware of the benefits of community involvement;

4 key individuals should be identified to form a task force to address the implications of increased community involvement;

5 the use of a force field analysis would raise issues, which could be communicated to staff and provide a framework for discussion (Figure 10.1).

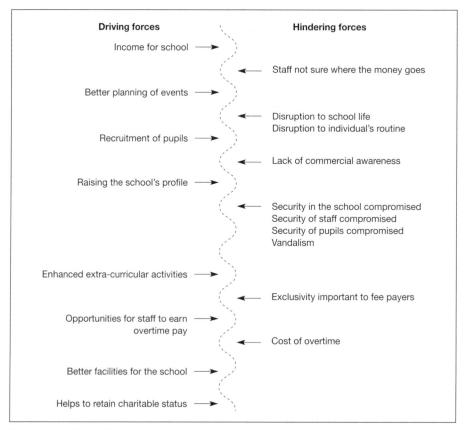

Figure 10.1 Force field analysis of attitudes to community involvement

The bursar's force field analysis raised many issues for discussion by the task force set up to promote community involvement in the school. In particular fears about security and disruption to the school's life would need to be allayed and the benefits to the school communicated more openly.

The bursar's contribution: discussion

As a member of the senior management team, the bursar was in an ideal position to understand the school's policy and strategy and to contribute to the development of community involvement using expertise gained in the service industry prior to taking up the post. Marketing was this bursar's responsibility along with motivating staff, making arrangements for receiving visitors and for the admission of new pupils. The questionnaire the bursar designed covered aspects of internal and external marketing, and its content would also act as an instrument to raise initial awareness of the issues. By using a force field analysis, the bursar gained an understanding of the issues supporting and impeding the new developments on which recommendations could be based for involving staff in the development of community relationships in the school. Membership of the senior management team by the bursar was also essential for dissemination of the information at a strategic level.

Case study 10.2: Determining the reasons for a falling school roll

School

London, Catholic, GM, mixed school, 700+ pupils, secondary phase with sixth form.
45 teachers, 8.8 support staff.
Bursar from accountancy and consultancy background.

Context

A review of pupil numbers in feeder primary schools indicated that the number of pupils in the school would increase in future years by just over a quarter and a new eight-classroom wing had been built to accommodate the anticipated change. In 1997, however, there was a decrease in pupil numbers and an open evening for the following year's intake indicated that a further shortfall was likely. The governors created a marketing working party to improve the school's image and began by preparing questionnaires for parents and pupils in order to analyse the market. A time frame of one year was proposed for collecting and analysing the initial data.

The bursar's role in the project

After reviewing trends and anecdotal evidence, the bursar determined that various factors could be responsible for the downturn in pupil numbers and that these should be evaluated for accuracy before working to improve the school's image. The factors he suggested for investigation were that:

1 the downturn in numbers was a minor 'blip' and of no significance;
2 parents were disaffected with the school;
3 staff themselves were not positive about the school.

There was no hard evidence that any of the above statements was true, so the collection and analysis of relevant data would provide the senior management team with information with which to assess the situation.

Understanding the mission statement

The bursar began by trying to ascertain whether the staff in the school subscribed to its mission statement, which due to its religious affiliations, emphasised pastoral care. The bursar considered that pastoral care was a particular strength of the school, but suggested that the school initiate a review of the mission statement. This review should involve all staff, governors, students, parents and other stakeholders to help ensure commitment to a new mission. The bursar believed that commitment would be further improved by:

1 displaying the mission statement 'with pride' around the school;
2 allowing sections of the school to rewrite the mission statement to reflect their areas of interest/expertise;
3 openly accepting failures to maintain high standards and regarding corrective action as a positive and communal act;
4 reviewing the mission statement in a 'spirit of continual improvement' at a later date.

He suggested that discussion groups be formed to share views and ideas, which would be presented to the governing body. There would be three stages to the consultation process as illustrated in Figure 10.2.

1 The first groups would hold meetings to agree their key ideas on the mission statement and pass these on to the marketing working party.
2 The ideas of the first groups would then be rationalised, and after further consultation and agreement, presented to the governing body.
3 The deliberations of the governing body would be communicated back to the various groups before a final decision was made.

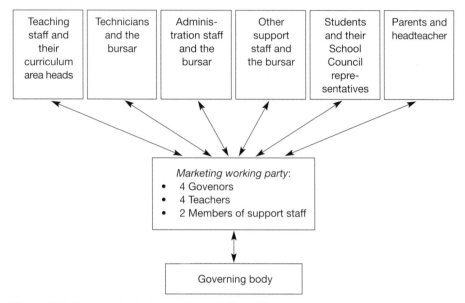

Figure 10.2 Proposed mission statement discussion groups

Marketing working part

Once the mission statement had been agreed and recognised, the bursar suggested a five-point action plan, which could be followed for marketing the school to its clients, who were identified as pupils, parents, future employers, other educational establishments and the community (Figure 10.3). The action plan entailed five stages.

1 Identify the school's information needs incorporating:

- the needs of current and potential pupils;
- the expectations of current and anticipated clients;
- the clients' perceptions of the school including, image, present provision, quality of education, also determining if there had been a change in attitude by current and prospective stakeholders;
- monitoring clients' attitudes to competitor schools;
- monitoring the current environment of the school locally and nationally including identifying clients, potential for growth or decline, resource/income generation, monitoring competitor schools' activities, successes and failures.

2 Once the school's information needs had been identified, a plan for the gathering of primary and secondary information for market research would require development. Suggestions included:

- administering questionnaires to determine clients' perceptions of behavioural control, quality of teaching and satisfaction with the school;

Figure 10.3 Action plan for marketing the school

- determining which school records would provide useful information, e.g. the postcodes of each year's intake;
- searching central and local government documents, books, journals and the media for appropriate and relevant information.
3 Collecting and analysing the data.
4 Reporting the results of the findings.
5 Developing a marketing plan linked to the findings, which plans for the future and establishes a regular monitoring procedure.

After analysing the data a strategic marketing plan was suggested, which would also incorporate information gathered from an analysis of the current position of the school using the Boston Consulting Group matrix; SWOT analysis; political, economic, social, technological, legal and ethical (PESTLE) analysis, objectives for the future; a plan of action and establishing controls to monitor performance. The marketing plan would be part of an ongoing process.

The bursar's contribution: discussion

In this case study, the bursar was in receipt of enough anecdotal evidence to suggest that improving the school's image externally would not alleviate its recruitment problem as it was possible that disaffection within (parent, pupils and staff) was causing the image of the school to deteriorate. The bursar, therefore suggested that the whole school become involved in deciding which factors were important to it by redefining the mission statement. As leader of two support staff teams, the bursar would represent their views within the marketing working party. The bursar was also in a position to oversee the gathering and analysis of information, most of which would be held in the administration office. As a member of the marketing working party the bursar would also disseminate the information gathered and was in a position to explain findings. The suggestions made by the bursar for the use of a variety of strategic management tools for analysing the data would ensure that the best use was made of the wealth of information available.

Case study 10.3: Developing a marketing plan after consultation with the school's stakeholders

School

Home Counties, GM, mixed school, 200+ pupils, primary phase.
11 teachers, 14 support staff.
Bursar from teaching and local government background.

Context

The school is a GM infant school, which shares its site with an LEA-controlled junior school. An extra classroom was added in 1996 to accommodate rising pupil numbers. The school day begins at 0900 and finishes at 1500. A 20-minute break is taken at 1030 and lunch is taken between 1200 and 1300. All children eat a packed lunch at the same time using the hall and three class-rooms. The school had provided a resources room and extended the administration area and refurbished quiet areas. The school was then consid-ering the conversion of the kitchens for nursery provision.

At the time of this case study, discussions during senior management team meetings about increased provision had led to an exploration of the nature of the present school day, other possible uses of the school building and the provision of after-school activities. The benefits of a change to the school day and the inclusion of after-school activities were then presented to the governors' Finance and Premises Committee. The governing body consid-ered that learning could be improved by focusing major curriculum activities in the morning, commencing at 0830 and reducing the lunch-break time to half an hour. They were, however, concerned about the effect of these changes on working parents. A further major consideration was the impact these changes would have on the junior school.

Formal marketing of the school was limited to the production of a school prospectus and some contacts with the local community. The school's Ofsted inspection report had highlighted a significant minority of parents who felt that there was inefficient communication and consultation between the school and themselves. Thus, marketing needed attention.

The bursar's role in the project

The bursar began to explore the school's overall marketing approach by conducting a SWOT analysis, the outcomes of which are shown in Figure 10. 4.

Strengths	Weaknesses
1 Resources available	1 Poor communication between school and customers
2 Governing body's increased awareness of school (post-Ofsted)	2 Limited awareness of external market
3 Associate staff	3 Poor internal communications
4 Safe school environment for pupils	4 Morale of teaching staff post-Ofsted 5
Some links with local community	5 No formal marketing policy
Opportunities	**Threats**
1 Review and change of current practice as a result of Ofsted	1 Other local schools affecting the roll
2 Forge new links with parents	2 Ofsted report – special measures
3 Development for improvement	3 Two year period to 'get it right'
Rebuild from scratch	4 Teaching staff morale low – threat 4 of resignations
	5 External market reaction to Ofsted

Figure 10.4 SWOT analysis of the school's marketing position

The bursar then considered the school's relationship with the shared-site junior school and other schools in the area, particularly in relation to implementing a new school day and after-school activities. As a member of a bursars' forum, which met to discuss local and national issues the bursar was able to take the opportunity to carry out a survey of the activities of the six other schools represented and extend it to include the partner junior school and two other LEA schools. The local press was also searched for information about after school activities in schools and newsletters of the local competitor schools were collected. The bursars discovered that all schools, except the partner school were involved in, or considering implementing extra-curricular activities, which had been extended to include the periods before school and during the lunch break. The variety of activities on offer was also investigated. Activities were heavily dependent on the skills and willingness of individual staff members. Teachers and parents ran most activities on a voluntary basis, although external providers were also involved.

In order to clarify the situation, and using the information gathered, a force field analysis was carried out comparing the driving and hindering forces for change in relation to changing the pattern of the school day and the school's activities (Figure 10.5).

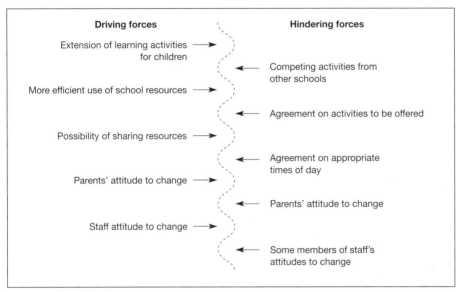

Figure 10.5 Force field analysis of attitudes to community involvement

The bursar's subsequent analysis identified that there was pressure for change coming from all areas but, paradoxically, some resistance from within the school by parents and the community as illustrated in Figure 10.6.

A strategy was then proposed by the bursar for improving marketing, which included:

1 developing the prospectus and reviewing its mode of presentation;
2 advertising;
3 informing the media of school activities;
4 holding open evenings and other related events;
5 exploring other communication techniques;
6 researching how other schools are marketing themselves.

The bursar also brought in a consultant to further assess the implications of a new school day and after-school activities. After reviewing the situation

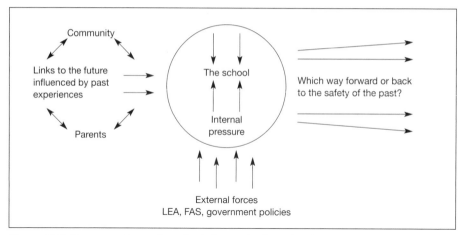

Figure 10.6 Pressures for and against change in the school

together, it was agreed that an incremental approach to the extra-curricular changes envisaged would be more acceptable to all those involved. Further benefit could also be derived from the development of a home/school strategy and greater community involvement in the school, especially if parents were also encouraged to take part in activities. It was suggested that a selected number of activities be introduced over a set period of time. An added benefit would be that any problem areas could be dealt with at a local level and would be easier to handle.

The bursar's contribution: discussion

The school in this case study was characterised by a forward-looking and dynamic senior management team, which had not considered the effects the changes it was making were having on its own school community. The bursar's use of a SWOT analysis highlighted the areas where communication could be improved, and his use of a force field analysis demonstrated the complex pressures between the school and its stakeholders.

The use made of the bursars' forum and consultant demonstrates the value of outside agencies in providing varying information. The bursars' forum was used to gather and share information about other schools in the area, and provided similar support for bursars to that which heads enjoy in their local groups. The consultant was brought in to provide an independent, alternative perspective when discussing the proposed changes.

The final suggestion for marketing the school was comprehensive and the recommendation that the changes in provision of extra-curricular activities be incremental was in direct response to the need to communicate and build up a relationship with the school's stakeholders. The following mnemonic, which was developed by the bursar as a reminder for keeping the process going is evidence of this responsive attitude:

Keep the direction moving forward.

Effective management.

Encompass the whole environment.

Participation of all involved in the school.

INform and pass on necessary information.

THE school's vision is shared.

Plan for the future.

Involve the community at all levels.

Communicate at all levels.

Tend to the needs of the customer.

Unify within and without.

Relate to others' needs.

Establish working relationships.

Case study 10.4: Recommendations for a school marketing plan linked to the operational budget

School

Welsh, independent mixed school, 300 pupils, sixth form only.
36 teachers, 99 support staff.
Bursar from military background.

Context

Independent schools are more dependent on marketing to attract pupils than state schools. This school is one of an international group, which generates approximately 90 per cent of its income from student funding, much of which is through sponsorship of its pupils rather than directly by student fees as would be the case for most independent schools. The school was marketed by use of its high-profile patronage and by providing UK secondary schools and LEAs with information. Due to the success of the school it was in need of more funds to support the sponsored pupils. The challenge to the bursar was to develop a marketing policy that would attract more sponsors and fee-paying students who fulfil the school's admission criteria without compromising the values set out in the mission statement.

The bursar's role in the project

The school has a policy that no more than 25 per cent of its students will be fee paying. The bursar had to bear this in mind when considering any marketing policy. The relationship between the operating budget and student numbers was therefore examined to determine the numbers of fully funded and sponsored students necessary to achieve a balanced budget. The current marketing policy of the school was then reviewed in the light of the school's financial plan. Information at the bursar's disposal included surveys of students attending for interview which determined where they had heard about the school, names of sponsors and their contributions, operating costs and the balance of fee-paying and sponsored pupils.

A PESTLE analysis and a brainstorming exercise with school staff was suggested by the bursar to agree long-term objectives. As a starting point, the bursar explored the micro-environmental factors that had the potential to have an immediate impact on the school. The findings are illustrated in Figure. 10.7.

The bursar also warned that in the light of the school's core values, some areas were more important than others and this should be borne in mind when

Competitors	• State schools • Independent schools • Sister schools • The School's International Office
Customers	• Students • Parents • Industry and commerce • Universities • National governments
Suppliers	• International Baccalaureate Board • National committees • Industrial and commercial sponsors • Charitable trusts and individual sponsors
Intermediaries	• The School's International Office • Feeder school headteachers • Parents • Alumni

Figure 10.7 Micro-environmental factors for discussion

making decisions. A suggestion was made that the marketing plan focus on fund raising, improving contributions from current sponsors, attracting students whose parents could contribute to their education and managing the image of the school individually rather than as part of a group. A further suggestion was that the school should focus on what makes it unique when promoting itself.

The bursar's contribution: discussion

In this case study the bursar used financial expertise to inform the school's marketing policy. Due to the unique nature of the school and its particular emphasis on values especially when recruiting pupils, it was not possible to raise extra funds by increasing the number of fee-paying students alone. The bursar carried out a detailed income analysis related to the school's budget, paying particular attention to marginal cost accounting, thus linking resources to educational needs. Once the numbers and ratios of fee-paying to sponsored students had been determined, a marketing policy could be devised which bore these factors in mind.

Case study 10.5: Market research and the sixth form centre

School

Urban, GM, mixed school 800+ pupils, secondary phase with sixth form.
57 teachers, 40 support staff.
Bursar from a military background.

Context

The school was established in the early 1950s originally as separate boys' and girls' schools sharing the site. The mixed sixth form was opened five years later, the schools amalgamated in 1985 and gained GM status in 1993. The college was inspected by Ofsted in 1997 and the following findings relevant to the sixth form were cited.

1 By the age of 19 pupils' attainment matches national expectations in most post-16 subjects with the exception of English and Design Technology where they are below national standards.

2 The number of pupils taking A-level is relatively small. The average points score for pupils taking two or more A-levels has in the last three years been 8.7 – well below the national average but in line with schools

of a similar nature. The performance of pupils in intermediate GNVQ programmes in 1996 was at the national average.

3   The school has recently introduced a monitoring scheme for individual pupil performance through setting minimum target grades. This is beginning to have a positive effect on standards, particularly in the sixth form.

4   Financial difficulties still remain and much needs to be done to improve standards of attainment and the quality of education overall. The school therefore at present does not give value for money.

5   The attendance of those sixth form pupils who continue their studies is barely satisfactory. The keeping of accurate records is difficult as many pupils do not attend registration, some because they have negotiated home study. Not all subject teachers keep detailed records of attendance at lessons.

The SMT had invested heavily of their time and in providing resources for sixth form students to give a broad and balanced curriculum entitlement and this had raised the profile of Years 12 and 13. During 1997 the sixth form was relocated into the main site from its previously detached building across the road. This involved substantial expenditure and there was a need to ensure that sufficient students would be attracted to the sixth form to safeguard its long-term viability. The bursar wanted to find out what the perception of the sixth form was by present and potential customers and determined that this needed a detailed market research survey.

The bursar's role in the project

After discussion with the SMT the bursar decided that the aim of the survey was *'to critically review post sixteen education in the school with a view to identifying a model of best practice for the twenty-first century in terms of customer expectation and satisfaction and the utilisation of resources to achieve value for money'*. In order to choose an appropriate strategy for carrying this out the following objectives were set:

● to ascertain the causal factors which contribute to the reduction in the post-16 roll;

● to evaluate resource use in value for money terms using best practice identified through historical, current and comparative data and models of cost-effectiveness from Ofsted and FAS;

● to identify the expectations of potential customers and the satisfaction of present customers through market research based on current studies into the psychology of post-16 students;

● to develop short- and medium-term decision-making and budgeting plans and long-term projections through an analysis of the findings of the market research;

- to draw conclusions from this analysis which will form the basis for recommendations to move towards best practice in the twenty-first century.

The bursar then needed to select appropriate methods to implement these objectives and resolved to employ both questionnaires and interviews to obtain the best picture of students' perceptions of the sixth form. An idea of the issues and historical data was needed to design the questionnaire. A literature review of post-16 education, cost-effectiveness and efficiency in education, performance indicators, marketing and quality identified 'excellence as the purposive factor in educational management' and the following equation based on an holistic approach to management:

$$Excellence = Quality + Effectiveness + Equity + Efficiency + Empowerment$$
(Caldwell and Spinks, 1992)

Interviews were carried out with the Head of Post-16 Education, the Examinations Officer and other senior and middle managers to gather further data and incorporate their suggestions into the focus, format and desired outcomes of the research. From this wealth of information a pilot survey was drawn up consisting of a 16-item, Likert scale questionnaire (five options from strongly agree to strongly disagree) and circulated through the sixth form tutors to students in Years 12 and 13. As well as providing valuable data about current perceptions this also identified further issues which would need to be addressed in the main survey of Year 11 which took place a month later.

The bursar's main survey was designed to complement the Year 11 interviews being concurrently conducted by SMT members and focused on several issues.

- How many current Year 11 students intend to continue their education?
- For those that did, which courses did they intend to choose?
- Where did they intend to study these and why?
- For those not continuing their education, what did they intend to do and why?
- The attitudes of all students towards factors affecting their choice of a post-16 institution.

A great deal of thought was put into the design and layout of the questionnaire as well as the logistics of its distribution and return (for example, precoding the forms, colour-coding each of the batches of questionnaires to the eight tutor groups, ordering the questions so they progressed from easier to harder questions and mixing closed and open response items). The bursar arranged for time to be allocated in form tutor periods for pupils to complete the questionnaire and briefed the form tutors. As a result the response rate was nearly 66 per cent.

Given the interest in cost efficiency as well as market research, the bursar also estimated the cost in time and money spent on the investigation (Figure 10.8).

Cost of survey		Hours
Cost in personal time:	Design of survey	6
	Reproduction	2
	Distribution	2
	Completion and return	1
	Analysis and use of SPSS	24
	Completion of report	48
	Total	**83**
		£
Cost in financial outlay:	Time @ £10 hour x 83	830.00
	Literature survey	60.00
	Reproduction @ 162 copies	24.30
	Printing final report	10.00
	Total	**924.30**

Figure 10.8 Cost of market research to the school

The outcomes

A great deal of data and analysis was generated by the bursar, the main findings of which were:

- a much larger percentage of students who opted to go to a FE college could be attracted back into the school's sixth form centre through appropriate action;

- very few students cease education at 16 and those who do have had valid reasons. It was considered unlikely that they could be attracted back into education;

- student attitudes in the school towards the sixth form centre did not differ from those found in other geographical areas;

- the limited internal marketing activities did not appear to be addressing the main areas of student concern;

- students were generally not in favour of either school uniform or community duties but would like to be seen as role models. This would suggest that there was some misunderstanding of the term 'role model'.

From these findings the bursar made the following recommendations to the SMT.

- There should be a clear commitment to ensuring all Year 7–11 students follow a path into the sixth form centre.

- There needs to be a high level of internal marketing to ensure all students are aware of the positive aspects of the sixth form centre.

- Internal marketing should also address the factors that influence the students' choice of a post-16 institution.

- Smart casual dress might be an alternative to uniform acceptable to both post-16 students and to the school.
- Community work should be an option available for those who wish to do it.
- The school needed to be aware that students valued the secure, orderly environment and co-operative relationships with teachers, and should build on these positive factors.

In addition to these valuable suggestions for future action in the school, the bursar also identified two areas where further research would add insights. These were the relationship between gender, tutor group and cognitive ability test scores (CATs) and post-16 choices and attitudes; post-16 competition in the area.

The bursar's contribution: discussion

There are many lessons to learn from this very detailed piece of market research carried out by the bursar. First, we have identified in this book the potential for tension between the emerging role of the bursar and those of senior and middle managers in the school. This study shows that the bursar's role can be complementary to other management roles. The bursar drew on a wide range of data from various persons at different levels and added expertise in questionnaire design and statistical analysis to produce a detailed picture of students' perceptions of the value of the sixth form. The questionnaire generated a great deal of information, which the bursar learned to analyse through the Statistics Package for Social Science (SPSS) software and to present in tables, pie charts and histograms. The package also gave the mean, median and mode values, standard deviation and skew of each question item. In all, the bursar collected an immense amount of data through the literature review, interviews and the two questionnaires, and this made a useful counterfoil to the information gathered by the SMT from individual pupil interviews. Additionally, because of the bursar's interest in value for money, the analysis of the cost in time and money makes the important point that all too often senior management fail to realise the operational cost of strategic decisions.

Final thoughts

The five bursars in the case studies were all members of their senior management teams. Their contributions were characterised by operation at a strategic level and by their decision to accumulate data, which helped them and the senior management team to understand the views of the schools' stakeholders and their schools' strategic position. As leaders of the support and administration staff, they had the time and expertise to gather, analyse and disseminate data to inform decision making. They were also willing to use expert advice from outside the school whenever possible. Notably, the advisers and consultants they used were free, as favours were returned in kind rather than through making payments out of the school funds. There is evidence that the bursars' position within the support staff and as front-line communicators with parents and the community made them aware of the viewpoints of others, and it was this insight that they used to determine the strategy for gathering information. A final characteristic in the bursars' approach to marketing was that they combined factors, which were important to the marketing of the school but might not normally have been considered, such as determining the link between resources and policy before deciding on a marketing strategy.

11
■ ■ ■

Learning: the Bursar and Aspects of the Curriculum

Introduction

This last chapter in Part Three covers perhaps the most contentious aspect of the bursar's role – involvement in teaching and learning. In times of turbulent change it is vital for an organisation to keep a focus on the core business and for schools this is teaching and learning. There is also the need to focus on the future to help the school stay ahead of the game. The case studies outlined here illustrate how bursars can explore teaching and learning strategies in different contexts and can determine the costs and benefits of developing new approaches to teaching and learning.

The case studies

11.1 *A stratgeic plan for cognitive acceleration through science education.* The bursar took a strategic planning role in investigating the costs and benefits of adopting cognitive acceleration in science as a solution to failing results in GCSE and a poor take up of the subject in the sixth form.

11.2 *Evaluation of an integrated learning system in mathematics.* The bursar moved from strategic planning to an evaluative role in reviewing the impact of a trial of an Integrated Learning System (ILS) in mathematics on the learning environment in order to identify the operational implications of expanding this provision.

11.3 *Alternative educational provision for disaffected Year 11 students.* As part of an incoming SMT, the bursar reviewed the origin and evaluated the outcomes of an alternative educational provision for disaffected Year 11 students with a view to developing a longer-term strategy.

11.4 *The development of a whole-school learning and information centre.* The school decided to embark on planning an ICT-based centre for sixth form teaching and learning with the bursar playing a leading role in securing the resources and widening the brief to develop a learning and information resource centre.

Case study 11.1: A strategic plan for cognitive acceleration through science education

School

London, Catholic, GM, mixed school, 700+ pupils, secondary phase with sixth form.
45 teachers, 8.8 support staff.
Bursar from accountancy and consultancy background.

Context

The school's science department consisted of six teachers in six laboratories supported by 2.5 full-time equivalent (FTE) technicians. The subject is resource hungry but achieved relatively poor exam results at GCSE compared to those in English and humanities. Science had not been popular with sixth form students; results were deteriorating and there was a key business imperative to rectify this situation. Alongside this issue were those of the underachievement of pupils and the cost-effectiveness of science education which together gave, in the bursar's judgement, unsatisfactory value for money. In a search for alternative strategies, the bursar was alerted to an intervention programme that claimed remarkable improvements in GCSE results – the Cognitive Acceleration through Science Education programme (CASE). The key features of this programme were:

- **Cognitive conflict**: children develop their ability to think when they confront and struggle with intellectual problems
- **Reflection/metacognition**: reflection by the learner on his/her own thinking processes ('learning to learn')
- **Bridging**: building bridges from the science-like activity to other subjects in the world outside – applying the same principle to new contexts
- **Reasoning patterns**: higher level thinking is characterised by reasoning which enables the control of variables, proportionality, equilibria, ascrib-

ing probability values to cause and effect relationships and comprehending a correlational relationship between variables. These cannot be taught directly but the teacher who is aware of them will be better equipped to help pupils develop such reasoning patterns for themselves. (Adapted from Adey, Sheyer and Yates 1990: 2)

CASE is included in the science teaching programme as a series of 30 lessons over two years (one 'thinking lesson' every fortnight) and has been shown to increase the proportion of students gaining five or more GCSE grades A* to C by some 20 per cent compared to control groups. The bursar therefore decided to investigate the possibilities of CASE for the Key Stage 4 curriculum.

The bursar's role in the project

The bursar first established the nature of the school climate into which CASE would be introduced as this would provide a valuable pointer to subsequent strategic planning. The bursar carried out a force field analysis to identify the driving and hindering forces as illustrated in Figure 11.1 and as a further tool used micropolitical mapping to plot the relative power/influence and concern/support of the SMT.

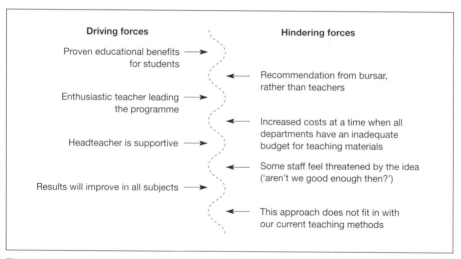

Figure 11.1 **Introducing cognitive acceleration in science – the bursar's force field analysis**

Having ascertained the school climate and the stances of the SMT, the bursar then visited four schools and interviewed the co-ordinators about their experiences of implementing CASE. They all confirmed that the pupils had gained from introducing the programme. The co-ordinators stressed the need for:

- adequate training for staff who were to be involved;
- the additional cost of the teaching materials;
- substantial extra photocopying;
- the requirement to purchase new apparatus.

In order to determine the full costs of introducing the scheme, the bursar's next step was to produce a programme budget for the costs of the scheme to be presented to the SMT.

Figure 11.2 shows the total new costs to be £5300, which would need to be spread over two financial years (£3100 in year 1 and £2200 in year 2). Eventually CASE would become self-financing in five years as the numbers of students grew but for the additional annual costs, students could be given a much improved basis for lifelong learning.

This case was presented to the SMT, the bursar pointing out that the science department could significantly enhance its contribution to the whole school if they were able, through the use of CASE, to give lessons in learning to the students. This might be reinforced if the maths department were to adopt CAME (Cognitive Acceleration through Mathematics Education). Thus, although there were financial costs, senior management commitment and teaching methods implications, the bursar considered that the benefits to the whole school would be significant in terms of the improvement in children's learning skills and the marketing value of improved examination results. This, in turn, would attract additional pupils to take up spare capacity in the school and improve the cost-effectiveness of the scheme.

Plan item First academic year	Teaching staff	Support staff	Training consultant	Other	Total
1 Training consultant			1600		1600
2 Existing technician time		(1250)			(1250)
3 Additional technician time		1200			1200
4 Teacher INSET	1200				1200
5 Technician INSET		550			550
6 Apparatus/materials				500	500
7 Thinking Science course				100	100
8 Reprographics (pupils)				45	45
9 Reprographics (staff)				8	8
10 Contingency				97	97
Total Existing costs		(1250)			(1250)
New costs	1200	1750	1 600	750	5300

Figure 11.2 The bursar's programme budget for the costs of introducing CASE (1997 prices, £)

The bursar's contribution: discussion

This case study illustrates the strategic planning role that the bursar can bring into play, which in this case, was powerfully put as the bursar was able to draw on previous experience as a management accountant about the importance of analysing the organisational climate before presenting plans. The holistic approach and consideration of the educational/learning issues, as well as the more traditional finance and resource aspects, show how a bursar as school business manager can act both in gathering information from outside sources and in preparing and presenting a coherent case to the SMT.

Case study 11.2: Evaluation of an integrated learning system in mathematics

School

Mixed 11–18, GM, comprehensive in Wales, 1300 pupils.
Bursar: from a teaching background in business studies/commerce.

Context

The school became a GM school in 1993 and, after gaining control over all its own finances, it channelled resources into what it believed to be the most appropriate areas to create a learning environment allowing children to reach their full potential. The school has a good standing in the community and excellent relations with local businesses, which often provide sponsorship and other assistance. The school has excellent academic results, which improved year by year.

The school won a 'most improved school' award, is oversubscribed but resists the temptation to be academically selective, preferring to retain its role as a community school, drawing its intake from designated local feeder schools and giving siblings of existing pupils priority in admissions. The issue for the bursar was the evaluation of an Integrated Learning System brought into the school to support the teaching of mathematics and enhance the ICT provision.

The bursar's role in the project

Stage I

The bursar's starting point was a review of the school's trial of an ICT Independent Learning System for mathematics in order to inform the consideration of extending this into other subjects. As well as an analysis of the costs of the system (purchase and maintenance), the fact that the ILS system includes a student progress-monitoring facility impacts on the work of support staff and the effects of this needed to be identified. Also the 'open access' possibilities of the system questioned the traditional roles of teacher and technician and the siting of the hardware in various parts of the school had security, room utilisation, health and safety implications.

The bursar carried out an evaluation of the SuccessMaker ILS system. This system is computer based and manages the delivery of curriculum materials to pupils in short daily bursts of intensive activity so that they are presented with individual programmes of work over a number of months. The system provides immediate feedback to the pupils on their progress as they work, adjusting the level of the next activity to reinforce, remediate or challenge them. There are also detailed records of individual and group results, which the teacher can access.

The key influences determined by the bursar in the analysis of the reasons why the school had decided to trial the ILS system revolved around the report of the Phase II ILS pilot by the National Council for Educational Technology (NCET, 1996). This report contained the belief that the evidence available fully justified the continued exploration of possible benefits from the use of integrated learning systems, specifically that SuccessMaker developed positive attitudes to learning and that these were being transferred to other classroom activities. The greatest benefits were found to be with the most and least able pupils. The senior management and the bursar therefore concluded that pupils in the school would improve their performance in mathematics at Key Stage 3 and decided to pilot the ILS SuccessMaker system for mathematics.

Stage II

The next stage in the evaluation was for the bursar to investigate the nature of the practice of mathematics teaching before and after the introduction of the system to determine the key differences and their potential effect on the learning environment. Prior to the purchase of the ILS, pupils spent their mathematics lessons receiving instruction from their teacher and undertaking a limited amount of computer-based mathematics exercises, mainly for reinforcement or remedial learning. Following the installation of the ILS system into one of the mathematics classrooms, pupils received their mathematics tuition via the interactive computer system allowing them to progress according to their ability and aptitude. Able pupils and less able pupils happily sat alongside each other, concentrated fully and worked purposefully, even pupils who were previously disaffected with mathematics. Interestingly, the denial of access to the mathematics room is now seen as a powerful sanction whereas previously exclusion from the classroom was only seen by the pupils as a deterrent in that they had to go to the 'disruptives' area'. The system kept records of their progress which were available to pupils and their teachers; this saved much time when analysing progress prior to school reports being collated.

The outcome of the bursar's analysis determined that there were significant effects on the pupils and teaching staff and the support services, the main ones of which were:

- improvement in pupil performance, especially with most able (enrichment) and least able (self-esteem);
- access to system out of hours (better plant utilisation – possible income generation);
- possible replacement of teacher by paraprofessional to manage system (but pupil supervision implications);
- assessment data can be analysed and prepared by support staff, releasing teachers to work with pupils, while still having instant access to the database (at present only on the administrative computer in the office);
- assessment records in business studies and technology can be integrated with the mathematics results and other subjects as they come on stream (e.g. ILS in English and languages);
- linking pupils' assessment records to the main administration network will enable access to all authorised staff for diagnostic and formative purposes.

Furthermore, the bursar identified the specific implications for the support services that such changes in the technology of teaching would have on the learning environment:

- more IT technicians will be needed, especially as real-time assistants (rather than behind-the-scenes preparation and maintenance);
- INSET will need to be available as an intrinsic cost (both at installation and as software and hardware are upgraded/replaced);
- changes in the pattern of resource use (e.g. less use of reprographics, more use of scanners, digital cameras, compact disks [CDs] etc.);
- the library/resource area, both for pupils and staff, will become a crucial central facility with Internet access, compact disk read-only memory (CD-ROM) and other audio-visual and ICT resources;
- the increase in ICT-based learning will require revisions in site services and security provision both physically, to prevent theft and vandalism, but also to protect unauthorised access to data through, for example, password protection and controlled gateways;
- support staff will need to consider how system generated assessment information (a feature of SuccessMaker) is kept up to date, accessible on-line and used to produce reports to parents and records of achievement by pupils themselves;

- such changes will require reallocation of duties and new job descriptions which will affect working routines and hours of duty to cover the extended day and term.

Finally, before proceeding to the preparation of an operational plan for expanding ILS provision, the bursar identified the overall benefits of adopting the ILS system by conducting a political, economic, socio-cultural and techno-logical (PEST) analysis (Figure 11.3).

Political/legal	**Economic**
Change of government could affect future funding levels for GM schools	Increase in support costs Changes in energy costs Reduction in the costs of hardware
Socio-cultural	**Technological**
Increase in pupil numbers Greater use of ICT in the home (Internet) Changed attitudes to work/leisure time	New developments in ICT Rates of obsolescence Speed of technology transfer

Figure 11.3   Introducing ILS – a PEST analysis

Having evaluated fully the outcomes of the trial period for the learning environment and the socio-political context of the school, the bursar then mapped out the key items which the SMT and governing body needed to consider in taking the decision about the future direction of ILS and ICT provision in the school. The bursar took into account both aspects of the core business of teaching and learning as well as the administrative issues required to put into practice the strategic intent of a move to more ILS provision. The main features of the bursar's three to five year implementation plan were:

1 produce a two-year costed projection of the resources required to provide ILS systems in mathematics, English and modern languages and present this to the governors for approval;

2 network the school to enable the administrative system to be accessed throughout the school, with appropriate password access and restricted gateways;

3 widen the use of paraprofessional support staff, possibly from those who take early retirement, to enable real-time classroom support;

4 obtain Special Development grants to train ICT technicians and teaching staff on the new systems and support staff on ILS information management;

5 maintain an asset register of soft and hardware to upgrade and replace resources when and where necessary;

6 educate parents on the new teaching techniques to gain their support.

The bursar's contribution: duscussion

This case study shows the bursar fulfilling a key strategic role in the planning stage but moves beyond this to exemplify a clear appreciation of both the learning and support staff aspects. A detailed physical and human resource analysis was conducted as well as a thorough review of the changes in the teaching and learning styles as a result of the experience with the ILS system. In the style of the report, there are leadership, learning and whole-school overtones which indicate operation well above the technician/resource specialist level. The bursar, as a member of the SMT, does work closely with senior management and the governing body and has developed a holistic view of the project being analysed here.

Case study 11.3: Alternative educational provision for disaffected Year 11 pupils

School

Provincial, locally managed, mixed comprehensive, 400 pupils.
Bursar from a school administration background.

Context

The school is a 12–16 LEA maintained mixed comprehensive of 407 students. It draws its pupils from an area with the highest indicators of social disadvantage in the region. There is a high proportion of slow learners in each year group.

In 1995, prior to the recruitment of a new senior management team, there was a deficit of £80 000 in the budget, truancy was high with an unauthorised absence rate of 3.5 per cent and the school was at the bottom of the local league table with only 10 per cent gaining five A*–C grades at GCSE. The Ofsted report in 1994 was poor. It identified underachievement in several areas of the curriculum and thus the need for teachers to raise their expectations of what students are capable of, ensure that learning tasks are matched to the ability of the students, improve rates of attendance and the provision for SEN pupils.

The incoming SMT conducted a SWOT analysis to determine ways of beginning to tackle the issues. One of the strategies chosen to improve both the image of the school and attack the issue of underachievement was the identification of six Year 11 students who were unlikely to complete their final year at the school. The area had been included in a Single Regeneration Budget plan (SRB – a European Union programme for socio-economically deprived areas) and the funding enabled the school to offer these pupils a more positive alternative for preparing them for adult life than the traditional academic atmosphere in the school. If the alternative action of permanent exclusion had been taken, they could have become a menace to the community, causing general disruption and participating in petty crime. The six students identified were to attend the New Careers Training (NCT) centre where they would be given a foundation training in various construction skills. They would continue to be taught the core curriculum of English and mathematics but 'college taster' courses, work experience and extra careers guidance was also offered. In return the students were expected to attend NCT as they would have school. After the project had been running for two years, the bursar had to decide whether this strategy had been effective and what the most cost-beneficial solution would be for the future.

The bursar's role in the project

The bursar first researched the context of the proposal through a 'dead document' survey reviewing the original SWOT analysis, the 1994 Ofsted report and subsequent Action Plan, the School Development Plan and the SRB plan. The bursar then conducted a structured interview with the headteacher in order to clarify the findings, background history and culture of the school. The evidence was consolidated with a brief questionnaire to all school staff designed to establish how well the school had informed all the staff and managed the change.

As part of the original review, the SMT had selected 14 elements, which it believed could be implemented to raise the level of students' achievement, the six relevant to the disaffected students' project being:

1 it could be implemented without needing extra staff time;

2 the SRB bid provided financial support;

3 the disaffected students needed alternative options;

4 national and local government policy encouraged schools to avoid excluding students;

5 the LEA had no alternative placement for these students if they were permanently excluded;

6 there was a benefit to the local community if these students remained in the education system.

The outcome of the bursar's documentary review revealed very little in terms of formal recording of agreements relating to the background of this decision. It did, however, show that the school had initially developed a vision and mission statement prior to the SWOT analysis, identified a strategic intent and then progressed to strategic planning drawing on relevant local and national government documents. Combined with the whole-school staff development days on developing the mission and building self-esteem throughout the school, this indicated a focus on creating a supportive and optimistic culture in the school and bringing the staff together under the new SMT.

A financial statement was also prepared by the bursar to identify the out-turn cost to the school of the project (Fig. 11.4). This demonstrated that the school had not needed to subsidise the project but had made a surplus, though the costs in terms of co-ordination and senior management time had not been accounted for.

Item	Income	Expenditure	Balance
£2112 per pupil	£12672		
SRB Funding	£3600		
Cost of NCT Training		£3970	
			£12302

Figure 11.4 Costs analysis of the disaffected students project

The bursar's analysis of the questionnaire to all staff showed that everyone was in agreement that removal of these students from the classroom had benefited the school. There was, however, an initial concern about the cost implications and the possibility that the students would see the option as a reward for bad behaviour. The staff had been reassured by the SMT and this had led to unanimous support.

Now the bursar needed to establish how the project had turned out in practice. The approach taken was to conduct open-ended interviews with the three teachers most directly involved with the planning, implementation and evaluation of the course for disaffected students; this gave a good picture of the outcomes of the project over a two-year period. The first year was a clear success but the decision to modify the second year to bring some of the teaching back into the school brought the original problems back and ended in the core staff having to use their non-contact time to tutor the students. The issue that the bursar and the SMT was left with, therefore, was how the project should develop in its final year of funding under the SRB and how the school could produce an exit plan to enable the lessons learned to be incorporated into main stream approaches.

To summarise the position and to inform the debate on the subsequent stage in the development of the initiative, the bursar then drew up a 'best fit' table, which illustrated the potential benefits to the school across a number of areas (Figure 11.5).

Level of 'fit'	Finance	Human resource	Outside support	School culture	Competition/ market needs
High	Outside funding	Quality of leadership and management Staff commitment Expertise of outside agencies	County TEC NCT centre	Pastoral care ethos	Nature of catchment area
Medium		Staff willingness to change	The LEA careers service Local community	Student attitudes	Government initiatives encouraging alternative ideas
Low	School budget The LEA	Staff time		Perception of students' abilities	No competition

Figure 11.5 "Best fit' analysis of the project

The bursar thus thoroughly evaluated the history, costs and outcomes of the choice of this alternative provision for disaffected Year 11 students. Clearly the removal of the students from normal classes has been successful but evidence from the interviews with the project teachers indicated that the students had difficulty coping in the less protective and less caring climate of the NCT. Their needs had not been as well served as had been planned – indeed the second cohort began to replicate the first cohort's disaffection with non-attendance at the NCT centre.

Although the SMT had now to decide, with the help of the bursar's report, how to take forward the project after the third (current) year, there were a number of related outcomes for the Key Stage 4 curriculum. The experience led to the starting up of a vocational option for Year 10 and close negotiations with the local FE college to explore the provision of GNVQs in various local trades. There was a well developed engineering and boat-building tradition in the region and the school already had strong links with the business community. One option the bursar had identified for the school would be to establish a craft-based education for disaffected students within the security of the school.

The bursar's contribution: discussion

For the NCT project, the bursar was involved in the initial costing and negoti-ations and helped to set up the continuous feedback between the centre, students and teachers which ensured that ongoing modifications were made as necessary. Targets were set at the end of each year and the success of the course assessed from these achievements. The strategic analysis, however, raised this involvement to more of a leadership role as the evidence gathered enabled the preparation of a wide ranging evaluation, using a number of com-plementary tools, which the SMT could use in determining the future development of the initiative. This case study shows how the bursar can per-form a crucial role in an aspect of alternative learning provision as part of a recovery plan from a poor Ofsted report.

Whereas these three case studies focused on particular areas of the curriculum, the final case study tackles wider issues that impact more generally on the learn-ing environment and the pupils across the school. It is indicative of the way in which the bursar can perform a more whole school leadership role.

Case study 11.4: The development of a whole-school learning and information centre

School

South-east, GM, mixed, 11–18, comprehensive school with 1500+ pupils.
100 teachers, 25 support staff.
Bursar from a school secretary background – long serving in this school.

Context

The school Vision Plan included the aims of enabling pupils and students:

1 to become independent lifelong learners;

2 to be confident and competent users of ICT.

The school became more acutely aware in the early 1990s of its responsibil-ity to educate its pupils for the information and knowledge society of the twenty-first century and decided to investigate the building of a learning and information centre to provide the means to this end. In the 1980s, ICT was hardly evident at all in the school but the targeted funding available for ICT through the extension of the Technical and Vocational Education Initiative (TVEI) gave a significant boost to the purchase of computer hardware and software. At the end of this initiative the school was faced with a series of dilemmas. The school had inadequate accommodation for any increase in computer facilities, the curriculum needed to take into account the provision required for ICT under the National Curriculum but the teachers in the school were inadequately experienced or trained to teach ICT. Decisions about the future ICT provision and approach in the school were required and the bursar and the SMT decided to tackle these urgently.

The bursar's role in the project

The bursar, together with members of the SMT, first decided to analyse the context of the issue by conducting a SWOT analysis which showed that the opportunities and strengths far outweighed the weaknesses and threats, and that even the latter could be overcome by the development of innovative strategies.

The bursar and colleagues in the SMT then carried out a 'best practice' analysis. Members of the SMT visited a number of sixth form, technology and further education colleges known for their use of ICT in an innovative way and reported back examples of best practice. Successful colleges were found to be using ICT to underpin all of their courses, particularly GNVQ. The priority was to provide resources for the sixth form students who had no suitable accommodation for private study in the school and no ICT facilities other than those in the business studies department. As universities were now requiring ICT skills from their students, the bursar felt it was important that students were not disadvantaged in their higher education through their lack of such skills.

The bursar supported the extension of the initial strategic plan to finance a purpose-built sixth form ICT centre to include the improvement of facilities for lower school pupils. Builders' estimates indicated that the cheapest option was a brick-clad, preconstructed unit and this offered the potential of a larger whole school development, extending the school vision plan to all pupils and students. In presenting this analysis to the governors, the decision was made to pursue this aim and it was agreed that the school should set aside, over a period of three years, reserves, which would be translated into the bricks and mortar of the building and the purchase of equipment. The Funding Agency for Schools was approached by the bursar to agree this as permission had to be obtained to carry over funds in excess of 10 per cent of the Annual Maintenance Grant to future financial years. Consideration had been made of the possibility of seeking funding through bidding for technology college status but the governors and SMT determined that the school should continue to provide a broad and balanced curriculum with ICT as a tool for delivering this rather than it being the only focus.

The bursar, in conjunction with other colleagues on the SMT then drew up a business plan considering the key issues. They were confident that, once the centre was up and running, funding via sixth form numbers would be secure as staying-on rates had been steadily increasing. An advertisement placed by the bursar in the local newspaper offering sixth form courses to external applicants proved that there was a need for a co-educational school providing a variety of post-16 courses together with good ICT study facilities. A prudent approach was taken to this, however, by staffing and resourcing at the minimum level and using the additional funding from excess recruitment to accrue reserves for the project. Similarly, lower school numbers were due to rise annually for the next five years as part of a FAS expansion programme to meet basic need and this not only strengthened the funding base but gave stability over the building and purchasing period.

The school had also been part of the FAS state of school buildings survey and this did not identify any serious weaknesses or areas that required urgent attention. Thus the bursar considered that the maintenance budget could be cut for one year to attend to minor repairs and health and safety issues. Only a further structural survey commissioned from a private contractor confirmed that the school's listed building, always a potential financial 'time bomb', was considered safe for the foreseeable future. The bursar was therefore happy that the scene was set for the concerted and concentrated effort of bringing the learning centre into fruition.

Other measures taken by the bursar with the SMT ensured expenditure across the school was carefully monitored and savings identified which could be transferred into the project without jeopardising the delivery of the curriculum and services to pupils. All contracts were scrutinised for value for money; in one case the bursar brought in a consultant to audit the school catering contract. The consultant was able to identify savings in excess of £10000. A change of the school's banker also enabled higher rates of interest to be gained on the reserves being accrued. Added to this was a major review of the overall management structure, which resulted in the abolition of a deputy head post and a saving of a further £30000. The bursar worked with the headteacher to restructure the premises and site team to create a maintenance team with sufficient specialist skills, thus obviating the need to call in expensive contractors to attend to plumbing, carpentry and decorating. Finally the creative use of the timetable enabled the use of an extended school day which maximised the deployment of teachers and released further funds from the staffing budget.

These measures released the necessary funds for the building and equipping of the learning and information centre. Planning permission and local residents' problems were overcome and the project went ahead.

The bursar's contribution: discussion

Since the centre's opening in June 1995, a number of issues further refined the thinking of the bursar and the SMT about students' learning and the management of the facility. A big culture change began to occur as teachers became aware that a CD-ROM costing £45 would contain as much information as £500 spent on books. The school began to write its own CD-ROMs, software and study guides for pupils to use as independent learning units.

The introduction of such alternative learning strategies could be seen as a potential threat to teachers' status and jobs, particularly as individual learning, supported self-study and computer assisted learning are introduced. With the recruitment of teachers becoming more difficult, however, the purchase of ILSs and the use of paraprofessionals and support staff skilled in the various software packages can be seen as a cost-effective way of providing an IT learning environment. The bursar's experience in the school showed that two and a half support staff could be employed for the cost of one teacher and they could assist a large number of pupils at the same time in the centre. There is, however, also the consideration of who will oversee and manage these non-traditional ways of providing the learning experience.

Final thoughts

These case studies showed the bursars adopting increasingly proactive stances to innovations in learning environments. In the first case study, the bursar examined a fundamental change in the style of teaching and learning based on the psychology of cognitive development and also brought a range of professional expertise to bear on the issue by mapping out the costs and potential benefits for colleagues in the SMT which should result in a more informed decision.

The second case study also has implications for teaching and learning. Integrated learning systems are the technology of the future and the bursar identified significant changes in the relationships not only between teacher and pupil but also between teaching staff and support staff in areas such as maintaining the learning environment and handling the increasing amount of assessment data. In this case, the role of the bursar moved beyond the presentation of a strategic plan and a whole-school approach was adopted in evaluating a trial project and identifying the key operational implications for the learning environment and the role of support staff of a more technology-rich approach.

The third case study brought together both approaches with the bursar taking a strategic analysis and evaluation role as well as projecting this forward as part of a development plan to improve the school's image and performance in the future. This not only addressed one pressing area in the development strategy but also began to model a way in which bursarial and teaching staff could work together to bring synergy into the school's approach to a very difficult client group – the disaffected school leaver.

The final case study showed the bursar playing both a technical and advisory role in strategic decision making and, as project manager, researching, co-ordinating and delivering a new learning environment. The argument put forward in Chapter 1 that the real value of bursars and support staff resides in the extent to which they can relieve the teaching staff of the burden of administration begins to look overcautious on examination of bursars' relationship with the core business of learning evidenced in these studies. Given that senior teachers in leadership positions in schools find their time taken up with more and more administration and management, it is only to be expected that bursars might get involved in teaching and learning, though this is by no means common as yet. Decisions need to be taken about whether or not this extending 'cross-over' of tasks should continue or if bursars and senior teaching leaders should instead focus solely on their specialist roles. In Part Four we discuss such possibilities as we debate the future of bursarship.

Part Four

■ ■ ■

Future Development: Leading Resource Management for the Learning Community

12
■ ■ ■

The Past and the Future

Introduction

This chapter of Part Four first summarises the position which bursarship had reached at the end of the twentieth century, reflecting on the evidence emerging from Parts One to Three of this book. The growth in the numbers of bursars and the developments in their business manager roles up to 2000 arose first from the increase of the tasks which schools had to undertake and, second, from the need to allow senior teaching professionals to concentrate their activities on directly enhancing the quality of teaching and learning. Both of these continue into the twenty-first century but there are likely also to be developments in the nature of schooling which will influence the direction of school business management. We have, therefore, speculated on these futures and on how bursarship might be reengineered by them, a theme which is also continued in Chapter 14. These speculations need to be viewed in the light of associated changes which are likely to occur in the teaching, support and senior management of schools since the emergence of bursarship cannot happen independently of other variables. This forms the final topic of this chapter.

Bursarship now

Reviewing the evidence from Parts Two and Three of this book, revealed bursars with roles currently spanning the four-stage model we introduced at the end of Chapter 1.

1 All bursars were rooted in the established position of being service providers who indirectly maintain the smooth provision of teaching and learning. This includes, e.g. accounting services, chasing up the delayed

provision of lawn mowing, making sure there is a catering service, and many other tasks which are sometimes dismissed as 'administrivia' yet without which no organisation can function smoothly. We categorised this as the first stage of our model but this is not to denigrate it. It remains an essential part of the bursarship role.

2   Most of the bursars who participated in this research, had added to this first role (or it had been added for them) that of becoming the source of management information for strategic decision making by monitoring, evaluating and reporting on their areas of responsibility. Their supervisory roles evolved as they formed and managed teams to provide an effective and efficient service.

3   Some bursars had moved into their schools' senior management teams. They became accepted as partners in the strategic decision-making process and were recognised as integral to school leadership which, prior to the mid-1980s, was almost entirely the concern of education professionals.

4   Finally, there were possibilities for some bursars to contemplate a move to a post of chief executive, or headship, or to a shared senior executive role.

Bursarship future – the school context

The position of an individual bursar in these models was, and is, much influenced by the extent to which their schools were, and are, externally controlled. We conceptualised the control of schools as being at points on a continuum between almost total dependency (for example, in US School Boards or English Education Action Zones), and virtually total autonomy (for example, schools in the independent sector or England's city technology colleges, or GM schools, 1991–9). The intermediary stage is that of local, or regional management (such as the regions of the Australian states or the community and foundation schools, from 1999, in England which were all managed by local education authorities).

Diagrammatically, we represent this continuum on a sliding scale (Figure 12.1). Within each category, a school's placement on the continuum is likely to

Figure 12.1 Conceptualisation of school levels of autonomy

be influenced by its success in achieving government-set norms, including the raising of student achievement. Hence a locally managed school deemed to be effective by government inspectors might find itself with virtually all the powers of a site-based school. A site-based school deemed to be failing, could be operating in the style almost of a locally managed school with temporary principals and governors drafted in to save the school from its problems. The bursar's role could similarly fluctuate according to the position of the school on the continuum and the extent to which a school's failure might be attributable to its business management.

The end of the twentieth century saw most schools in England and Wales in the locally managed category but with significant elements of site-based control and strong intimations that this would continue to be the direction of the movement in the structure of the school system. Given that development, the significance of bursarship was assured. There were, however, some slight contra-indications in the first questioning of the value of site-based management to effective teaching and learning that had not been satisfactorily proved by the end of the twentieth century. Were site-based management to prove a failure in improving the outcomes of schooling, then bursarship might be seen as no longer required. None the less, the political value to central government of dismantling the effective power of the local education authorities at the end of the twentieth century was sufficiently strong to ensure the continued movement to site-based schools with a need, therefore, for a business manager to take the role previously provided by LEAs.

Within this system of control of schools, the role and powers of a bursar are likely to be affected by impending educational and societal developments. The future environment for schools is likely to be complex, turbulent and characterised by accelerated change building on the developments between 1986 and 2000. Socially, future schools would subscribe to a community ethos. They would aim to enhance their understanding of the cultural needs of stakeholders and their awareness of the interdependence of the different groups with whom they are involved as well as promoting their well-being. The entrepreneurial focus of schools would result in increased responsiveness to pupils and parents and the building of links with businesses and the community as well as greater emphasis on the effective use of resources including the most appropriate use of technology. In order to respond to the complexity of the environment, all school staff would be involved in a continuous learning process, leadership would be distributed and information gathered, analysed and disseminated from global to school level. These features are summarised in Figure 12.2.

From these generalised expectations, we developed an imaginary school of the future in which an education resource manager (ERM – the title which we have selected as most likely for the successor to the bursar of the twentieth century) could be operating. We have presented this below in a similar format to that used for the case studies in Part Three.

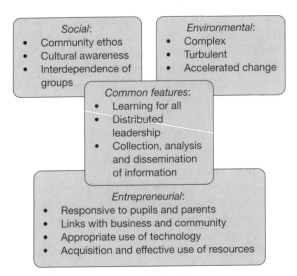

Figure 12.2 Characteristics of the school of the future

School 2020 and its context

Ages 0–100+. It serves a learning community of 5000 people. Pre-school provision from birth. Lifelong learning access for those of post-compulsory school age with redeemable vouchers to claim schooling as and when required. Basic, vocational, academic and leisure education are provided linked to higher education providers through a national education grid. Individualised learning programmes are designed for each learner. All students have their own ICT technology bases in their own homes, linked to the school. Social learning opportunities are provided to encourage learning competition and learning from one another in basic curriculum subjects and where group work is vital as in sports and the performing arts. The school buildings consist of what were a twentieth-century secondary school, two feeder primary schools and an adult education centre. The adult education centre is now the technology control centre. The primary learning areas house pre-birth to Key Stage 2 provision with classrooms for basic curriculum work. The old secondary school on the site has been upgraded for lifelong learning. There are purpose-built sports and performing arts facilities established in 2000 with the aid of a National Lottery grant. These are jointly managed with community groups. The small administrative centre links to the homeworkers who provide clerical and record-keeping functions. The grounds are extensive and include the amphitheatre which can be roofed in bad weather. What remains of the original secondary school is a series of rooms whose sizes can be readily changed to meet the varied needs of the school's learning community preparing to acquire academic qualifications.

Each of our Part Three case studies involved a problem on which the bursar's advice and action was necessary. Here the problem is that the management structure of School 2020 had grown from a pre-2000 secondary school and had been adjusted *ad hoc* as the numbers of learners increased and the demands for lifelong education grew. The senior team, which includes an ERM, decided to review the leadership patterns for the school and to plan new strategies. The ERM was asked to reflect particularly on the business management of the school and its support. The 2020 working pattern of the daily activities of the ERM can be seen in the predictions of Chapter 4 (Figure 4.5).

Bursarship future: restructuring proposals

Following are the proposals suggested by the ERM to the senior team of our imaginary school. Each proposal involved all school staff, not only the ERM or the support staff. Each of them represented evolution from trends in the late twentieth century though some would require more of a leap to achieve them than would others. It was possible that some might operate concurrently.

The company executive

The first two proposals (Figure 12.3 and 12.4) were designed as a small step structurally from the *ad hoc* situation that had already arisen at School 2020. The two possible restructurings proposed would place the resource and business management functions of the school on an equal level with the teaching management function with the possibility of the business management function even gaining primacy. In both of the two scenarios a career route for bursarship to leading executive has become overt.

In the proposal in Figure 12.3, a post of chief executive would be created. This was to signify the significance of general management to the school with the central role being that of the strategic planner. The chief executive would also

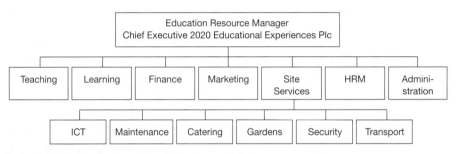

Note: Only the Site Services Branch has been detailed as an exemplar

Figure 12.3 School management in 2020, the ERM as Chief Executive

be responsible for oversight of monitoring and evaluating outcomes in order to ensure responsiveness to clients (government, pupils and parents). Each area of the school's activities would have its own section head. Teaching and learning would be considered equal to the other aspects of management thus creating several senior posts likely to require bursarial backgrounds.

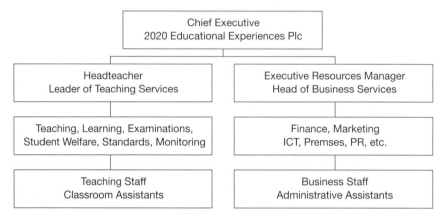

Figure 12.4 School management in 2020, the ERM as Head of Business Services

In the second proposal (Figure 12.4), running the school as a business would be given equivalent status to running the school as an educational organisation. Hence there would be a headteacher and a head of business services, each responsible for their own areas. Both of these would be responsible to a chief executive who might come from a teaching or from a business background.

The ERM reported that both these ideas had originated in the concept of the professional-as-administrator. This was first considered in an education management context by Meredydd Hughes in 1973 and he related the idea to the future of the school principal. He saw the role of principal as encompassing the role of the business manager, or administrator. The ERM of School 2020, however, considered that the concept of the professional-as-administrator was now more applicable to the ERM role. Noteworthy was the realisation that, not only had the concept moved from the principal to the ERM but also that it had reversed, becoming the administrator-as-professional. The administrator of the late twentieth century was becoming the professional educational manager of the early twenty-first century. The administrator was seen to be able to embrace the responsibilities, roles and values of the professional educator principal.

The 1973 concept of the 'professional-as-administrator' was proposed by Hughes as a way to resolve 'accommodation between the organisation's emphasis on superordinate control and the professionals' desire for colleague control' (Hughes, 1973: 174). Both of these were issues identified by the ERM of School 2020 as challenging in the development of strategies for leadership development. In the 1973 Hughes's model, the head was the professional-as-administrator who aimed to align the needs of teaching colleagues for professional autonomy with the needs of an organisation for control. In our 2020 model, the business manager could be seen as the 'administrator-as-professional'. This person would be able to align the needs of different groups of colleagues from both teaching and support services. Each group is committed to its professional autonomy but in the interests of the organisation and its students, these need to be combined. The ERM as chief executive was best placed to engineer this combination.

Multi-skilled operatives

In this model the ERM proposed that all staff (or more staff) would become significantly interchangeable thus reflecting the development of more flexible organisations and of the totality of a learning and teaching community. The outcome of multi-skilling would be no differentiation among types of staff. Each staff member would be regarded as available for teaching, administration, cleaning, leadership or catering, etc. so that staff could be moved to meet shortages in growth areas as needed.

In the late twentieth century, the ERM reminded the senior team, there had been moves to retain and emphasise the differences between teaching and support services but, despite this, teachers had continued to provide a substantial amount of non-teaching services such as secretarial and classroom assistance tasks. Meanwhile, support staff had given some help with direct teaching as, for example, teachers of business studies, providing classroom guides for differentially abled students or instructing in the use of ICT equipment. The division between teaching and support staff had become increasingly difficult to justify as differentials in qualification levels between 'support' and 'teaching' staff had considerably decreased. From 2005 onwards, it was estimated that 75 per cent of all 18 year-olds were progressing to higher education, hence the possession of a first degree had become an accepted part of almost everyone's general entitlement to education. Thus a newly qualified administrator would have the same basic accreditation as teaching staff taking up employment at the school.

Multi-skilling would also enable staff to develop an holistic view of education, This would potentially be the end of a specific resource manager *per se* just as there would be the end of specific teaching and support roles. Some hierarchy would be retained but roles in the senior team could be distributed on a rotation basis and/or as workloads rose or fell with the rapid developments which all expect in the educational service. All staff taking up employment at School 2020 would need training in teaching skills, management and leadership skills, business services and the technicalities of, for example, catering, maintaining computers, clearing up litter, examination invigilation, counselling or writing reports. Organisational knowledge would be retained, transmitted and accessible to any staff from computers; individuals would not be needed as experts.

Teamworking

The ERM offered two notions of team restructuring for School 2020 staff.

Functional teams

Figure 12.5 Support staff as separate functional teams

The first team model built on to late twentieth-century developments when the support staff themselves were first internally 'teamed', each team having clear responsibility for achievements in specific areas (Figure 12.5). The underpinnings were a belief in the value of the team being united in its pursuit of tight targets. In the early years of the twenty-first century, these had emerged as, for example, benchmarking and performance-related pay for such achievements as 90 per cent litter-free days per semester, no exclusions of differentially abled students and ten minute turnaround responses to teachers' requests for photocopying. In this structure, the ERM emerged as leader of an administration team which gradually acquired, somewhat *ad hoc*, all responsibilities for human resource management, for public relations and, of course, finance. The advantage was the elevation of the administrative service as the lead body for all support staff.

The format of teaming proposed for School 2020 by the ERM would mean that groupings of support staff would be clearly demarcated. This would range from the cosmetic to the more dramatic.

School dinner providers and supervisors, for example, would be obviously categorised in relation to what they do. The school dinner service provision is often separate and may be out-sourced. Whether or not this is the case, renaming it as Catering Services with its own targets and management might not make much difference to what has always happened. The ERM of School 2020 expected, however, that tight teaming and goal setting would encourage greater entrepreneurship, a wider range of services and better identification of team members with outcomes. The School 2020 Catering Service, for example, might come to unite dinners, breakfasts, catering for special events, tuck shops, supervision of students' nutrition, responsibility for those students with eating disorders, franchising of food outlets to national chains and the establishment of a shopping mall. Similar semi-autonomous teams would develop and maintain the buildings and grounds, or provide a wide range of reprographic, publishing and ICT services. Classroom assistants, SENs, laboratory technicians and language assistants would be the specialist curriculum support team.

The remit of the ERM would thus gain an elevated role over considerably extended services requiring extensive specialised knowledge regarded as equal to that required to teach students. The teaching service of the school would benefit from an enhanced range of services, more professionally provided.

Integrated teams

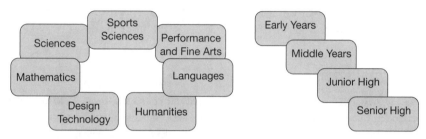

Figure 12.6 Support staff in integrated curriculum or age cohort teams

In the second 'team' model (Figure 12.6), all staff would be allocated to particular curriculum areas, or to particular year groups or sets of students. The team responsibility would be for the 'whole student' from entry to leaving school. The team would feel attached to its own students and would thus be more committed to ensuring their success. Each team would have its own teachers, business manager, parent co-ordinator, caterer, cleaner, ICT technicians, counsellor, examination administrator etc., or could operate with the multi-skilling detailed above.

This teaming is built on industrial production models of the late twentieth century which found that teams with full responsibility for a product both increased the numbers of units produced but also improved the quality of the outputs. It also resurrected older, nineteenth- and twentieth-century schooling notions of having an educational organisation divided into 'houses' which would encourage loyalty largely engendered by making the 'houses' compete for school trophies. Such 'houses' used to include only pupils and teaching staff but the new model included the support staff and made the 'houses' virtually self-contained.

The ERM role would be to allocate members and budgets to teams and to audit, monitor and evaluate each team's outputs. The ERM would be the strategist who set specifications for services (including academic targets) and the operationalist who dealt with contracting for both internal and external teams.

Bursarship future: revolution or evolution?

The 2020 school we envisaged above was based on expectation of change, though the models of bursarship suggested for the school of the future ranged from those which would require incremental change to those which would need more fundamental developments for both schools and for their business managers. Any of the ideas suggested would, of course, need to be adapted to the circumstances of particular schools, but here we need to assess what might be the general factors in the educational system and its schools which might predispose schools to adopt one model rather than another. This section therefore discusses educational futures, educational continuities, attitudes of teaching and of support staff and changes in school hierarchies.

Educational futures

In its seventy-fifth anniversary edition, the *Harvard Business Review* invited five recognised 'thinkers and observers' in the business world to present their vision of the organisation of the future (Drucker *et al.*, 1997). Drucker suggested that it was possible 'to identify and prepare for the future ... [by acknowledging] major events that have already happened, irrevocably, and that will have predictable effects in the next decade or two' (Drucker *et al.*, 1997: 20). These included:

- turbulence and accelerated change in organisations and the economy (Drucker *et al.*, 1997; Senge, 1997);
- a rapid shift in information requirements, concentrating more on gathering and analysing information from outside the institution (Drucker *et al.*, 1997);
- greater response to feedback from customers within and outside the organisation and proactivity in gathering data which will inform decisions related to customers' needs (Dyson, 1997);
- the rise of the community organisation which enriches the life of its workers (Handy, 1997);
- institutional learning arising from research, the development of the individual's capabilities and the development of practices and interrelationships within the organisation (Senge, 1997);
- the rise of the knowledge worker (Drucker *et al.*, 1997);
- distribution of leadership (Senge, 1997);
- a greater recognition of the benefits and particularly the limits of technology (Saffo, 1997).

Many of these expectations could affect the future role for bursarship as Figure 12.7 indicates.

Organisational details	Managerial skills/qualities
Complex, turbulent, uncertain	Problem solving
Accelerated change	Flexible
Information gathering	Analysis and dissemination
Community	Moral awareness
Learning	Learning
Distributed leadership	Self-co-ordination
Responsive to the customer	Delegation
Responsible use of technology	Time management

Figure 12.7 The attributes of the manager working in the future organisation

Developments in information technology, the widespread resourcing of schools with computer hardware, rapid strides in teaching and administrative software and the diaspora of the Internet were all much vaunted as likely to lead to dramatic changes in schooling in the twenty-first century such as that envisaged in our School 2020 model above. In this some learning becomes home based and it is only the social subjects which bring students to the relatively few remaining school buildings. The rest is a 'virtual' school. If this happens, one can imagine a more powerful role for bursars or their successors, our mythical ERMs. The 'virtual' organisation can be much larger than the predecessor physical school and thus could need more effective administration, management and leadership in which an ERM would be of great importance. In any organisation, power arises from knowledge and bursars/ERMs are likely to be one of the most knowledgeable about the information technology which controls the system.

Dramatic changes for schooling were also anticipated by the post-modernist theorists of the late twentieth century from the 'deschooling' movement of the 1960s (e.g. Illich, 1970; Husen, 1979), the subjectivisim of Greenfield in 1974 (Greenfield and Ribbins, 1993) to the chaos theorists (e.g. Gleick, 1988). In these envisaged worlds of discontinuities, one might see a bursar/ERM surviving as the calm place, necessary to the administration in the midst of a storm. Equally, one might decide that administration, management and leadership are all impossible and unsuited to a time in which the post-modernist individual is self-determining.

Thus the educational scene appears set for major changes. One must ask, however, how likely these are in view of factors which could predispose the system to slower, more incremental changes. These factors are discussed in the next section.

Educational continuities

In assessing the future shape of bursarship, we must take into account the continuities of education. Teachers are essentially a conservative profession; schools are charged by society with passing on their culture to new generations; students need to be socialised into citizenship; parents and politicians have expectations of education formed from their own time at school. Hence, for example, the end of the twentieth century saw the reintroduction of various features of nineteenth- and early twentieth-century education – school governors' powers (1986), a national curriculum (1988), whole-class teaching and literacy and numeracy hours (1997) and education for citizenship (1999) (Thody, 2000).

All these forces support, not some 'space-age technological whizz kid' but, traditions of leadership from past generations. The traditional pattern of leadership is that of a single headteacher who has emerged from a teaching background and has gained experience in levels of school management concerned mainly with teaching and learning issues directly. In the late twentieth and early twenty-first century, as in the latter part of the nineteenth century, these traditional expectations are reinforced by the pressures on schools to be accountable to their students, parents, communities and to politicians, for their expenditure of public monies. One particular demand from these groups is that standards of achievement must be raised. This is deemed necessary because we are no longer achieving the standards of the past nor meeting the standards of our international competitors. Hence, for example, GCSE is not seen as being as demanding as were O-levels. How often do we hear politicians claiming that everyone learnt to read and write effectively when they were at school whereas today we need a National Literacy Hour to achieve this again? It does not matter that evidence can be advanced to disprove these claims, there is a perception that the past was better. Note also its reincarnation in Ofsted reports on school leadership. 'Strong' leadership is praised, just as it was in nineteenth-century inspectors' reports.

In making changes for the future shape of school leadership, we must, therefore, be aware that change is likely to be evolutionary rather than revolutionary, incremental rather than total. There must be continuity in line with what society anticipates. This 'continuity in change' model appears to stress the centrality of the individual head but in achieving the model successfully, we would suggest that one of the keys is the leader's support systems, and these include bursars with an enhanced role and position with the possibility of bursars themselves becoming headteachers. In addition, the solo, 'hero-innovator' headteacher model emerged from nineteenth-century independent schools and in these schools, 'bursars' have long held a wider role remit than in the state sector; their example may, therefore, be carried over into the state sector.

Teacher attitudes

The beginning of the changes of bursars' roles to that of the education resource manager has been wrought by the senior educational professionals in the school. The bursar role was introduced to relieve headteachers of work and this has been achieved but it has brought into being the bursar as a new contender for power in senior school management. Headteachers, being at the pinnacle of their profession, would have little reason to be concerned about competition for power from a newcomer into senior management.

For teaching staff, however, the issue may be less clear-cut. The bursar's value to their daily activities may be less obvious than to the tasks of the headteacher. The presence of a new member in the senior management team may appear to reduce promotion opportunities to deputy head posts. The acceptance, in the senior management team, of a bursar as business manager who does not have the same type, nor extent, of qualifications as themselves may lead to questioning of their managerial competences. The status of the business manager in the senior team is a recognition of the importance of support services to the success of teaching and learning. This may appear as a threat in a period of ICT developments which can replace 'face-to-face' teaching.

Were teachers to be questioned about these fears, it is unlikely that they would be overtly expressed, or even acknowledged, but in the management of change they need to be understood. Teachers will need to cope with major changes in the way they 'teach' in the first years of the twenty-first century and in making such changes, will need to pass through feelings almost of bereavement as they leave behind much that was well known to them. In these circumstances, the business manager, leading a support staff taking over some of the roles previously done by teachers, may appear less as a welcome helper and more of a threat to the profession of teaching. On the face of it, a business manager who organised a more efficient reprographics service would be, apparently, ideal but there are teaching staff for whom standing by the photocopier dashing off last minute visual aids serves as a relaxation from more stressful, high-level tasks of teaching. In moving to a higher level of business management, the value to all teaching staff has to be strongly demonstrated. The appreciation of the business manager and support staff to the centrality of teaching achievements will come gradually and only if it can be managed without appearing to threaten the position of teachers.

Support staff attitudes

Bursars are usually categorised as part of the support staff, a designation which was just beginning to be questioned at the end of the twentieth century. It was unlikely, however, that teaching and support staff categories would be merged into one 'staff' very quickly but there were indications that support staff had gained consciousness of their importance to educational outcomes.

Reciprocal recognition by teachers began to develop first through reliance on the technocracy of paraprofessionals in science, ICT and school financial management. Policies of inclusion (of students previously considered ineducable in mainstream schools) raised the numbers of support staff as many of these students needed personal supervisors. Classroom assistants, previously somewhat denigrated as a 'Mums' army' gained their own specialist qualifications. Catering and cleansing services were contracted out to businesses. Corporate, executive uniforms, lunch supervisors and estates management staff displaced the older, less businesslike stereotype of the 'dinner lady' or the 'caretaker'. The resultant feelings of integration and significance of support staff would undoubtedly affect the bursar who had become *de facto* or *de jure* leader of the support staff.

Flatter hierarchies

Structural models being suggested for future school management stress the general principles of having a flatter hierarchy, flexibility in job descriptions with staff moving across previously rigid boundaries and various versions of team organisation, all of which would accord with some of the developments in the roles of bursars. In 2000, however, these are still largely in opposition to the hierarchical gradings of both teaching and support staff salaries and responsibilities found in most schools. If changes in hierarchies are the future for management, then their introduction needs care. Such changes can seem to mean only loss of career prospects in the short term. For support staff, their career routes are already short, uncertain and with fewer opportunities for senior posts than those with teaching qualifications. If hierarchies are flattened, therefore, the already slim chances of promotion for support staff appear to be further reduced.

Conclusions

This chapter has considered the forces for change within and around schools which may affect the development of the bursarship role, first in a general acceptance of the notion of a bursar and then movement beyond it as the role is interpreted. The bursars themselves are, however, part of the change mechanism.

Their personal driving force for change must be the 'professionalisation' of bursarship through its education and training provision, and the acknowledgement of its status through members' associations and their national establishment. These issues are discussed in the following chapter.

13
■　■　■

The Professionalisation of Bursarship

Introduction

We raised the issue of the professionalisation of the role of the school bursar in Chapter 1. We briefly outlined the increase in the numbers of bursars who have been appointed to state schools as a result of the 1986 and 1988 Education Acts and contrasted this with the much longer tradition of bursarship in the independent sector. We identified the main routes into the post and indicated that bursars have commonly taken up the role as a second or third career. This chapter outlines our thinking and provides evidence that maps out bursarship as a profession at the beginning of the twenty-first century, and describes the advent of a growing coherence in induction, on-the-job training, skills enhancement courses and professional development at postgraduate and masters level.

The first issue which this chapter explores is that of professionalisation itself. There is little doubt that senior educational leadership can make a valid claim to being a profession (especially with the introduction of the National Professional Qualification for Headship and the accompanying National Standards). Eraut (1994: 223) considered that the key characteristics of a profession are that it creates and maintains a specialist knowledge base, remains autonomous and largely self-directing, controlling entry and qualification, and has a strong tradition and sense of public (or client) service. Often these features are embodied in a code of conduct for members of the profession. Bursars, therefore, joined the senior leadership of schools just at the time when the Teacher Training Agency had formally codified the roles and responsibilities of senior and middle managers. An appraisal system specifically linked to pupil performance targets had also been introduced as had a General Teaching Council. The possibility of establishing a staff college for school headteachers was being discussed.

By the end of the twentieth century, in contrast to middle and senior leaders generally, the bursarship role had been more clearly defined at school level. In staking out their claim for a distinctive place in school leadership and management, however, it was in bursars' interests as a profession to come to a swift consensus as to the constituent parts of the role. In so doing, bursars had the undoubted advantage of being able to draw on the work of bodies such as:

- the Teacher Training Agency (TTA);
- the Management Charter Initiative (MCI);
- the National Council for Vocational Qualifications (NCVQ);
- Royal Society of Arts (RSA).

All of these bodies had drawn up competence standards for middle and senior administrative and management posts. At the same time, after some ten years of state school bursarship, various local and national groupings of bursars, and LEA administrative staff had accumulated considerable expertise in identifying and designing training courses for the key skills, knowledge and attributes required for successful school bursarship.

Bursarship was thus at a crucial 'cusp point' in the development of site-based school administration in 2000. Was there a sufficient understanding and will in the senior leadership of schools to recognise the proper contribution that bursars can make to school achievement alongside headteachers, inspectors/advisers, educational psychologists and education officers? For the future development of bursarship, therefore, there is a need to achieve a necessary level of consensus as to:

- the body of specialised knowledge;
- the routes into the post;
- the hierarchy of qualifications;
- the sense of service.

This chapter will explore these issues as a prelude to our concluding chapter, which looks into the future for site-level educational administration.

Bursarship as a profession

There are as many definitions of what constitutes a profession, as there are writers on the subject. Indeed it is difficult to envisage a common definition which would encompass the traditional occupations such as doctor, vicar, army officer, civil servant as well as the 'wackier' end of post-modern specialisms for example, media image consultant, outplacement adviser or business process reengineering analyst. Given this huge range, Glover and Hughes (1998: 3–5) devised a framework which could be adapted for the emerging profession of bursarship. This consists of a description of the main characteristics of a profession, the nature of the expertise with which professionals 'profess' and the sense of responsibility and public duty that they have.

Characteristically, professions are self-governing, exercising discipline over their members and controlling the entry of candidates into their ranks, often through some test of expertise and experience in both the distinctive body of knowledge and the necessary practical skills. They are also typically organised into a professional association, which is accepted by the members as competent to recognise them, represent them, and is considered valuable to them personally in their career development. In turn employers and relevant others recognise membership of the body as evidence of competency, often through provision of accredited courses leading into the profession and suitable arrangements for structured practical in-service experience and post-qualification education, development and training.

This issue of competency and its effect on professionalisation became particularly relevant given the direction of management development in the 1990s. In the USA and UK, this followed divergent paths. The US experience involved specific management training. It dates back to the 1920s and the scientific management school founded by Frederick Taylor, the principles of which resulted from reducing shopfloor work functions to time and motion equations thus removing the human factors which could result, literally, in 'spanners in the works'. Business schools and postgraduate schools of management science taught these principles to managers so there has been a long tradition of a trained and regularly updated force of managers in the USA and a symbiotic relationship between captains of industry and the world of commerce and business.

In the 1970s, sociology and psychology became more influential in the attempt to diagnose those elements of competency which distinguished the 'best from the rest' – i.e. the attributes of superior managerial performers. This accompanied the 'excellence' movement characterised by Peters and Waterman's (1982) classic text. Much work has been done by such as the American Management Association and Hay McBer (Esp, 1993: 23) to identify the generic competencies that underlie such superior performance.

In the UK, by contrast, there was not the same tradition of training for managers, either in the business/commercial world or in education, the emphasis being on learning through experience on the job. The focus was, therefore, on specific vocational skills validated by bodies such as the National Council for Vocational Qualifications and often demonstrated through the submission of a portfolio of experience. The MCI developed a three-level scheme for first line supervisors, middle managers and senior managers, which focused on the demonstration of 'can-do' functional skills and competencies. Similarly, the RSA middle and senior management standards, validated at NVQ Levels 4 (first degree equivalent) and 5 (postgraduate), required the provision of evidence of managerial performance in a detailed range of vocational tasks.

It was not surprising, therefore, that the emphasis in bursars' courses tended to be on the operational and functional aspects of the role. As part of their National Standards for School Bursars the NBA brought together the wide range of operational areas in six key areas of bursarship (Figure 13.1). These standards developed alongside the TTA's framework for initial teacher training and continuing professional development to bring coherence to INSET and progression to training and development opportunities. The first stage was

---

The National Standards for bursars are in five parts:

1 **CORE PURPOSE OF SCHOOL BURSARSHIP:** *to provide professional leadership and management of support services enhancing effectiveness, success and improved efficiency, thereby ensuring a higher standard of learning in schools resulting in improved standards of achievement.*

2 **KEY OUTCOMES OF SCHOOL BURSARSHIP:** *effective bursarship results in high quality support to teaching staff valued as partners in the joint enterprise of education and where the team spirit permeates all school employees regardless of job or qualification.*

3 **PROFESSIONAL KNOWLEDGE AND UNDERSTANDING:** *e.g. effective budget procedures, premises management, health and safety, personnel, marketing, contracts/external agencies, and support staff appraisal.*

4 **SKILLS AND ATTRIBUTES:** *leadership, decision making, communication, self-management.*

5 **KEY AREAS OF BURSARSHIP:**

   a **Administrative management:** promoting the effective functioning of the school in its interaction and communication with persons and agencies within and outside the school community.

   b **Financial resource management:** applying the best practices and highest standards of financial management to optimise value for money and to maximise efficiency.

   c **Human resource management:** managing the school's personnel function effectively and sensitively to best effect.

   d **Facility and property management:** developing and maintaining the physical assets of the school to maximise their effectiveness as an environment conducive to learning.

   e **Information management:** ensuring that high quality information is effectively managed to ensure its deployment in support of decisions made by governors and senior management.

   f **Support services management:** managing all services within the school that support learning, such that the headteacher and teaching staff can concentrate on and facilitate the pupil learning process in a safe, secure and well supported environment.

Figure 13.1 National Standards for school bursars

Source: Adapted from NBA (1998).

the implementation of a range of competencies for students undertaking initial teacher training. This was followed by the drawing up of a list of tasks and abilities required at the headteacher level. These headteacher competencies were accessible through the Headteachers' Leadership and Management Programme (HEADLAMP) from 1995 for newly appointed headteachers and the NPQH for aspiring headteachers from 1997 (Figure 13.2).

To some extent the Key Areas identified in the National Standards for headteachers and bursars in Figures 13.1 and 13.2 reflected the managerial emphasis on operational functions in the UK. The first four parts of each set of National Standards, however, located these key areas within a wider professional responsibility as a whole. Indeed, the framework put forward by Glover

---

The National Standards for headship are in five parts:

1 **CORE PURPOSE OF HEADSHIP:** *to provide professional leadership for a school which secures its success and improvement, ensuring high quality education for all its pupils and improved standards of achievement.*

2 **KEY OUTCOMES OF HEADSHIP:** *effective headship focuses on high standards of school ethos, teaching, pupil progress, parents' partnership, governors responsibilities, efficient/effective use of resources.*

3 **PROFESSIONAL KNOWLEDGE AND UNDERSTANDING:** *in areas such as quality, data handling including ICT, curriculum, assessment and teaching, leadership and management, political/legal framework, governance.*

4 **SKILLS AND ATTRIBUTES:** *leadership, decision making, communication, self management.*

5 **KEY AREAS OF HEADSHIP:**

   a **Strategic direction and development of the school:** headteachers, working with the governing body, develop a strategic view for the school in its community and analyse and plan for its future needs and further development within the local, national and international context.

   b **Teaching and learning:** headteachers, working with the governing body, secure and sustain effective teaching and learning throughout the school, monitor and evaluate the quality of teaching and standards of pupils' achievement, and use benchmarks and set targets for improvement.

   c **Leading and managing staff:** headteachers lead, motivate, support, challenge and develop staff to secure improvement.

   d **Efficient and effective deployment of staff:** headteachers deploy people and resources efficiently and effectively to meet specific objectives in line with the school's strategic plan and financial context.

   e **Accountability:** headteachers account for the efficiency and effectiveness of the school to the governors and others, including pupils, parents, staff, local employers and the local community.

Figure 13.2 National Standards for headteachers

Source: Adapted from Teacher Training Agency (1998).

and Hughes (1998) emphasised that professionals, in carrying out their responsibilities, have a duty to 'profess' through the provision of expert advice, information, ideas, specialist services, help and support. In doing this they would develop and maintain a sense of responsibility to their clients, the community and society. It is these last issues, those of professional expertise and responsibility to both a range of communities and recourse to a 'higher authority' (religious or secular) which points to an area of considerable potential for tension, particularly for the role of the bursar. Headteachers and deputies have developed a strong line of support through their professional organisations (the Secondary Heads Association and the National Association of Headteachers) both of which act as guardians of the professional integrity of headteachers and deputies as well as a trade union. Although the many publications of these two associations do give a great deal of advice on probity and ethical dilemmas, the ethical dimension is not made specific in the National Standards for headteachers.

The importance of this ethical dimension (the recourse to a higher authority referred to by Glover and Hughes and addressed in detail by Bergenhene-gouwen, 1996) for the claim to be a professional is crucial. Bursars are often put in a difficult position as guardians of public resources and can have split loyalties to their headteacher, the governing body and their own sense of professionalism. This split loyalty has led, in some cases, to the suspension of the headteacher or the bursar where impropriety or incompetence is suspected. It is often preceded by a period of time when bursars may have privileged knowledge (for example, regarding the inappropriate use of public funds for personal or non-educational purposes) which puts them in a very invidious position. In the case of the National Standards for bursars, guidance on avoiding or dealing with such ethical dilemmas is given in the Code of Conduct (see Appendix II, Section 6). This is not sufficient on its own to ensure that professional standards are upheld – it needs the 'higher authority' to provide a framework of discipline and sanctions which is accepted by the members of the profession themselves.

There are two main bodies in the profession of bursarship which fulfil this purpose: the National Bursars Association for the state sector and the Independent Schools' Bursars Association for the private sector. Although with both the NBA and the ISBA the school is the member and the bursar is the delegate, there is a crucial difference between the two organisations as bursars can become individual members of the NBA, whereas at the time of writing they could not be individual members of the ISBA. Therefore bursars do not have access to independent professional advice in the ISBA, nor do they have a professional code of conduct. Both organisations, however, offer a wide service for their members and are increasingly using the educational press and Internet to promote their activities. The NBA's website can be accessed at <http://www.nba.org.uk>. It gives information on joining the NBA, its regional structure, opportunities for training and development, a list of approved suppliers of equipment and services, a facility for advertising job vacancies and a range of pages for members including a bulletin board for exploring contentious or difficult issues and a help-line service. Additionally the NBA issues a termly professional journal that incorporates into a loose-leaf developmental handbook and has negotiated legal protection insurance and a career development loan service for bursars. The ISBA issues a review magazine three times a year, quarterly bulletins for guidance on current issues, advice documents on specific management issues and a bursars' guide book. It also runs an annual induction course for new bursars, courses on current issues and a high-profile annual conference. Other services offered by the ISBA include legal protection insurance for bursars, membership of purchasing consortia and the use of its network of skilled practitioners to provide information and advice to those who contact the central office with queries and problems.

Professional competence

Following the approach to leadership which determines the 'best from the rest', there were a number of more generic frameworks for school managerial competencies developed in the late twentieth century. Lyons and Jirasinge (1996) developed and validated a framework which had its roots in the work done by Saville and Holdsworth in the occupational psychology field. In a study commissioned by the TTA, the Hay McBer organisation identified 15 key characteristics of effective headteachers identified in Figure 13.3.

Personal values and passionate conviction
- Respect for others
- Challenge and support
- Personal conviction

Creating the vision
- Strategic thinking
- Drive for improvement

Planning, delivering, monitoring, evaluating and improving
- Analytical thinking
- Initiative
- Transformational leadership
- Teamworking
- Understanding others
- Developing potential

Building commitment and support
- Impact and influence
- Holding people accountable

Gathering information and gaining understanding
- Social awareness
- Scanning the environment

Figure 13.3 Fifteen key characteristics of effective headteachers

Source: HoC (1998: para. 18).

Although the list of competencies in Figure 13.3 contained an element of for-ward looking to the twenty-first century, they were essentially drawn from the best of current experience. In contrast, Figure 13.4 shows the areas of compe-tency agreed by experienced bursars in a series of focus groups and interviews asking them to identify skills, qualities and knowledge which they felt would be necessary for school business managers in the next century.

The development of personal skills was felt to enable bursars to interact with confidence in a turbulent environment and learning skills would provide them with the capacity to understand the complexities of the world around them. Organisational skills were deemed to increase bursars' awareness of political and social allegiances within the school and their understanding of educa-tional and resource allocation issues would optimise the learning environment. As bursars have been conscious of the tensions between teach-ing and support staff, the development of social skills would be particularly important. Increased communication skills and leadership qualities would especially benefit bursars if they wanted to promote the contribution of sup-port staff to the school.

Area of competency	Skills, qualities and knowledge
Personal	• Problem solving • Flexibility • Self-management • Self-esteem • Decision making • Confidence • Enthusiasm • Motivation
Learning	• Independent thinking • Data gathering • Critical analysis and dissemination • Development of transformational mindsets • Reflection • Lifelong learning • Experiential learning • Clarity of thinking
Organisational	• Social awareness • Political awareness • Corporate ethics • Understanding of educational issues • Resource allocation
Social	• Co-operation • Communication • Leadership • Delegation

Figure 13.4 Areas of competency for bursarship in the twenty-first century

To enhance the development of bursarship as a profession, education and training are needed for these competencies and for areas of functional and technical expertise. These include an understanding of business and management topics and subjects such as accountancy and the use of information technology. Bursars also need to develop an awareness of educational and learning issues in order to contribute effectively to the resource management and development of the school. We now need to consider the current and future arrangements for their training and development.

Education and training

The means by which bursars will become viewed and valued as education professionals include development and training leading to recognised qualifications and/or professional registration. Bursars themselves quickly recognised this and training for bursars developed as a response to requests from bursars as individuals rather than from the schools in which they worked. In general, this fragmentary training was either specifically functional/technical in areas such as administration, finance, marketing and health and safety, or more management orientated and included strategic and development planning, auditing and evaluation, total quality, change and project management.

In the 1990s, training providers included the school itself, LEAs, colleges and universities. Most bursars attended short courses provided by LEAs and/or received training within their schools. This training was mainly functional in character and usually included familiarisation with software packages, ICT skills, personnel, finance and clerking governors meetings. Some schools inducted bursars into the ethos of the school by familiarising them with missions and visions. In general, bursars financed further development and training themselves when they attended courses run by colleges of further education and universities. These courses included the vocational, such as HNCs, NVQs and professional qualifications or provided the mainstream qualifications of first degrees, postgraduate certificates and diplomas or masters degrees including MBAs. The University of Lincolnshire and Humberside was the first university to offer an MBA specifically for bursars in 1996 and the NBA awarded its first licentiates (Licentiate of the National Bursars Association – LNBA) in 1999 to bursars who could prove considerable expertise in two areas and competency in a further two areas of the National Standards for bursarship.

The range of training and development provision available throughout the 1990s is illustrated in Figure 13.5 in the first column, where its fragmentary nature becomes apparent. A whole-school alternative for the twenty-first century is proposed in the second column, which would provide a coherent development programme for both teaching and support staff including the bursar.

In-service training (1990s)	Professional development (2000)
Fragmented *'ad hoc*-racy': rarely co-ordinated within a strategy, funded from many sources, TECs, LEAs, school budgets etc.	**Professional development plan:** all schools and colleges will have a balanced and co-ordinated strategy for staff development linked to the Development Plan and outcomes from appraisal.
Top down needs identification: by governors, headteachers, SMT and central government.	**Systematic bottom-up process for needs identification:** which will enable individual staff to articulate their needs within school, LEA and national priorities.
Menu-led INSET courses: leaflets, booklets published and advertised in specialist press: *Liberty, QED, Resource Manager Today* and NBA/ISBA journals.	**Business-led professional development programmes:** tackling content and process issues, as well as learning and leadership strategies.
INSET participants are mainly enthusiastic volunteers: often pursuing personal career and skills development through award bearing courses – NVQ, AAT, IPD, DMS, MBA.	**All staff have access to professional development:** enthusiastic volunteers plus others not previously involved identified through needs audits. Confluence of staff development and school and LEA needs.
Little institutional involvement: in identifying types of training needs, individual support-staff for training and following up on outcomes of training.	**Schools at the centre of the process:** in identifying needs, targeting development priorities, contracting delivery, following up and evaluating outcomes at operational level.
Little individual support staff involvement: in identifying their own needs, deciding how best to meet them within a school framework. Many support staff left out entirely.	**Systems ensure involvement of all staff:** in all stages of the development cycle as collaborative learning participants.
Little or no systematic evaluation: or concern about the effect of training on the individual or school and none on the ultimate effect on pupil's educational experiences. No attempt to measure the cost-effectiveness of training.	**Monitoring and evaluation built in to the process:** at all levels. Staff development events are evaluated at the point of delivery. Outcomes are evaluated in terms of their effect on the school and its community and the lessons fed back into the process. There will be a careful scrutiny of the cost effectiveness of staff development.
INSET regarded as *ipso facto* a 'good thing if you can get it' but largely unmanaged, unco-ordinated, *ad hoc* and reactive.	**Staff development carefully managed as a rolling programme within a stated development plan at school, LEA and government levels.**

Figure 13.5 Scenarios for professional development at the beginning of the twenty-first century

The 'professional development' approach illustrated in the second column of Figure 13.5 was gradually put in place in many schools for the teaching staff in the 1980s and 1990s. Bursars and support staff, however, were generally not included in these whole-school approaches and they developed their functional and operational skills as they individually perceived their training requirements. There was no systematic guidance from the profession, which was at the embryonic stage, and very little from schools or LEAs. By the late 1990s the NBA had lobbied successfully for training and educational programmes for bursars and had identified a more coherent route from initial training to doctorate level.

A chart proposing levels of training and education against the different levels of bursarship can be seen on the training and development section of the NBA's website <http://www.nba.org.uk>. A range of organisations including the DfEE, Ofsted and Investors in People supported this initiative. Figure 13.6, adapted from the NBA's 1999 chart, considers NVQs, other professional qualifications, prior learning and mainstream qualifications at the various levels that signify the career progression from initial appointment at the lowest level to education resource/school business manager.

No single column offers the range of training required for a bursar to operate effectively at the highest level, functionally, technically and strategically. Thus any bursar in the early twenty-first century is likely to have achieved learning or gained qualifications from more than one of the columns and possibly all of them.

1 *NVQs*. NVQs not specifically targeted at bursarship are provided by many colleges around the country and concentrate on developing functional and technical skills such as administration and finance. The NBA also negotiated the provision of NVQs directly relevant to bursarship in 1997, which incorporated management skills. These courses were residential and as such encouraged the exchange of ideas and knowledge among bursars that are incumbent on the development of bursarship as a profession.

2 *Professional qualification equivalence*. These courses are usually sponsored by professional bodies and develop skills in technical areas. The most common qualifications are in accountancy, personnel management or health and safety, although there are other areas of expertise depending on the previous background of the bursar and the principal requirements of the posts. Other areas of expertise include marketing, management or engineering.

3 *Accreditation of prior learning*. Until 1999 there was no official means of accrediting prior learning, although within the profession, bursars were aware of those who were operating effectively within their posts. The advent of the registration scheme for bursars has provided a vehicle for those without formal qualifications to gain masters-level Credit Accumulation and Transfer Scheme (CATS) points and to be entered on the National Register of Licensed Bursars as LNBAs. The NBA is also offering courses specific to bursars in recruitment, report writing and leadership skills.

4 *Mainstream qualifications*. Bursars who have taken the route of formal qualifications up to degree level, possess qualifications in a range of subjects which demonstrate competency in learning but these are not always specif-

Level of bursarship	NVQ level	Professional qualification equivalent	Accreditation of experiential learning	Mainstream qualification
Office assistant	NVQ 1 Administration	RSA Book-keeping Certificate in Office Studies	Evidence of secondary education	2 x GCSE
Clerical officer	NVQ 2 Administration and Finance	RSA 2/3 Book-keeping ONC Business Studies	Previous work experience at clerical level	4 x GCSE
Finance assistant/ administrative assistant	NVQ 3 Administration and Finance	Association of Accounting Technicians Intermediate level Institute of Management	Work at supervisory level including financial responsibility	Certificate in Management
Finance manager/ administration manager	NVQ 4 Management	Intermediate/ Final Certificate/ Diploma of professional accounting body Certificate of Management or similar	History of work at first line manager level including decision-making authority	Certificate in Management and/or A-levels
Support services manager	NVQ 5 Management	Full membership by examination of a professional accounting or management institute	History of work at senior management level including strategic management	Diploma in Management and/or First Degree
School business manager		Fellowship or equivalent by exam of a professional institute in appropriate discipline	Evidence of strategic level expertise/ experience in educational management and NBA registration	Second or Masters Degree in subject relevant to school bursarship, probably through CATS
Education resource manager			Recognised by peers as exhibiting substantial expertise and experience in senior educational leadership	Doctorate in Educational Leadership or PhD

Figure 13.6 Chart of approximate qualification routes for bursars

Source: Adapted from NBA model developed by James Welsh (1999)

ically relevant to the role. Such qualifications are often supplemented by professional qualifications in a specialist area such as accountancy. There is now a growing number of bursars who hold postgraduate diplomas or MBAs and some hold these qualifications specifically in education management. It is also possible for bursars to continue their education and achieve PhDs or EdDs in educational leadership.

There are three main implications that can be derived from Figure 13.6. There is an emphasis in the first three assistant levels on gaining knowledge in functional areas, in particular finance and administration. This knowledge is essential for the running of the school but does not develop management skills nor an understanding of the core business of the school, i.e. it is operational and functional. The managerial levels from finance/administration manager upward recognise the need for development of supervisory and decision-making skills. At this point the bursar's knowledge enables them to operate at a more tactical and strategic level. In so doing they are more likely to make use of the specialist knowledge of others in building an effective support service team to deliver a high-quality educational learning environment. Bursars at the highest level are educational leaders, combining practical expertise in educational resource support systems with an understanding of the impact of their role on education and teaching and learning. Increasingly they will be qualified to doctoral level. This interplay of theory and practice (praxis) will enable them to continually consider how their role and that of their support staff can evolve to promote an effective and efficient learning environment in the school.

While there are strands of leadership and management which run right through the different levels of bursarship each of the distinctive levels outlined above will need specific training and development opportunities.

The future of bursars' education and training

The chapters in Part Two of this book, which highlighted the range of bursars' responsibilities and their position either inside or outside the senior management team raised issues about their training requirements. Bursars need functional/technical training, which can be provided by LEAs, the school, colleges and professional bodies, but they also require management training. NVQs provide a basic understanding of management subjects but more advanced development is best achieved through postgraduate diplomas or an MBA. A fully integrated training programme would provide functional organisational training, personal competency development, management training, an understanding of educational issues and an awareness of social and political issues within the school, its community and on a global level as illustrated in Figure 13.7.

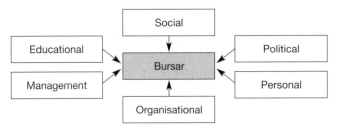

Figure 13.7 Areas identified for the development of the bursar

Throughout their career, bursars should achieve specific levels of development and education to enable them to operate effectively in their role. Those in their early career, up to the level of administration manager, need to concentrate on accumulating functional knowledge that increases their personal competencies and understanding of procedures in developing and working within organisational structures. This development would enable them to work effectively at an operational level. A more experienced bursar or support services manager would progress to acquire supervision skills, the ability to measure efficiency and an understanding of decision-making processes and systems. Such a person would also develop a critical awareness of the educational core business in which they were operating at a tactical level. The school business manager would develop an interpersonal synergy, which enabled him or her to operate effectively within the culture and ethos of the school at a strategic level. Political understanding, including diplomatic abilities, would augment this level of operation and enable an effective lobbying ability of all school stakeholders.

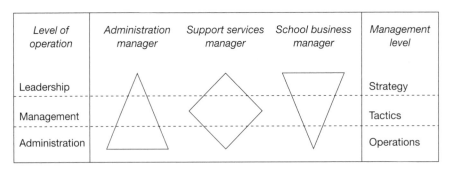

Figure 13.8 Bursars' levels of operation and management

Looking at the levels of operation of bursars we can see three ideal types for whom different education and training is needed. Figure 13.8 illustrates the three 'ideal types' of site-level resource manager representing these three levels. Level 1 can be characterised as the administration manager, not a member of the senior leadership team, carrying out routine clerking and servicing the needs of teaching staff on request. At this level they would not be expected to have a direct contact with teaching and learning as such but may well provide significant information for the educational decision-making process. Level 2 would be the support services manager, leader of the support staff, a member of the senior leadership team but still subordinate to senior teaching staff. There may well be friction and tension between the site-level resource manager and senior teachers.

Finally there is the ideal type of the school business manager as a full member of the school leadership team. Alongside the headteacher and deputy heads he or she is active in strategic development and establishing procedures ensuring they are communicated and realised in the school. Her or his understanding of the education process facilitates the building of flexible, interactive systems and support learning teams. As a leader of 'associate staff' (Mortimore *et al.*, 1995), she or he ensures that administration, finance and premises management are efficiently and effectively carried out by staff who feel valued and able to interact with and support teaching staff. Through an understanding of their own role, the school's values and the needs of educators to facilitate learning, the school business manager ensures the school is a living and adaptive learning environment, which anticipates and responds to change.

At the beginning of the twenty-first century bursars have laid the foundations for developing their own profession. They have defined their role and competencies and have defined a code of ethics for their working practice. They have also actively influenced the training and development that is available to them and, by registering bursars into associations and more specifically as licentiates, are beginning to control entry to, and define the different levels of, their profession. The profession, however, is very young and has yet to engender the debate among its members that will enable it to mature and evolve.

In the final chapter, we will assume the foundations of the role of school business manager have now been well laid. We will thus review the future development of the various roles of the bursar and take the opportunity to speculate on the emergence of a fundamentally new type of role – the education resource manager.

14

■ ■ ■

Leading Onwards

Introduction

In Chapter 1 we concluded by presenting a four-stage model describing the 'ideal types' of bursars which we have identified in our work on school bursarship. This typology represents the various ways in which bursars interface with their tasks and the senior management in the school. The four types are illustrated in Figure 14.1.

Type	Role	Description
1	Administration manager	The bursar as outside the SMT, seen as an administrator servicing the needs of teaching and management staff on request.
2	Support services manager	The bursar as an adviser to the SMT and usually, but not invariably, the leader of the support staff.
3	School business manager	The bursar as a fully accepted part of the SMT, leader of the support staff with some human resource management responsibilities for teaching staff and managing outsourced contracts.
4	Education resource manager	The bursarship role is an integral part of the SMT, with a post equivalent to, or higher than, that of a deputy head with responsibility for all human resource management as well as all functions which affect the provision of a high-quality learning environment.

Figure 14.1 A typology of bursars' roles

In Part Four we have so far discussed the changes in structure and autonomy taking place in schools at the turn of the twentieth century and mapped out the response of bursars as professionals to some ways in which schools may develop in the future. In so doing we have focused mainly on the first three of the above stages. This chapter will develop a conceptual model relating the roles played by bursars to the levels of autonomy schools either have or wish to achieve. As yet there are few bursars who could be said to be operating at the fourth stage of education resource manager, so the final part of the chapter will explore how this role-type, which we conceive to be of a whole different order of operation, namely a strategic leader in partnership with the head-teacher, might develop.

School autonomy and the bursar's role: a new model

The first three stages in the above typology can be broadly related to three levels of management performance.

1 *Reactive, functional*: at this level of performance, the bursar is fully competent within the role and doing a satisfactory job which includes a primary focus on administrative tasks such as personnel and financial record keeping, premises and school office management.

2 *Active, systems specialist*: as well as the activities in level 1, the bursar will also have the ability to evaluate their own personal strengths and weaknesses and how they affect the organisation. The bursar would be supervising teams of specialist functional operatives. The office staff would be managed to ensure that administrative tasks are effectively and efficiently carried out. Other major management activities would include ensuring the school is operating legally and working at optimum resource levels, providing information for policy decision making and promoting the school within the business and local community.

3 *Proactive, site leader*: at this level the bursar would be supervising other staff, stepping in when needed to carry out functional tasks but also facilitating their own and others' professional development. Such bursars would also have the opportunity to operate in a leadership capacity as they would be members of the senior management team and hold designated responsibility for the school's support staff teams. They would, therefore, contribute to setting the ethos and policies of the school and communicating them to their staff. They would also lead the implementation of their staff development to enable them to operate as effective individuals working collaboratively with all staff in the school.

We can now relate the autonomy/dependency model developed in Chapter 12 (Figure 12.1) directly to that in Chapter 13 (Figure 13.8) describing the different role bursars play in schools. Thus in Figure 14.2 the three 'ideal types' of site-level resource manager are identified against the level of autonomy enjoyed or desired by the school. A school that is largely dependent on its district (or LEA) and therefore reactive rather than proactive to policy imperatives will need an administration manager who is strong on routine data processing, has some ability and expertise in managing the site-level team and who is happy with a limited leadership role. Where the school has a larger degree of autonomy the support services manager needs to have a greater expertise in team management but still retain some facility for routine clerking (to remain in touch with staff carrying out such functions on site) as well as an increased capacity for leadership. For the school of the future, with a high degree of autonomy, the school business manager needs to have the highest level of expertise in strategic leadership as the level of devolved funding enables the buying in (or outsourcing) of support staff who will carry out the routine operations and will also have some ability to manage their own teams.

This model enables schools to determine their actual or desired level of autonomy and thence to identify the optimum characteristics of their site-level resource manager. Of course, we have already stated that no school can be completely autonomous or dependent and so will need to consider the linkage between the levels of leadership, management and routine operations at the site level and those of the district/LEA as the funding authority.

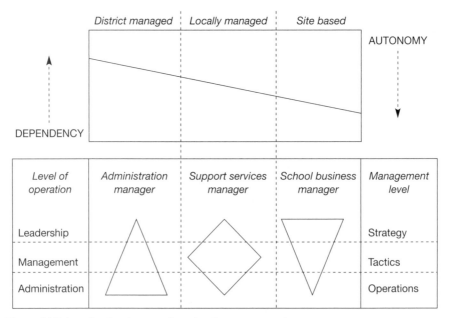

Figure 14.2 Levels of autonomy in school management

The educational resource manager:
a new role for school bursars

The fourth role in the typology (Figure 14.1) is that of the education resource manager which will develop as more schools take up the opportunity to manage more of their support services for themselves. This role will increase the focus on leadership in the context of the community learning centre. A parallel debate has been taking place in the role of the headteacher where the plans for the setting up of the National College for School Leadership at the beginning of the twenty-first century became the physical embodiment of the shift in emphasis from management to leadership.

The result of such thinking enables a new conceptual structure of school leadership to emerge. On the teaching side are the deputy headteachers with, for example, curriculum and pastoral responsibilities and parallel to these is the education resource manager as leader of the support staff; both are linked in the SMT and in responsibility to the headteacher (*see* Figure 14.3).

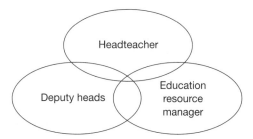

Figure 14.3 The school senior management team

Where, in the past, strategy was set by top management leaving the operational aspects to middle managers, indications are that future leadership will be distributed throughout the school (Maxcy, 1995). Thus, each person in the organisation will be responsible for some strategic as well as operational thinking. Such a site-based management system means that strategic *and* operational decisions will need to be taken with the devolution of educational resources. The challenge for education resource managers of the future, therefore, is to play a full part in senior leadership as well as leading their teams in a way which respects the contribution all can make to a supportive learning environment.

The rise of site-based leadership in schools

The rise of site-based management in the UK parallels the move to more responsive customer oriented organisations with flatter management structures in the business environment (Davies and Ellison, 1997). As education organisations respond to the increasing pace of change (Fullan, 1993) and become more like businesses of the future, the structure of their administration will need to reflect this change in orientation (Sawatzki, 1997). Such a reconceptualisation takes into account the difference in emphasis from administration to leadership, developments in thinking about the way we learn (Gardner *et al.*, 1996) and how this might be mirrored in approaches to successful leadership (White *et al.*, 1996).

Over the past century industrial and educational organisations tended to develop as hierarchies. They have been characterised by a line management structure where boundaries were difficult to cross horizontally and vertical movement only occurred through promotion. In this structural modernist world, schools were rational entities that operated within clearly defined rules, teachers taught and someone else, usually outside the school at the district or LEA level, was responsible for management and administration. Schools today need to respond to increasing uncertainty characterised by rapid global changes, parental and government pressure and a variety of social problems. To increase school responsiveness, reform proposals have included:

- an emphasis on student achievement;
- increased autonomy at school level;
- emphasis on community involvement;
- teacher and staff development programmes accompanied by appraisal;
- results driven accountability (Maxcy, 1995: 77).

Additionally, education has been characterised by complexity in the form of:

1 *ambiguity*: autonomy of site-based management versus centralised decision making in the form of the National Curriculum where in the UK guidelines for literacy and numeracy are particularly prescriptive;

2 *turbulence*: rapid access to information, communication and technological developments that could radically alter the way the curriculum is delivered worldwide;

3 *uncertainty*: in the search for accountability and higher standards, traditional routes to senior leadership have become both more fragmented and less attractive professionally and remuneratively (Lashway, 1998).

The highly structured organisation, which was more effective in a stable industrial age is no longer appropriate for the complex environment of the information age, with its emphasis on accountability; this requires a more flexible, flatter, organisational structure. In such a context professional responsibility and leadership roles are defined by current needs and not historical tradition.

In the post-modernist era, characterised by complexity and constant change, the manager as controller and administrator of the *status quo* is ill equipped to respond to turbulence, ambiguity and uncertainty. Rather than reacting to change, those who wish to be successful and effective in their chosen field, must lift their eyes to the horizon to anticipate and prepare for the future (Bennis, 1985: 7). Effective school leaders, therefore, need to develop an awareness of the immediate and global environment and the ability to respond to the future through scenario planning before creating a vision that can be communicated and supported by their colleagues and staff.

Such leaders need the ability to draw on a wider range of ways of thinking. Rather than the more traditional rational approach focusing on 'making the numbers' they would use intuitive insights and interpersonal skills. Leaders in this futures oriented approach will be operating at the level of 'artist', as distinct from 'technician' (Pedler and Boydell, 1985). They will be characterised not by an approach to job tasks which drills them in narrow functional skills and rigid National Standards (the competence model epitomised in the UK by National Vocational Qualifications, the Management Charter Initiative and the National Professional Qualification for Headship) but by one based on more generic attributes which distinguishes the 'best from the rest' (Hay McBer, in Esp, 1993; Davies and Ellison, 1997).

At first sight it would seem that, if headteachers are to be encouraged to develop these more strategic approaches (e.g. through the UK government's National Programme for Serving Heads), then the routine clerking duties could fall to others in the senior leadership team, i.e. the site-level resource manager. Such a modernist solution, however, could lead to a fragmentation of responsibilities and may not be in the school's best interests. An alternative post-modern solution would be to ensure that, while allowing for a degree of division of labour in the senior leadership team, each member carried out some of the generic leadership tasks of the senior team as a whole – this would be more in tune with the flatter management structures of the responsive organisation.

We now turn to how bursars themselves see their role developing in the future. The next section describes the outcome of a series of focus group discussions with bursars to investigate how leadership teams were responding to increased site-level administration, particularly in the nature of tasks and responsibilities of the education resource manager.

The education resource manager of the future

In order to project the current picture of bursarship into the future, focus groups of school bursars were held to brainstorm the future role and the attributes that would be needed. The methodology can be seen in Appendix I. The first meeting, discussed the issues related to supporting learning, human resource management, information and communication technology, health and safety and the effective use of buildings. This was facilitated by a card-sort exercise based on an amalgamation of National Bursars Association key areas of bursarship and Surrey LEA's headteachers', curriculum leaders' and teachers' accountabilities. The groups sorted the responsibilities into those carried out by bursars and those by others in the school, each pile was then categorised into 'families' of duties. The groups agreed on six general support areas:

1 finance;
2 marketing and promotion;
3 human resource management;
4 strategy;
5 premises;
6 administration.

Two of the three groups added teaching and learning/curriculum to their responsibilities. These responsibilities included helping to develop strategies to support the learning of pupils and ensuring that their line-managed staff understood the teaching and learning plan. The responsibilities proposed by the groups as essential to bursars are listed in Figure 14.4.

These responsibilities illustrate the role of the education resource managers of the future as contributing to the development of school policy and leading their teams to put this into practice. In particular they would be developing the areas for which they had overall responsibility by monitoring and evaluating current practice and linking it with the school's development plan. They would also provide specialist knowledge and manage contracts. Their relationships with the school's stakeholders were seen as being important in promoting the school's ethos and interests and representing the views of the support staff. In general they would be establishing and maintaining a purposeful working environment.

Nine months later the same focus groups met again to discuss current issues in leadership development and in particular the current government agenda for education, national standards for management and leadership, factors involved in high performance, successful continued professional development and leading learners. They were asked to discuss and list:

1 the key roles of the site-level resource manager of the future;
2 how the site-level resource manager should relate to non-support staff groups;
3 what the site-level resource manager can do to contribute to building school achievement.

The key roles for the education resource manager of the future were envisaged as contributing to the school's vision and participating in strategic development and planning. They considered that they should be change facilitators who interpret the school's vision in practical terms and promote and deliver the school's aims. Although they would concentrate on leading the business side of the school, they felt that they were also key players in the learning envi-

Finance
1 Lead the team responsible for finance which includes budgeting, planning and control
2 Lead the development of sound financial systems

Human resource management
1 Develop human resources
2 Manage the performance of the school's support staff through the provision of appropriate procedures for appointment, induction, appraisal and development
3 Manage the deployment of support staff
4 Evaluate the support staff development programme
5 Develop working relationships with support staff
6 Create the opportunity for colleagues to learn from one another
7 Represent the views of colleagues within area of responsibility
8 Know about relevant human resource legislation
9 Manage support contracts

Premises
1 Establish and maintain an attractive and purposeful working environment
2 Ensure conformity with health and safety legislation
3 Establish and monitor a site security policy
4 Manage support contracts

Marketing
1 Articulate the curriculum philosophy of the school
2 Obtain support for school purposes, objectives and policies
3 Create and maintain relationships among all members of the school community
4 Develop supportive relationships with parents
5 Develop relationships with relevant agencies to secure support for the school
6 Develop relationships with community to secure support for the school

Strategy
1 Help develop school purposes, objectives and policies
2 Articulate and implement all school policies
3 Lead and manage a team of colleagues in developing strategies to put agreed policy into practice
4 Assist in the design and implementation of strategies for development and change where required
5 Evaluate strategies with a view to promoting continuous improvement in quality throughout the school
6 Develop and monitor management structures, processes and procedures to ensure that the school achieves its curriculum and pastoral aims through the fulfilment of the development plan
7 Initiate and manage change and improvement in pursuit of organisational goals

Administration
1 Ensure that administrative requirements are fulfilled in order to facilitate the smooth running of the school
2 Oversee systems to monitor and record achievement
3 Carry out record keeping procedures to satisfy school policies and national inspection (Ofsted) requirements
4 Observe colleagues at work to inform future developments

Figure 14.4 Essential tasks for bursars of the future – response from focus groups

ronment and in providing a consistent management approach and professionalism in their field.

In relation to non-support staff, the education resource manager would be a
professional of equal status offering a different perspective. Their expertise in
their own area would be used to inform, support and contribute with integrity
to the development of the school. They also saw themselves as a link between
stakeholders such as governors, teachers and support staff.

The education resource manager's contribution to school achievement would
be through the creation and continuous improvement of a learning environment and the provision of a financial overview and effective support service.
They would lead high-performing support staff who would understand the
vision of the school and would be welcoming to the community. In order to
provide an optimum service to the school, they would need to develop a wider
perspective by keeping up to date with education initiatives and agencies
external to the school.

In Chapter 5, we reported on the outcome of a series of observations of bursars in action which showed the proportion of time spent on administration
(47 per cent), management (46 per cent) and leadership (7 per cent), although
the last figure did include a range from no time spent on leadership activities
to over a quarter of their time. This contrasts markedly with an analysis of the
responses of the focus groups, looking towards the future role which indicates
a significant shift from administration to leadership activities as shown in
Figure 14.5.

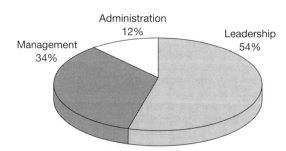

Figure 14.5 Future levels of operation from focus groups

Implications for the future role of bursars

The key change for schools in England and Wales at the beginning of the
twenty-first century is that of the change of status and funding that will
enhance the opportunity for autonomy as well as bringing all state schools
under a common regime for strategic planning. In this context we will also see
the future development of the role of the headteacher both in terms of the

training for aspiring heads and the development programme for serving heads which were put in place by the Teacher Training Agency in the late 1990s. The final section of this chapter will examine the outcomes of our research in the light of these proposals and identify key issues for the operational and strategic role of bursars.

The experience we have gained from a decade of site-based management of schools across the world needs to be built on as we move into the twenty-first century. The main areas concern:

1   the leadership and management of the increasing number of both administrative and learning support staff;
2   achieving the optimum value for money in the specific balance of resources for learning at the site level;
3   the roles and relationships in the senior leadership, particularly the potential overloading of heads and deputies with administrative and site/premises-related responsibilities.

Leading support staff

One of the most significant changes in schools in the late 1990s has been the increase in numbers and variety of support staff; in the school office, as premises maintenance staff and in the classroom as teaching, learning or pupil support assistants. Indeed, as we have noted above, the 'head count' of such staff may well exceed that of the teaching staff. These also need to have clear job descriptions, a designated team leader or line manager and agreed arrangements for performance management and professional development. This is especially important as many, if not most, will be on part-time, teaching term only or short-term contracts.

These groups of staff, though they have an obvious operational link to the teaching staff or other team leaders, need strategic management and human resource development. Many schools have recognised this in appointing the bursar to lead the support staff team, in some cases in partnership with team leaders for the various functional groupings. The challenge for the twenty-first century is to develop this experienced and valuable group into an integrated multi-skilled team which can respond flexibly to the learning needs of the pupils and the teaching requirements of the teaching staff.

Value for money and economies of scale

Up to the 1990s, value for money was not a concept that figured very highly at school level. The economies of scale which LEAs could obtain through their bargaining power and bulk purchasing seemed the most obvious way of keeping costs down. In practice, however, LEAs set up complex arrangements for the management of their support services and this often appeared fragmented at the school level where each service had independent lines of communication. There was also the strange phenomenon of national and local government taking on more administrators to deliver a devolved service!

At the school level, however, Ofsted reports are demonstrating that the vast majority of schools are delivering satisfactory or good value for money. In effect schools are trading off the economies of scale of a centrally planned economy against the particular mix of resources needed by the more entrepreneurial school responding to the specific needs of the pupils. Senior leaders in schools have also become very experienced in bidding for and coherently managing a whole variety of grants (e.g. TVEI, Grants for Education Support and Training [GEST], National Curriculum resources, technology grants, Standards Fund etc.). The net effect is that the resources work harder for the pupils of the school as they are more carefully targeted to pupils' needs. Bursars again are playing a crucial role in achieving this economy of scale at the school level as well as ensuring value for money. This is not only an issue for the individual school but has wider implications. As bursars develop their support networks, they will need to be more proactive in their strategic liaison with local and national authorities and thus engage more vigorously in the education political economy (Swanson and King, 1997).

Bursars and school leadership

In responding to the increased pressure of responsibilities that have come with site-level management, schools have turned to the appointment of bursars to organise the support staff into coherent teams. Certainly there is evidence of the overload of senior management as a result of having to cope with LMS/GM and Ofsted, to name but two, hence the initiative of the NPQH to train potential headteachers more effectively and the deliberations of the House of Commons Select Committee on Education and Employment into the future role of the headteacher (HoC, 1998; 1999).

Experience from working with bursars in schools indicates that, although they bring substantial solutions to the problem of overload, there is a potential for tension in their relationship both with senior leaders and with other support staff, for example, the person who controls the school finances is seen as having power. Add to this the fact that many bursars manage more support staff than the number of teachers in the school and there is considerable scope for conflict and disharmony. In some schools, this has been tackled by bringing the bursar into the SMT as an equal partner, though, as some bursars also act as clerk to the governors, they could be seen as being more equal than others!

From bursar to education resource manager

This book has shown how the establishment of the role of the professional bursar has led to a better recognition of the importance of managing the administrative function at school level. Bursars themselves need opportunities to learn more about the core business of learning and their colleague senior managers need to appreciate the complementary role that bursars and their support staff can play in the enhancement of school achievement. The responsibility for the first steps towards achieving this rests with leaders and bursars in schools. We suggest the starting points should be as follows.

School leaders should:

- provide clear job descriptions for bursars, related to other senior managers;
- develop coherent line management for support staff;
- recognise that all school leadership, including that of the bursar, is focused on the core business of improving achievements in teaching and learning;
- consider the incorporation of the bursar into the senior management team;
- support career development for bursars.

Bursars need to:

- mentor support staff in their career routes to bursarship;
- participate in discussions on developing further the practice and theory of bursarship;
- share as fully as possible in all aspects of school life;
- understand the value of training and education in achieving personal professional development;
- ensure that their training includes the study of how children learn, and of best practice in teaching, so that bursars can better develop appropriate support services.

These are the first steps on the route to the transformation of the bursar into the education resource manager of the twenty-first century. Some schools will already have climbed these steps; others will not yet have begun the ascent. The challenge, after completing the initial steps, will be to debate the ways in which the education resource manager can become a whole-school leader. This book has reviewed the route so far and begins the contributions to the next stage in bursarship development.

Appendix I:
Research Methodology
■ ■ ■

Introduction

The research reported in Parts Two and Three of this book is the outcome of a pilot case study into school bursarship. As this is a very under-researched area, we chose to employ an exploratory design (Adams and Schvaneveldt, 1991), characterised by a multiple method approach to collecting and analysing data. The case study was chosen as the most appropriate methodology to accommodate this research design (Yin, 1989) and featured:

- a phenomenological approach of generating theory and sampling small numbers (Easterby-Smith *et al.*, 1991);
- a strongly ideographic philosophy, placing 'considerable stress upon getting close to one's subject and exploring its detailed background and life history' (Burrell and Morgan, 1979: 6);
- a holistic perspective involving a qualitative research design of observations and interviews as well as a normative analysis of archives and documents including job descriptions and application forms.

Research frame

Defining the research question

Several aspects were considered to explore bursars' contribution to schools and their career histories, responsibilities and operational levels. In order to develop an understanding of these areas of investigation, a range of research questions were considered and four specific areas selected for the pilot study. The areas of exploration were:

1   the career experiences and qualifications of bursars;

2   the roles, activities and responsibilities of bursars;

3   the relationships of bursars with teaching professionals, governors, pupils and other school stakeholders;

4   the position of bursars in relation to their senior management teams.

Selecting the research sample

The sample (Fig. I.1) included bursars from locally maintained, GM and independent schools in England and Wales. Their schools catered for between 230 to 2040 pupils aged from four to nineteen. This group formed an opportunity sample of 34 bursars who attended the University of Lincolnshire and Humberside's MBA in Education Management for Bursars run by the International Educational Leadership Centre (IELC). Data was added from a further two bursars who applied for but did not attend the course.

As an opportunity sample was used, the data gathered should be seen as providing indicative rather than representative findings. The sample had the advantages of being readily accessible, willing to participate, emanating from a variety of schools and interested in developing the profession of bursarship. Over half the sample were from GM schools, the principal features of which were transferred to all state schools from 1999. The disadvantages of using an opportunity sample were that almost all were from secondary schools; in addition it is difficult to estimate the extent to which their potential interest in bursars' professional development (evidenced by their willingness to undertake a higher degree) is replicated among all bursars.

Selecting the methods

The research design incorporated a range of methods to build a holistic picture of bursars. Primary and secondary data was collected from:

1   literature on support staff and a wider review of school management sources (Chapter 2);

2   an analysis of job descriptions, application and enrolment forms collected from the sample group (Chapters 3 and 5);

3   observation of six bursars at work (Chapter 4);

4   interviews with the sample group including questions on the nature of the bursar's role and its development (Chapters 3, 5 and 6);

5   focus groups discussing the future role of the bursar (Chapter 14);

6   case studies developed from data provided by MBA participants (Part Three).

School type	Age range	Pupil nos	Gender	Area
Locally maintained	11–16	640	Girls	London
	11–16	750	Boys	London
	11–16	800	Mixed	London
	11–16	900	Mixed	London
	11–18	1010	Mixed	London
	12–18	1150	Mixed	London
	11–16	1040	Mixed	South
	12–16	400	Mixed	South
	11–18	770	Mixed	South
	11–18	1180	Mixed	South-west
	11–18	2050	Mixed	South-west
	11–16	760	Mixed	East Midlands
	11–18	1170	Mixed	North
	11–18	770	Mixed	Wales
GM	11–18	1170	Mixed	London
	11–18	1340	Mixed	London
	5–7	230	Mixed	Home counties
	11–16	560	Mixed	East
	11–16	820	Mixed	East
	11–19	920	Mixed	East
	11–18	740	Mixed	South-east
	11–18	800	Mixed	South-east
	11–18	1450	Mixed	South-east
	12–18	1190	Mixed	South
	11–18	990	Mixed	South-west
	11–18	1350	Mixed	South-west
	11–16	560	Mixed	Midlands
	11–18	660	Boys	Midlands
	11–18	570	Mixed	Wales
	11–18	570	Mixed	Wales
	11–16	560	Mixed	Midlands
Independent	4–18	340	Girls	South
	4–18	670	Girls	East
	16–19	370	Mixed	Wales

Figure I. 1 School details of the main sample group of bursars

Primary data

Finding out what the school business manager is supposed to do

Job descriptions, person specifications (and explanatory letters attached to them) from bursars were used to provide a descriptive analysis of bursars' roles and an indication of how those employing the bursars envisaged the post. The job descriptions provided an introduction to the bursar's role using easily accessible data in readily analysable forms, while the bursars' additional explanatory letters were valuable indications of how the sample group thought their roles had developed in practice. This helped to meet Clerkin's objection to using job descriptions, which 'can only offer a single snapshot at a particular time in a school's history' (Clerkin, 1994: 19).

In contrast with the views of the bursars themselves provided in interviews and with the views of researchers observing the bursars, job descriptions were used to indicate the expected roles, responsibilities and activities to provide an overview of the role. The job descriptions did not cover the same areas nor did they follow a standard format and, therefore, some researcher categorisation had to be imposed to facilitate comparisons. A total of 35 bursars were asked to provide their job descriptions, and 23 responded, all of them from secondary schools. It is difficult to estimate the significance of a 66 per cent response rate as some of the non-returnees may not have had job descriptions and others said they were too busy to respond.

The data was analysed both quantitatively and qualitatively to provide a normative description. The quantitative analysis used headings found in the job descriptions or suggested by the literature. All items within the job descriptions were ticked off as they were assigned to a particular heading, although some were used more than once if they could be considered to be relevant to different aspects of the post. The headings chosen were finance, HRM, premises, pupils, external relationships, information technology, meetings and skills. Each heading was further divided if appropriate sub-headings became apparent. After analysis and categorisation of the data, subheadings were listed in a spreadsheet package using the highest number of times an item appeared in job descriptions. The information was then represented as a 'radar' diagram (Figure 3.1). This circular chart is divided into sectors corresponding to the categories with the most frequent items plotted closest to the centre.

The qualitative analysis was carried out by importing the job descriptions into the data analysis software package, Non-numerical Data Indexing, Structuring and Theorising (QSR NUDIST), and assigning the data to different headings derived from the literature search. Key headings used were finance, administration, premises and HRM. Marketing and information technology were added from the job descriptions as activities that had not been found in the literature. All areas of work were categorised under roles, responsibilities and activities. A range of stakeholder relationships were also used including teaching staff, support staff, headteacher, governors, pupils, parents, businesses, local community and government agencies. Finally, management roles were explored using leadership, management and the senior management team as headings. Further data was extrapolated using the key words, insurance, contracts and health and safety, which had been highlighted by the quantitative analysis.

Finding out what school business managers actually do

Bursars were observed in their work environments to investigate their actual responsibilities and activities. The job descriptions had provided a view of the expected roles, levels of responsibility and relationships but they were historical in their application as evidenced by comments from the bursars.

Job description vintage 1993 – needs updating!

(Male bursar, GM school, East, 1998)

The observations were chosen as a means of verifying (Strauss and Corbin, 1990) or falsifying (Popper, 1972) the job descriptions, particularly as they would provide examples of the actual activities of bursars. This research method also provided an additional perspective to bursars' views of their posts as given in interviews.

It was felt that the sample chosen for observation should represent primary and secondary phase schools, independent, local and GM funding, church schools, a variety of geographical locations and of different job titles. The final combination of categories for the bursars chosen is illustrated in Figure I.2.

The sample bursars were contacted by phone and asked if they would take part in the research and all those approached, agreed. The phone call was followed by letters to the bursar and the headteacher explaining the research project and the form of observation including a sample of the observation sheet. After receiving a letter of agreement from the school, a further letter was sent to the bursar stating the date of the observation, how the observation would be carried out and offering to withdraw if any sensitive issue arose during the period of observation. The bursar was asked to estimate expected arrival and departure times so the observer could be present for the same period. They were also asked to provide their job descriptions, school prospec-

School	Phase	Funding	Church school	Location	Job title
1	Primary	GM	No	Home Counties	Bursar/ administrator
2	Secondary	Independent	No	Wales	Bursar
3	Secondary	Locally maintained	No	North England	Administration officer
4	Secondary	Locally maintained	No	Midlands	Registrar
5	Secondary	Locally maintained	Yes	London	Bursar
6	Secondary	GM	No	East	Bursar

Figure I.2 Profiles of schools chosen for direct observation

tuses, numbers of pupils, staff and line-managed staff details, last annual report to parents and the summary of the last Ofsted report.

Each of the three researchers undertook two observations, each lasting one day. In order to standardise their recordings the following procedures were agreed.

1 The observation would be carried out using forms, ring bound in books of 50 forms. The form allowed for recording the start and finish time of each activity, who the bursar met, where the bursar was and the overt purpose of each activity. There was a space to record a full description of each activity and the changes of activity were numbered for later reference. An activity was defined as 'an identifiable single event with an observable beginning and ending' (Duignan, 1980: 10).

2 Clarification would be sought during the day, whenever possible, if the meaning and details of an activity were not self-evident to the recorder. Alternatively, time would be used at the end of the day to summarise the activities and ask questions.

3 The researchers would draw a plan of the bursar's office, its furnishings and contents and estimate its size. If possible the headteacher's office would be drawn for comparison. A record would also be made of the location of the bursar's office in relation to the headteacher, senior management team, support staff and teaching staff.

4 The bursar would be observed from the time of arrival to the time of leaving work. The researcher would stay with the bursar throughout the day, taking comfort and lunch breaks at the same time. If it was not possible for the observer to stay the full length of the day, the bursar would be asked to record when the working day ended and what work was done in the period after the researcher left.

Although bursars were asked to ignore the researchers during observations, in all cases the bursars explained their activities and took the opportunity to talk about how they were apppointed, what their role entailed, their interaction with staff and the loneliness of the role. Sometimes other members of staff or visitors would talk to the observers even though they had been asked not to communicate with them. During one of the observations, the bursar's contact with staff in the school was relatively slight, which the bursar said was atypical. It was subsequently realised that the observer had been sitting in the immediate line of visibility of the door, thus visitors had assumed the bursar was already in a meeting and had not entered.

As the researchers had agreed standard procedures before commencing the observations and had used the same data capture forms, the information had been recorded with the minimum of variation, thereby providing consistent material for analysis. The observation sheets, which were typed before the outcomes were compared, were analysed by:

- categorising the data under the same responsibility headings as the job descriptions;
- calculating the length of the bursars' working days;
- determining the number of tasks undertaken during the day and the length of time spent on each task;
- calculating the number and range of people with whom the bursar interacted;
- assigning responsibility levels to each activity.

The data was also searched for indications of the future role of the bursar as educational resource manager.

Finding out about bursars' careers

International Educational Leadership Centre records

Initial analyses were made using the records of 36 students who had applied to attend the IELC, MBA in Education Management. Application forms provided information, which was used anonymously on gender, qualifications, school details, work titles, number of years in post, previous posts and membership of professional bodies. The data was analysed to establish if there were particular career routes to bursarship, a 'typical' bursar or if relationships were indicated between particular types of schools and the career backgrounds of bursars.

The genders, ages, work titles and number of years in bursar or bursar-related posts were analysed quantitatively and detailed analyses were also made of bursars' qualifications, career experiences and career levels. Each element was categorised into specialist areas and then further analysed using gender and job title, school phase, funding and number of pupils. The number of career changes were also recorded using new posts rather than movement between companies as the criterion. The reasons that the bursars gave for applying for the course were also analysed quantitatively to provide an insight into bursars' attitudes to their posts and why they felt they needed further development, noting any comment demonstrating bursars' attitudes to their career, responsibilities or relationships.

The researchers were aware that application forms were not questionnaires specifically designed for research. Thus, while some provided a great deal of detail and listed any information they thought might be relevant, others gave the minimum possible. It was felt, however, that for this exploratory research, there was enough information on which to establish a framework for future research and to provide indications of likely career routes and futures.

Interviews

Direct, 15-minute interviews were held and structured questions posed as the interviews also had to be used to discuss bursars' reasons for applying for the course and their reflections on completing it. Bursars were first asked to describe their vision of the bursar's role. Subsequent questions relating to the course, elicited information on how they viewed their current roles and revealed their reactions to relationships and tasks in their schools. Thirty-three of the bursars in the sample were interviewed on entry to the MBA course and 14 of these discussed their reflections on completing it.

The interviews were transcribed on to a computer and then searched for comments on their career paths and their perceptions of the roles and status of bursars. The responses were then categorised and analysed quantitatively as well as their requirements for personal and professional development.

Finding out what bursars think they will do in the future

The role of the school bursar was considered by focus groups of bursars from two cohorts of the MBA course. The first cohort was divided into three random groups (Figure I.3). The focus groups were then repeated with 31 bursars from a second cohort. This larger second cohort was divided into six groups of five or six bursars. The groups were selected to reflect the funding source of the schools which gave one GM, one special, two independent and two local authority groups (Figure I.4).

All the groups were allocated separate rooms. They were then allowed 20 minutes to complete the first part of the discussion. Each group was given 104 cards listing responsibilities and tasks which might be appropriate to the

A	B	C
Senior administrative officer 11–16 LM city school (750)	Bursar 12–18 GM provincial school (1190)	Administration officer 11–18 LM provincial school (1170)
Administration manager 12–16 LM provincial school (400)	Bursar 11–18 LM provincial school (770)	Facilities manager 11–18 LM provincial school (2050)
School administrator 4–18 Independent provincial school (670)	Assistant bursar 4–18 Independent provincial school (340)	Bursar 11–18 LM provincial school (1180)
Bursar 11–18 LM city school (1010)	Administration team leader 11–16 LM provincial school (1040)	Bursar 11–18 LM provincial school (770)
Registrar 11–16 LM city school (760)	Bursar 11–18 GM provincial school (1350)	General manager 11–16 LM city school (900)

Figure I.3 The composition of the first focus groups

Group A (GM)

Bursar
11–16 (620)

Bursar
11–16 (570)

Senior administrative officer and bursar
Secondary (1160)

Bursar
11–16 (1200)

Business manager
11–18 (1200)

Group B (Independent)

Bursar
3–18 (350)

Bursar
3–16 (380)

Bursar
Multiphase (530)

School administrator
4–18 (820)

Business manager and bursar
3–18 (600)

Group C (Independent + LM)

Bursar
Secondary (270)

Bursar
Secondary (290)

Assistant bursar
7–18 (440)

Chief administrator
Secondary (1100)

Group D (LM)

Bursar
11–18 (1160)

Bursar
Secondary (1260)

Principal administrative officer
Secondary (1300)

Finance and administration manager
11–18 (1340)

Bursar
11–18 (1500)

Group E (LM)

Bursar
11–16 (450)

Bursar
11–16 (600)

Bursar
11–16 (740)

Bursar
Secondary (800)

Bursar
11–16 (1000)

Bursar
11–16 (1280)

Group F (Special schools)

Bursar
11–16

College manager
11–19

Bursar
8–16 (140)

Resources manager
Age range unknown

Bursar
2.5–19

Figure I.4 The composition of the second focus groups

bursar. They were then asked to categorise them into headings of their own devising and put the cards under each category in a separate headed envelope. The headings were listed on a sheet of flip-chart paper for use in a group discussion. The list of responsibilities and tasks had been drawn up using:

1 NBA key areas of bursarship taken from the following headings:
   - administration management;
   - facility and property management;
   - financial resource management;
   - human resource management;
   - information management;
   - support services management.

2 Surrey County Council headship, curriculum leader and teacher headings which had been listed under:
   - administration;
   - evaluation and quality;
   - management of financial and physical resources;
   - management of people;
   - management of teaching and learning;
   - policy and leadership.

Each group found their own way of sorting the categories. Some groups divided the cards between themselves and asked each person to categorise their own, before coming together to agree the headings. The other groups worked together to agree all cards. After the groups had assigned the responsibilities and tasks to different headings they reported back on how they had decided on these headings. The flip-chart sheets were attached to the wall next to each other. The group with the most headings reported back first and their headings were linked together in the light of the other two flip charts.

After a discussion about the categories, each group was then assigned separate areas of responsibilities and asked to decide which of their cards were essential to the role of the bursar in the future. Strategy, administration and learning were not included in the responsibilities, but the groups were reminded that they might like to check through all their cards after they had sorted those in the relevant envelopes. It was also possible for them to add new responsibilities if they felt the cards did not include something important. They worked in separate rooms again for a further 20 minutes and were assigned the following responsibilities:

A HRM;

B finance and premises;

C marketing and public relations.

After listing the responsibilities essential to the role of the bursar, the groups reported back and discussed their reasons for the allocations.

Secondary data

Literature

The topic selected for the literature search was 'the role of the bursar' using the parameters of the English language and bursars in compulsory full-time educational establishments in England and Wales (Figure I.5). The time period of 1988–98 was chosen to commence with the Education Reform Act of 1988 and to cover developments up until 1998. Most data was obtained on the Internet using COPAC as the main search engine and the descriptors of school + administration, education + administration, school + finance, school + personnel. Within the British Education Index, most journal articles were found under school-based management, school effectiveness, support staff and LMS. The *Education Authorities' Directory and Annual* (1997) was used to gather information about bursars' schools.

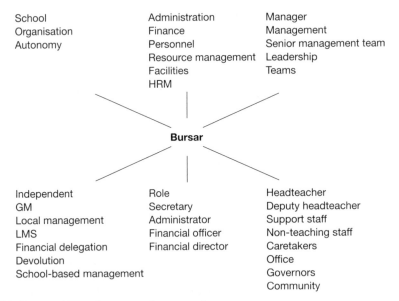

School
Organisation
Autonomy

Administration
Finance
Personnel
Resource management
Facilities
HRM

Manager
Management
Senior management team
Leadership
Teams

Bursar

Independent
GM
Local management
LMS
Financial delegation
Devolution
School-based management

Role
Secretary
Administrator
Financial officer
Financial director

Headteacher
Deputy headteacher
Support staff
Non-teaching staff
Caretakers
Office
Governors
Community

Figure I.5 Bursars' literature search parameters

Quotations and summaries from the books were analysed using the qualitative data software package, QSR NUDIST. The categories selected included:

1 roles, responsibilities and activities covering finance, administration, human resource management and site management;

2 relationships with headteachers, support staff, teachers, governors, parents and pupils.

More categories were attached, as new areas were found in the literature, thus businesses, communities and government bodies were added to the relationships. It also became apparent that separate sections would be needed for career history, qualifications, training and management activities.

The search revealed only one book and one article devoted to support staff which included bursars. Most information was found in areas that did not relate specifically to bursars. The majority of the information fell into the categories of finance, administration, human resource and site management. Relationships were recorded most often with headteachers, teachers and support staff. No literature was found involving bursars' relationships with pupils.

Case studies

The other main source of secondary data was the research reports carried out by the bursars on the IELC MBA. Participants were required to apply concepts/models from the literature in each topic area to their own schools and submit a management report. These reports were edited and condensed by the research team to represent the key features of each issue and then returned to the original author for comment. The resultant case studies are published in Part Three.

Commentary

As the design of the research was exploratory and issue seeking, the outcomes are to be regarded as indicative of the role of bursars in schools at the beginning of the twenty-first century. Further research needs to be conducted to make the findings more representative as well as specific to particular contexts.

There was a high degree of internal validity and consistency between the findings of the various aspects of the research. Bursars and other educational leaders to whom the methodology and research findings have been presented generally report that they see considerable face validity in the result.

Appendix II

■ ■ ■

NATIONAL STANDARDS FOR SCHOOL BURSARS

INTRODUCTION

These National Standards set out the knowledge, understanding, skills and attributes which relate to the key areas of school bursarship. They define expertise in school bursarship and are designed to serve as the basis for planning the professional development of both aspiring and serving school bursars. Whilst more experienced Bursars will have different needs from their newly-appointed colleagues, all Bursars are expected to provide leadership and management which secures high quality support and resource provision and which raises effectiveness in schools.

For the purposes of this document, the term "Bursar" is held to be interchangeable with comparable titles such as "Director of Resources", "Business Manager", "Administrative Director", etc..

The standards follow the structure of the National Standards for Headteachers produced by the Teacher Training Agency, and thus build on work done by that body and by higher education institutions, by OFSTED, by the Institute of Management, by the Association of School Business Officials (International) and on research commissioned by the National Bursars Association. They also reflect national management standards as defined by the Management Charter Initiative.

The standards are in six parts:

1. Core purpose of school bursarship
2. Key outcomes of school bursarship
3. Professional knowledge and understanding
4. Skills and attributes
5. Key areas of school bursarship
6. Code of Practice for School Bursars

1. CORE PURPOSE OF SCHOOL BURSARSHIP

To provide professional leadership and management of the support services of schools, thus enhancing effectiveness, success and improved efficiency, thereby ensuring a higher standard of learning in schools resulting in improved standards of achievement.

The Bursar is the school's leading support staff professional, and supports the Headteacher in his/her duty to ensure that the school meets its educational aims. Responsible to the Headteacher, the Bursar is in turn responsible for ensuring that the school as a physical entity operates as a harmonious and efficient organisation and that support services are provided in the most effective manner in the support of learning.

The Bursar is responsible for ensuring by precept and example that support staff work together with teaching staff in the best pursuit of their joint aim of achieving learning by pupils, developing principles of best practice through liaison with professional bodies, colleagues in other schools, and by taking initiatives to meet new situations.

Above all, the Bursar promotes the highest standards of business in the ethos of the administrative function of the school and ensures the most effective use of resources in support of the school's learning objectives.

2.   KEY OUTCOMES OF SCHOOL BURSARSHIP

Effective bursarship results in effective schools where:

(a)   the highest standards of business and administrative professionalism obtain in a mutually-supportive environment, committed to Quality in all its manifestations;

(b)   the most efficient and cost-effective use is made of resources in pursuit of the educational aims of the school and that best value for money is obtained in all decisions;

(c)   sound practices of budgetary development and control are followed in order to optimise the school's use of its financial resources;

(d)   the school premises are maintained in conditions conducive to learning and to the development of pride in the school's physical environment and are used to the maximum effect;

(e)   the health, safety, and security of all persons on the school site is perceived as an individual and collective responsibility;

(f)   the school's personnel function is managed such that all school employees regard the school as a good and caring employer, committed to enhancing the quality of the employer-employee relationship;

(g)   contracted and in-house services are effectively managed and integrated into the educational thrust of the school;

(h)   the school's relationships with external agencies and suppliers transmit positive images of the school's ethos and standard practices;

(i)   the school is marketed to its potential client base in such a manner as to recommend it as the school of choice;

(j)   the support staff are regularly appraised, thus identifying areas of professional and personal development, furthering their effectiveness within the organisation;

and where

(k)   the support staff provide high quality support to teaching staff and are valued as partners with the teaching staff in the joint enterprise of education and where the team spirit permeates all school employees regardless of job or qualification.

3. PROFESSIONAL KNOWLEDGE AND UNDERSTANDING

To carry out their responsibilities effectively, Bursars need specific professional knowledge and judgement and a range of leadership, management, administrative and personal skills and attributes which are applied across the key areas of responsibility identified later. The knowledge and understanding that Bursars need draws on sources both inside and outside education.

The following areas of knowledge and understanding are relevant to all schools, although some aspects in some schools will need to be interpreted differently. Bursarial expertise is demonstrated by the ability to apply this knowledge and understanding in each of the key areas of bursarship.

Bursars should have knowledge and understanding of:

(a) what constitutes Quality in the provision of support services within schools, and the close interrelationship between good support and good learning;

(b) how to use comparative data and benchmarking to develop best practice and best value for money strategies in the provision of support services;

(c) how to apply advice from bodies such as the DfEE, the National Audit Office, the National Bursars Association, and parliamentary commissions in the optimisation of support practices in pursuit of pupil learning outcomes;

(d) how to specify, select, deploy and develop management information systems such that the school's management team and the governing body are assured of high quality information;

(e) political, economic, social, religious and technological influences which have an impact on strategic and operational planning;

(f) leadership styles and practices and their relevance in different contexts within the school;

(g) the fundamentals of financial management and control, accountancy terminology and the ability to accurately interpret financial documents;

(h) human resource legislation, including employment law, personnel practices, remunerative practices, recruitment and selection strategies, and disciplinary proceedings;

(i) national and european health and safety requirements and in particular their impact upon the provision of a safe and secure school environment where learning can flourish;

(j) the role of national, regional and local bodies in the educational life of the country and in the day to day conduct of the school within its social matrix;

(k) the contribution made to the school by external advisers such as OFSTED teams, auditors, NAO advisers, Inland Revenue inspectors, and professional consultants.

4. SKILLS AND ATTRIBUTES

The skills and attributes which follow are essential, but are not all exclusive, to the Bursar's role. The Bursar is expected to apply them, singly and in combination, in relation to each of the key areas of bursarship identified later.

Leadership skills, attributes and professional competence: the ability to lead and manage people to work as individuals and as a team towards a common goal.

Bursars should be able to:

(a) create and secure commitment to a clear and shared vision for an effective organisation;

(b) initiate and manage change and improvement in pursuit of organisational goals;

(c) prioritise, plan, and organise;

(d) direct and co-ordinate the work of others;

(e) build and support a high-performing team;

(f) work as part of a team;

(g) devolve responsibilities, delegate tasks, and monitor outcomes;

(h) motivate and inspire support staff;

(i) set standards and provide a positive role model for support staff and pupils;

(j) seek advice and support when necessary;

(k) deal sensitively with people and resolve conflicts;

(l) use appropriate leadership styles in different situations and appreciate their impact.

Bursars should possess and display the attributes of:

(a) personal impact, presence and self-confidence;

(b) resilience, enthusiasm, energy and vigour;

(c) flexibility and adaptability to changing situations;

(d) intellectual ability;

(e) reliability, integrity and commitment;

(g) probity, justice and humility.

4. SKILLS AND ATTRIBUTES (contd)

Decision making skills: the ability to investigate, solve problems and make decisions:

Bursars should be able to:

(a) collect and weigh evidence, make judgements and take decisions;

(b) analyse, understand and interpret relevant information and data;

(c) think creatively and imaginatively to solve problems and identify opportunities;

(d) demonstrate good judgement.

Communication skills: the ability to make points clearly and understand the views of others:

Bursars should be able to:

(a) communicate effectively orally and in writing;

(b) negotiate and consult effectively;

(c) manage good communication systems;

(d) demonstrate a high level of computer literacy;

(e) develop, maintain and use an effective network of contacts.

Self-management: the ability to plan time effectively and to organise oneself well:

Bursars should be able to:

(a) prioritise and manage their own time effectively;

(b) work under pressure and to deadlines;

(c) be self-motivating;

(d) achieve challenging professional goals;

(e) take responsibility for their own professional development.

5. KEY AREAS OF BURSARSHIP

Expertise in bursarship is demonstrated by the ability to apply professional knowledge, understanding, skills and attributes to bring about planned outcomes. It is assumed that the Bursar will work in conjunction with the Headteacher and the senior management team in the following key areas:

A. Administrative Management:
Bursars promote the effective functioning of the school in its interacting and communicating with persons and agencies within and without the school community. This includes:
- (i) managing the administrative, clerical, and other support functions of the school;
- (ii) preparing and producing records and returns;
- (iii) managing information and communication systems;
- (iv) managing legal, public, statutory, and marketing matters.

B. Financial Resource Management:
Bursars apply the best practices and highest standards of financial management to optimise value for money and to maximise efficiency. This includes:
- (i) complying with sound principles of school finance;
- (ii) budgeting and financial strategy/planning;
- (iii) accounting, auditing, and financial reporting;
- (iv) managing cash, investments, and credit control;
- (v) developing, promulgating and maintaining sound principles of financial practice.

C. Human Resource Management:
Bursars, appreciating that the personnel resource is the school's greatest asset, manage the school's personnel function effectively and sensitively to best effect. This includes:
- (i) administering personnel and their remuneration;
- (ii) planning and supporting staff development;
- (iii) securing good labour relations through individual and collective negotiations;
- (iv) developing good human relations;
- (v) following clear and fair principles of recruitment, retention and discipline.

D. Facility and Property Management:
Bursars develop and maintain the physical assets of the school to maximise their effectiveness as an environment conducive to learning. This includes:
- (i) supervising the planning and construction processes;
- (ii) ensuring the safe maintenance and operation of all school premises;
- (iii) advising the Governing Body on the purchasing and disposal of premises;
- (iv) ensuring the continuing availability of supplies, services and equipment;
- (v) following sound practices in real estate management and grounds maintenance;
- (vi) maximising income through lettings and other additional activities.

5.   **KEY AREAS OF BURSARSHIP (contd.)**

E.   **Information Management:**
Bursars ensure that information is effectively managed and its analysis and delivery systems constantly developed to ensure that high quality information is deployed in support of decisions made by Governors and Senior Management.
This includes:
(i) participating in strategic planning;
(ii) conducting programme evaluation;
(iii) ensuring adequate and reliable communications;
(iv) reviewing management information systems;
(v) developing management information systems.

F.   **Support Services Management:**
Bursars manage all services within the school that support learning, such that the Headteacher and teaching staff can concentrate on and can facilitate the pupil learning process in a safe, secure, and well-supported environment.
This includes:
(i) managing risk/fire control, safe systems of work, health & safety, and medical aid;
(ii) ensuring the adequacy and safe operation of school transportation;
(iii) ensuring the adequate and efficient provision of food services;
(iv) supervising the caretaking and cleaning services;
(v) managing all support contracts to the school;
(vi) ensuring the maximum level of security consonant with the ethos of the school.

6.   CODE OF PRACTICE   (With acknowledgement to the Institute of Management)

GENERAL
At all times a member shall uphold the good standing and reputation of the National Bursars Association and the profession of Bursar. Members shall:

Have due regard for and comply with relevant law
Act with integrity, honesty, loyalty and fairness
Act within the limits of professional competence
Follow such guidance on professional matters as promulgated by the Council

REGARDING SELF:
At all times the member should, in addition to the above:

Pursue professional activities with integrity, accountability, and competence
Disclose any personal interest which might be seen to influence decisions
Practise an open style of management whenever possible
Take active steps for the continuing development of personal competence
Safeguard confidential information and not seek personal advantage from it
Encourage the development and maintenance of Quality in all activities

REGARDING OTHERS:
At all times the member should, in addition to the above:

Ensure that others are aware of their responsibilities, areas of authority, and accountability
Encourage and assist others to develop their potential
Consider the mental and physical health, safety and well-being of others
Have regard for matters of conscience of others
Have regard for the needs, pressures and problems of others and not discriminate on grounds other than those demonstrably necessary for the task
Establish and develop continuing and satisfactory relationships based on mutual confidence
Neither offer or accept gifts, hospitality or services which could, or might appear to, imply an improper obligation

REGARDING THE ORGANISATION:
At all times the member should, in addition to the above:

Uphold the lawful policies and practices of the organisation
Identify and communicate relevant policies, practices, and information
Regularly review organisation structure, objectives, procedures, and controls
Seek to balance departmental aims in furtherance of the organisation's overall objectives
Safeguard the assets and reputation of the organisation
Ensure truthfulness in all public communications
Seek to conserve resources wherever possible and preserve the environment
Respect customs, practices, and reasonable ambitions of other peoples which may differ from one's own

Appendix III

■ ■ ■

The two premier organisations for school bursars are the National Bursars Association and the Independent School Bursars Association.

They can be contacted as follows:

National Bursars Association
Secretary and Registrar
National Bursars Association
PO Box 12, Chard
Somerset
TA20 3YX
Tel/Fax 01460 65628
Email: peter-rickard@oakwell.sagehost.co.uk
Web address: <http://www.nba.org.uk>

Independent Schools Bursars Association
The General Secretary
5 Chapel Close
Old Basing
Basingstoke
Hampshire
RG24 7BY
Tel: 01256 330369
Fax: 01256 330376
Email: isbasing@compuserve.com

References

■ ■ ■

Adams, G.R. and Schvaneveldt, J.D. (1991). *Understanding Research Methods*. 2nd edn. London: Longman.

Adey, P., Shayer, M. and Yates, C. (1990) *Better Learning*. London: Kings College.

Anthony, P. and Pittman, R. (eds) (1993) *Head To Head: How To Run A School: Fifteen HMC Heads Offer Their Advice*. 2nd edn. Saxmundham: John Catt Educational.

Austin, B. (1975) 'Time analysis of a local government manager's working day', *Local Government Studies*, April, 61–72.

AZTEC (1994) *Case Study Melrose Special School*. Teacher Placement Service for UBI.

Bennis, W. (1985) 'Managing the dream: leadership in the 21st century', *Journal of Organizational Change Management*, 2, (1), 6–10.

Bergenhenegouwen, G.J. (1996) 'Professional code and ethics for training profession-als', *Journal of Industrial Training*, 20, (4), 23–9.

Bolam, R., McMahon, A., Pocklington, A. and Weindling, D. (1993) *Effective Management In Schools: A Report for the Department of Education*. London: HMSO.

Bowe, R., Ball, S.J. and Gold, A. (1992) *Reform of Education and Changing Schools: Case Studies in Policy Sociology*. London: Routledge.

Boyd, R. (1998) *Independent Schools: Law, Custom and Practice*. Bristol: Jordans.

Bullock, A. and Thomas, H. (1997) *Schools At The Centre? A Study Of Decentralisation*. London: Routledge.

Burrell, G. and Morgan, G. (1979) *Sociological Paradigms and Organisational Analysis: Elements of the Sociology of Corporate Life*. Aldershot: Ashgate.

Bush, T. and Middlewood, D. (eds) (1997) *Managing People in Education*. London: Paul Chapman.

Caldwell, B.J. and Spinks, J.M. (1992) *Leading the Self-Managing School*. London: Falmer.

Clerkin, C. (1985) 'What do primary school heads actually do all day?' *School Organisation*, 5, (4), 287–300.

Clerkin, C. (1994) 'Preparing job descriptions: the heads role' in Spear, C.E. (ed.) *Primary Management and Leadership Towards 2000*. Harlow: Longman.

Coulson, A.A. (1986) 'The Managerial Work of Primary School Headteachers' in *Sheffield Papers in Education Management*. No. 48, Sheffield: Sheffield City Polytechnic.

Curriculum and Management Consultancy (undated) *Surrey County Council Job Profiling*. Addlestone: CMC.

Davies, B. and Ellison, L. (1997) *School Leadership for the 21st Century: A Competence and Knowledge Approach*. London: Routledge.

Dean, J. (1993) *Managing the Secondary School*. 2nd edn. London: Routledge.

Dean, J. (1995) *Managing the Primary School*, 2nd edn. London: Routledge.

Deem, R. (1996), 'The school, the parent, the banker and the local politician; what can we learn from the English experience of involving lay people in site based manage-ment of schools?' in Pole, C.J. and Chawla-Dinga, R. (eds).

DfEE (1996) *Guidance on Good Governance.* London, Department for Education and Employment.

DfEE (1998a) 'Fair funding: improving delegation to schools'. Consultation paper. London: Department for Education and Employment.

DfEE (1998b) Unpublished letter to Chief Executive Officers of Local Education Authorities confirming decisions on the Fair Funding consultation paper, London, Department for Education and Employment, Consultation Paper.

DfEE (1998c) 'Teachers meeting the challenge of change', Consultation Paper, London: Department for Education and Employment.

Drucker, P.F., Dyson, E., Handy, C., Saffo, P. and Senge, P.M. (1997) 'Looking ahead: implications of the present, *Harvard Business Review*, September–October, 18–32.

Duignan, P. (1980) 'Administrative behaviour of school superintendents: a descriptive study', *Journal of Educational Administration*, 28(1), 5–26.

Dyson, E. (1997) in Drucker *et al.*, *Harvard Business Review*.

Earley, P. and Creese, M. (1998) 'Governing bodies: rationale, roles and reassessment, *Viewpoint*. London: Institute of Education.

Easterby-Smith, M., Thorpe, R. and Lowe, A. (1991) *Management Research: An Introduction.* London: Sage.

Education Authorities Directory and Annual (1997) Redhill: School Government Publishing Co.

Emerson, C. and Goddard, I. (1993) *Managing Staff in Schools.* Oxford: Heinemann.

Eraut, M. (1994). *Developing Professional Knowledge and Competence.* London: Falmer.

Esp, D. (1993) *Competencies for School Managers.* London: Kogan Page.

Evetts, J. (1996). 'The new headteacher: budgetary devolution and the work culture of secondary headship', in Pole, C.J. and Chawla-Dinga, R. (eds).

Fidler, B., Russell, S. and Simkins, T. (eds) (1997) *Choices for Self Managing Schools: Autonomy and Accountability.* London: Paul Chapman.

Foreman, K. (1997), 'Managing individual performance' in Bush, T. and Middlewood, D. (eds) *Managing People in Education.* London: Paul Chapman.

Fullan, M. (1993). *Change Forces: Probing the Depths of Educational Reform.* London: Falmer.

Gardner, H., Kornhaber, M.L. and Wake, W.K. (1996). *Intelligence: Multiple Perspectives.* London: Harcourt & Brace.

Gleick, J. (1988) *Chaos.* London: Cardinal, Sphere Books.

Glover, I. and Hughes, M. (1998) *The Professional-Managerial Class: Contemporary British Management in the Pursuer Mode.* Aldershot: Ashgate.

Greenfield, T. and Ribbins, P. (eds) (1993) *Greenfield on Educational Administration: Towards an Humane Science.* London: Routledge.

Hall, V. (1997a) 'Managing staff' in Fidler, B. *et al.* (eds).

Hall, V. (1997b) 'Management roles in education' in Bush, T. and Middlewood, R. (eds).

Hall, V., Mackay, H. and Morgan, C. (1986) *Head Teaches at Work*, Milton Keynes: Open University Press.

Handy, C. (1994) *The Empty Raincoat: Making Sense of the Future.* London: Hutchinson.

Handy, C. (1997) in Drucker *et al.* Harvard Business Review.

Harris, O. (1996), 'A review of the deployment of teacher support staff in a secondary school'. Unpublished MBA Educational Management Dissertation, University of Leicester.

Harrison, M. and Gill, S. (1992) *Primary School Management.* Oxford: Heinemann.

Harrold, R. and Hough, J. (1988) *Curriculum, Finance and Resource Deployment: Toward School Self-Evaluation*. Sheffield Papers in Education Management, Sheffield, Sheffield Polytechnic.

Hickcox, E.S. (1992) 'Practices of effective chief education officers: a preliminary discussion', paper presented at the CCEA regional conference, Hong Kong.

HMI (1992), *Non Teaching Staff in Schools: A Review by HMI*, London: HMSO.

HoC (1998) *Ninth Report: The Role of Headteachers*. Session 1997–8. London: The Stationery Office.

HoC (1999) Second Special Report, *Government's Response to the Ninth Report from the Education and Employment Committee of the House of Commons on the Role of Headteachers*. Session 1997–8, House of Commons Papers, Session 1998–9. London: The Stationery Office.

Hughes, M. (1973) 'Research report: the professional-as-administrator' in Strain, M., Dennison, B., Ouston, J. and Hall, V. (1998) *Policy, Leadership and Professional Knowledge in Education*. London: Paul Chapman.

Husen, T. (1979) *The School in Question*. Oxford: Oxford University Press.

Illich, I. (1970) *Deschooling Society*. New York: Harper and Row.

Johnson, G. and Scholes, B. (1993). *Exploring Corporate Strategy*. London: Prentice Hall.

Knight, B. (1993). *Financial Management for Schools: The Thinking Manager's Guide*. Oxford: Heinemann.

Lashway, L. (1998) *Trends and Issues: Training of School Administrators*, Internet site address: <http://enc.uoregon.edu/issues/training/index.html>

Lawton, S.B. and Scare, J. (1991) 'Inferring values from the physical culture of the CEO's office' in Leithwood, K. and Musella, D. (eds) *Understanding School System Administration: Studies of the Contemporary Chief Education Officer*. London: Falmer.

Lyons, G. and Jirasinghe, D. (1996) *The Competent Head: A Job Analysis of Head's Tasks and Personality Factors*. London: Falmer.

Macbeath, J., Moos, L. and Riley, K. (1998) 'Time for a change' in Macbeath, J. (ed.), *Effective School Leadership: Responding to Change*. London: Paul Chapman.

Markham, K. (1990) 'The role of a bursar', *School Governor*, November/December, 12–14.

Mavor, M. (1993) 'The management of change', in Anthony, P. and Pittman, R. (eds).

Maxcy, S.J. (1995) *Democracy, Chaos, and the New School Order*. Thousand Oaks: Corwin Press.

Middlewood, D. (1997) 'Managing appraisal' in Bush, T. and Middlewood, D. (eds).

Mintzberg, H. (1973) *The Nature of Managerial Work*. New York: Harper and Row.

Mortimore, P. and Mortimore, J. with Thomas, H., Cairns, R. and Taggart, B. (1992) *The Innovative Uses of Non Teaching Staff in Primary and Secondary Schools Project*: London: DfEE and The Institute of Education, University of London.

Mortimore, P., Mortimore, J. and Thomas, H. (1995). *Managing Associate Staff: Innovation in the Primary and Secondary Schools*. London: Paul Chapman.

Mortimore, P., Sammons, P., Stoll, L., Lewis, D. and Ecob, R. (1988) *Schools Matter: the Junior Years*, London: Paul Chapman.

Nathan, M. (1996) *The Headteacher's Survival Guide*. London: Kogan Page.

NBA (1998) *National Standards for School Bursars*. National Bursars Association.

NCET (1996) *Integrated Learning Systems*, National Council for Educational Technology.

Partington, J., Stacey, B. and Turland, A. (1998), *Governing Independent Schools*. London: Fulton.

Pedler, M. and Boydell, T. (1985) *Managing Yourself*. London: Fontana.

Peters, T.J. and Waterman, R.H. (1982) *In Search of Excellence*. London: Harper and Row.

Pole, C.J. and Chawla-Dinga, R. (eds) (1996) *Reshaping Education in the 1990s: Perspectives On Secondary Schooling*. London: Falmer Press.

Popper, K.R. (1972). *Objective Knowledge: An Evolutionary Approach*. London Hutchinson.

Potter, D. and Powell, G. (1992) *Managing a Better School*. Oxford: Heinemann.

Raddan, A. (1995) 'Associate Staff in Schools: Training Provision and Participation'. Unpublished MBA Educational Management Dissertation, University of Leicester.

Reid, K., Bullock, R. and Howarth, S. (1988) *An Introduction to Primary School Organisation*. London: Hodder and Stoughton.

Ribbins, P. and Marland, M. (1994) *Headship Matters: Conversations with Seven Secondary Headteachers*. Harlow: Longman.

Riches, C. (1981) 'Non-teaching staff in primary and secondary schools' in *Management in the School – Block 6 the management of staff, Open University E323*. Milton Keynes: Open University Press.

Riches, C. (1984) *The Management of Non-Teaching Staff in a School: A Methodological Exploration*. London: Harper and Row.

Saffo, P. (1997) in Drucker *et al*. *Harvard Business Review*.

Sawatzki, M. (1997) 'Leading and managing staff for high performance', in Davies, B. and Ellison, L. (eds).

Senge, P.M. (1997) in Drucker *et al*. *Harvard Business Review*.

Smith, D. (1993) 'The head and the bursar' in Anthony, P. and Pittman, R. (eds).

Somervell, R. (1935) *Robert Somervell for Thirty Three Years Assistant Master and Bursar at Harrow School*. London: Faber and Faber.

Spencer, M. (1991) 'They also serve ... team management and the deputy head', in Stevens, D.B. (ed.).

Stevens, C. (1992) 'Recognising the school administrator', *Times Educational Supplement*, 22 May, 13.

Stevens, D.B. (ed.) (1991) *Under New Management: Strategies for Secondary Schools in the 1990s*. London: Harlow.

Strauss, A. and Corbin, J. (1990) *Basics of Qualitative Research: Grounded Theory Procedures and Techniques*. Newbury Park: Sage.

Swanson, A.D. and King, R.A. (1997) *School Finance: Its Economics and Politics*, 2nd edn, White Plains, NY: Longman.

Szemeremyi, S. (1991) 'Money matters' in Stevens, D.B. (ed.).

Teacher Training Agency (1998) *National Standards for Qualified Teacher Status, Subject Leaders, Special Educational Needs Co-ordinators and Headteachers*. London: TTA.

Thody, A. (1997) *Leadership of Schools: Chief Executives in Education*. London: Cassell.

Thody, A.M. (1998) 'Training school principals, educating school governors', *International Journal of Educational Management*, 12(5), 232–9.

Thody, A.M. (1999) 'From political servant to community democrat', *Education Today*, 49(2),

Thody, A.M. (2000) 'Utopia revisited or is it better the second time around?', *Journal of Educational Administration and History*, accepted for publication in 2000.

Thomas, H. and Martin, J. (1994). *The Effectiveness of Schools and Education Resource Management: A Final Report to the Department for Education*. March, The University of Birmingham.

Thomas, H. and Martin, J. (1996) *Managing Resources for School Improvement: Creating a Cost Effective School*. London: Routledge.

Wallace, M. and Hall, V. (1994) *Inside the SMT: Teamwork in Secondary School Management*. London: Paul Chapman.

Warrington, M. (1992) *Managing Non Teaching Staff*. Leicester: Secondary Heads' Association.

Webb, R. and Vulliamy, G. (1996) *Roles And Responsibilities in the Primary School: Changing Demands and Changing Practices*. Buckingham: Open University Press.

Welsh, J. (1999) *NBA Website*: http://www.nba.org.uk/

West-Burnham, J. (1997) 'Reflections on leadership in self-managing schools', in Davies, B. and Ellison, L. (eds).

White, P., Hodgson, P. and Crainer, S. (1996) *The Future of Leadership: Riding the Rapids to the Twenty-First Century*. London: Pitman.

Whitehead, M. (1997) *Times Educational Supplement*, 2, 25 April, 23.

Wright, T. (1994) *Managing a Primary School in the Mid 1990s*. Tamworth: Bracken Press.

Yin, R.K. (1989) *Case Study Research: Design and Methods*. Newbury Park: Sage.

Index

accountability *see* job descriptions
accountancy qualifications 53, 192, 194
accreditation of prior learning 193
Adams, G.R. 210
administration
    definition 38
    future role 205
    job description 38–9, 48
    management role 62–3, 198
    model 15
    relationships with teachers/governors
        68–9
    teacher support 85–7
administration manager 15, 62–3, 169–70, 196,
    198, 200
admission and appeals procedures 86
advising governors/headteachers 39
alternative education provision 157–61
ambiguity 16, 172, 178, 202
appeals and admission procedures 86
appraisal systems 88, 106–7, 184
attitudes
    to community involvement 132–3, 139
    of bursars 25, 68–70
    of support staff 104–5, 109–10, 181–2
    of teachers 24–25, 68–70, 181
Austin, B. 46
autonomy 202
    levels of 170–1
    school autonomy and bursars' roles 8,
        199–200
AZTEC 27

Bennis, W. 203
Bergenhenegouwen, G.J. 188
Bolam, R. 22, 24
Bowe, R. 22, 25
Boyd, R. 3
Boydell, T. 203
British Triathlon Association 117
budgets 31–2, 141–3
    see also finance
Bullock, A. 22, 26
Burrell, G. 210
Bush, T . 21, 23, 25

Caldwell, B.J. 145
career aspirations 57–61
    research method 216–17
career experiences 54–5
CASE (Cognitive Acceleration through Science
    Education) 150–3
catering services 89–91
centralisation 4–5, 202
centralisation of curriculum 4–5
change
    attitudes to 181–2
    educational continuities 180
    educational futures 178–9
    future role of bursars 204–8
    restructuring proposals 173–7
    School 2020 172–3
    school context 170–3
    'Teachers meeting the challenge of change'
        6, 7
chaos theorists 179
chief executive position 173–4
classroom support 91–5, 100
Clerkin, C. 46, 213
Code of Conduct 188, 230
Cognitive Acceleration through Science
    Education (CASE) 150–3
community involvement 130–3, 139
company executive 173–5
competence standards 184, 185, 190
Conservative government 6
continuity in change model 180
contracts 30
    outsourced 89–91, 95, 108–9, 182, 198
    site 34–5, 108–10
    staff 32, 205, 207
Corbin, J. 214
costs
    energy costs 124–5
    of introducing CASE 152
    management of 31–2
    of market research 146
    and teacher effectiveness 97–101

Coulson, A.A. 46
Creese, M. 11
curriculum centralisation 4–5

daily activities 45–7, 48–50
data handling 95
Davies, B. 202, 203
Dean, J. 21, 22, 25, 26, 27
Deem, R. 26
deschooling movement 179
DfEE (Department for Education and
 Employment)
 'Fair Funding' 6, 8
 'Guidance on Good Governance' 11
 'Teachers meeting the challenge of change'
 6, 7
disaffected students project 157–61
Drucker, P.F. 178
Duignan, P. 46, 215
Dyson, E. 178

Earley, P. 11
Easter Schools 127
Easterby-Smith, M. 210
economies of scale 207–8
education see training and education
Education Acts 3, 7, 183
educational continuities 180
educational futures 178–9
educational resource manager 67–8, 170, 198,
 201, 209
 future role 203–6
 model 16
 relationships with teachers/governors 72
Ellison, L. 202, 203
Emerson, C. 12, 13, 21, 24, 27
energy costs 124–5
Eraut, M. 183
Esp, D. 185, 203
European Union (EU) grants 125
Evetts, J. 9, 26
extended school days 127

Fair Funding regulations 6, 8
falling school roll 133–7
female bursars 55–7
Fidler, B. 21
finance
 budgets 31–2, 141–3
 future role 205
 information provision 83–5
 information relevance 84
 job description 30–2
 management 27, 64, 65
flat hierarchies 182
flexibility 182

force field analysis
 attitudes to community involvement
  132–3, 139
 cognitive acceleration 151
Foreman, K. 15
Fullan, M. 202
functional teams 176–7

Gardner, H. 202
gender issues 56–7
Gill, S. 21, 22
Gleick, J. 179
Glover, I. 185, 188
GM (grant maintained) schools 3
Goddard, I. 12, 13, 21, 24, 27
governors 10–12, 40, 47, 49
 relationships with 4, 11–12, 24–6
Grant Maintained Schools Bursars Association
 59
Greenfield, T. 179

Hall, V. 21, 24, 25, 46
Handy, C. 81, 178
Harris, O. 25
Harrison, M. 21, 22
Harrold, R. 22
Hay McBer 189, 190, 203
HEADLAMP 187
headteachers 5, 6, 7, 9–10, 40, 47, 70
 characteristics of effective 189
 National Standards for Headteachers 187
 relationships 42, 44, 71
health and safety 32–34
 knowledge of 14, 39–40, 186
 qualifications 52, 57, 193
Hickcox, E.S. 46
hierarchies 182
history of bursarship 3, 4, 6–8, 20–1
HMI 12
Hough, J. 22
House of Commons Select Committee on
 Education and Employment 6, 7, 8, 9, 60
Hughes, M. 10, 174, 185, 188
human resources management 32–4, 64, 205
Husen, T. 179

Illich, I. 179
image see school image
importance of bursars 21–4
income generation 34–35, 36, 127, 129, 131
Independent Schools Bursars Association
 (ISBA) 14, 59, 188–9
induction 60
information and communications technology
 (ICT) 35, 99–100, 161–4
information provision 95
integrated learning systems 153–7

integrated teams 177
ISBA (Independent Schools Bursars
    Association) 14, 59, 188–9

Jirasinge 9
job descriptions 29–42, 64, 209, 212–13
    administration 38–9, 48
    advising governors/headteachers 39
    finance 31–2
    human resources 32–4
    information and communications
        technology 35
    levels of responsibility 38–40
    management activities 39, 48
    marketing 36–7
    personal skills and qualities 41
    policy-making decisions 40
    pupil interaction 35–6
    site/premises management 34–5
    status 40
    see also roles and responsibilities
Johnson, G. 81

King 9
Kingshurst City Technology College 26
Knight, B. 22, 23, 26, 54

Labour government 6–8
Langhurst City Technology College 24
Lashway, L. 202
Lawton 44
LEA
    delegation 8, 200
    service provisions 5, 6, 103, 110, 160, 207–8
    relationship with 72
    training 14, 28, 59, 184, 191–193, 195
leadership 40, 189, 199, 200, 201–3, 208
    definition 48
    educational leadership 112
    of support staff 70, 95, 207
learning
    integrated learning systems 153–7
    whole-school learning 161–4
levels of responsibility 38–40
library resources 98–9
Licentiate Registration Scheme 60, 61
LMS (local management of schools) 3, 5, 6
lottery funding 116–8
Lyons 189

MacBeath, J. 9
McKay, H. 46
Management Charter Initiative (MCI) 184, 186
management definition 48
management devolution 5

management information systems 86
management performance 199
management responsibilities 39, 48, 199
management training 195–6
market research 143–7
marketing 36–7, 205
    and operational budgets 141–3
    plans 137–43
    see also school image
Markham, K. 13, 21, 22, 23, 24, 25, 26
Marland, M. 24, 25, 26
Martin, J. 12, 21, 22, 24, 26
Master of Business Administration 60, 71, 191, 195
Mavor, M. 25
Maxcy, S.J. 201, 202
MCI (Management Charter Initiative) 184, 186
'Meeting the Challenge' Green Paper 6–7
meeting people 47
Middlewood, D. 21, 23, 25, 27
Mintzberg, H. 46
mission statements 134–5
Morgan, C. 46
Morgan, G. 210
Mortimore, J. 21
Mortimore, P. 9, 15, 20, 21, 22, 23, 24, 25, 26, 27,
    28, 55, 196
motivation of support staff 88
multi-skilling 61, 175

Nathan, M. 23, 24, 25, 26
National Bursars Association (NBA) 14, 59,
    60, 188–9
National Council for Vocational Qualifications
    (NCVQ) 184
National Curriculum 4–5
National Lottery funding 116–8
National Standards for Headteachers 187
National Standards for School Bursars 60, 61,
    186, 212–30
National Vocational Qualifications (NVQs) 14,
    193
NBA (National Bursars Association) 14, 59,
    60, 188–9
NCVQ (National Council for Vocational
    Qualifications) 184
New Careers Training (NCT) 158, 160
NPQH (National Professional Qualification for
    Headship) 58, 187
nursery provision 81–3
NVQs (National Vocational Qualifications) 14,
    193

offices 44–5, 86
Ofsted 95, 193, 208
    and support staff 94, 95

consequence of inspection 101, 138, 143–4, 157–161
operational budgets 141–3
outsourced contracts 89–91, 95, 108–9, 182, 198

Partington, J. 11
pastoral care 134
  see also catering
Pedlar, M. 203
performance appraisal 88, 106–7, 184
person specifications 41, 93, 212
personal characteristics 4
personal skills development 41, 190
personality 45
Peters, T.J. 9, 185
policy making decisions 31, 40, 204
Popper, K.R. 214
Porter, M.E. 81
Potter, D. 23
Powell, G. 23
premises see site management
private tuition income 127
professional development 192–3
professional qualification equivalence 193
professional qualifications 52–3, 194
professional-as-administrator model 174–5
professionalisation of bursarship 13–14, 183–97
  Code of Conduct 188, 230
  competence standards 184, 185, 190
  definition of a profession 184–5
  National Standards for School Bursars 60, 61, 186, 212–30
  personal skills development 41, 190
public relations 129
  see also marketing; school image
pupil interaction 35–6

qualifications 51–3, 193–5
  career experiences 54–5
questionnaires
  market research 145
  relevance of financial information 84

Raddan, A. 20, 27, 28
Reid, K. 22
relationships 68–72
  administrative manager stage 68–9
  educational resource manager stage 72
  school business manager stage 71–2
  with senior staff/governors 4, 11–12, 24–6, 66
  support services manager stage 70–1
  with teachers 25–26, 68–9, 70
remuneration of support staff 104–5
reprographics service 121–3
resource deployment 78–81

responsibilities see roles and responsibilities
restructuring proposals 173–7
  company executive 173–5
  multi–skilled operatives 175
  teamworking 176–7
Ribbins, P. 24, 25, 26, 179
Riches, C. 20, 27
roles and responsibilities 21–4, 30, 37, 44, 62–8
  administration 62–3, 198
  current position 169–70
  educational resource 67–8, 198, 201, 203–6, 209
  future position 170–3, 203–6
  restructuring proposals 173–7
  and school autonomy 199–200
  school business manager 65–7, 198
  support services 63–5, 198
  see also job descriptions
Royal Society of Arts (RSA) 184, 186

Saffo, P. 178
Sawatzki, M. 38, 202
Scane 44
scenario planning 95, 119
Scholes, B. 81
School 2020 172–3
school autonomy 199–200
school business manager 65–7, 198, 170, 200
  model 16
  relationships with teachers/governors 71–2
school image 129–48
  falling school roll 133–7
  market research 143–7
  marketing plans 137–43
  promoting community involvement 130–3
school roll 133–7
Schools Administrators Conference 59
Schvaneveldt, J.D. 210
secretarial qualifications 52–3
self-study areas 113–15
Senge, P. 178
senior management teams 9–10
  administration manager 69
  contribution to 66, 83
  decision making 8, 159–61, 162, 164
  educational resource manager 67, 72
  information to 32, 79–80, 95, 116, 152–3, 156
  membership of 15–16, 23, 107, 157, 198
  relationships with 66, 68–70
  school business manager 71–72
  support services manager 70
SHA (Secondary Heads' Association) 12
sigmoid curve 81

site management
    cost reductions 124–5
    and educational leadership 112
    effective use of facilities 126–8
    extended school days 79–80, 127
    future roles 205
    income generation 34–35, 36, 127, 129, 131
    job description 34–5
    optimum use of space 115
    reprographics service 121–3
    security 34–5, 119–20, 130–33, 205
    self–study areas 113–15
    sports facilities 116–21
    swimming facilities 118–21
site-based management 6–8, 201–3
sixth form centre 143–7
skills and attributes 226–7
skills development 41, 190
Smith, D. 28
Somervell, Robert 20–1
Spencer, M. 23
Spinks, J.M. 145
sports facilities 116–21
status 40, 44, 68
Stevens, C. 12
strategy 205
Strauss, A. 214
subjectivism 179
SuccessMaker ILS system 154
Summer Schools 127
support services manager 63–5, 85–7, 170, 198, 200
    model 15
    relationships with teachers/governors 70–1
support staff 12–13, 86, 87–8, 96–111
    appraisal 88, 106–7
    attitudes to change 181–2
    classroom support 91–5, 100
    and cost/teacher effectiveness 97–101
    effective utilization 93
    increasing numbers 97–101
    leadership of 4, 12, 15–16, 23, 70, 95, 207
    motivating 88
    remuneration 104–5
    reorganising for team effectiveness 102–4
    sites and premises teams 108–11
    SWOT analysis 88
Surrey County Council (Curriculum and Management Consultancy) 38
Swanson, A. 9
swimming facilities 118–21
SWOT analysis

catering services 91
marketing 138
nursery provision 82
support staff 88
Szemeremyi, S. 22

task lists 22–3
Taylor, F. 185
Teacher Training Agency (TTA) 38, 184, 207
teachers
    administrative support 85–7
    attitudes of bursars 25, 68, 69, 70
    attitudes to change 181
    teacher development 4–5
'Teachers meeting the challenge of change' 6, 7
teaching qualifications 53
teams 176–7
    reorganising for effectiveness 102–4
    site and premises 108–11
Thody, A.M. 10–11, 44, 46, 48, 180
Thomas, H. 12, 21, 22, 24, 26
titles 20, 68
training and education 27–8, 59–61, 191–7
    future of 195–7
    levels of 193, 196–7
    professional development 13–14, 192–3
    providers of 191
    qualifications 193–4
TTA (Teacher Training Agency) 38, 184, 207
turbulence 16, 172, 178, 202

UBI (Understanding British Industry) report 27
up-skilling 60

value for money 207–8
virtual schools 179
Vulliamy, G. 22

Wallace, M. 21, 24, 25
Warrington, M. 12, 22, 28
Waterman, R.H. 9, 185
Webb, R. 22
West-Burnham, J. 38
White, P. 202
Whitehead, M. 15
whole school learning and information centre 161–4
working day 21, 45–7, 48–50
Wright, T. 25, 26

Yin, R.K. 210